THE
GREYHOUND
STORY

THE
GREYHOUND
STORY
FROM HIBBING TO EVERYWHERE

By Oscar Schisgall

Published by J. G. Ferguson Publishing Company
Chicago
A subsidiary of Doubleday and Company, New York
Distributed to the trade by Doubleday
1985

Library of Congress Catalog Card Number: 84-82190
ISBN:0-385-19690-3

BY WAY OF DEDICATION

This is one way, however inadequate, to express my gratitude to some of the many people who so generously helped me with their time, their efforts, their memories. If I begin with Gerald H. Trautman it is in deep appreciation of his unfailing readiness to discuss the Greyhound history he so vigorously helped to shape. Once, when he mentioned the existence of personal scrapbooks, I thought it would be revealing to see them. I had no idea there would be 16 huge tomes, each weighing several pounds, and that Gerald Trautman himself would carry them into his office the next morning. Even before he regained his breath he telephoned me to say the volumes were at my disposal. This was so typical of his unstinting help that I record it with special appreciation.

At the same time I offer my earnest thanks to John W. Teets, and Frank L. Nageotte. Both of these men enriched the Greyhound story with personal experiences and recollections no one else could have had. And I am indebted to Frederick Dunikoski for his enthusiasm in collecting and preserving Greyhound lore and making his remarkable knowledge available to me.

Then there were retired Greyhound officers, Adam Sledz and Clifford Graves in particular, who contributed many glowing memories to these pages, and to them, too, I am profoundly grateful.

And finally I offer my thanks to Dorothy Lorant and Donald Behnke of the public relations department. They were my mentors, my colleagues, my guides. They opened doors whose existence I did not even suspect. Without their assistance this book could never have been written. I hope these few lines will convey to them some sense of my enduring gratitude.

Oscar Schisgall

Editor's Note

Oscar Schisgall died at his home in New York City on May 20, 1984, shortly after he had read and corrected the final galleys of his book The Greyhound Story.

PREFACE

The history of The Greyhound Corporation is, before all else, an unmatched commentary on the opportunities inherent in the economic system of the United States. It is the story of a few remarkable men who began their careers by driving people over the rutted roads of Minnesota, back in 1914, then catapulted their enterprise into the world's largest network of intercity motor transportation.

Today, seventy years later, the Greyhound story is also a record of wide diversification. The company has expanded in so many directions that to appraise its current activities presents an encyclopedic challenge. The corporation's chairman once spoke of these operations as "diversification within diversification" and characterized them as a hedge against economic buffeting. No doubt that is the accurate way to describe Greyhound's many facets. For most Americans, however, the very name, Greyhound, signifies the business of operating buses.

The reason is understandable. From the start buses have been the company's basic and abiding interest, the foundation on which everything else has been built. "Go Greyhound—and leave the driving to us" has for more than thirty years been one of the best known advertising messages in the land. Today some 3,500 streamlined, red-white-and-blue Greyhound coaches traverse the nation's highways, serving more communities than do railways and airlines combined. Swift, colorful, they carry the emblem of the running greyhound not only throughout this country but across the vast reaches of central and western Canada. No system of intercity bus transportation anywhere matches the more than 300,000,000 miles they cover every year, nor the 45,000,000 passengers they accommodate.

It has been said that a Greyhound traveler can see all of America slide past the picture window beside him—mountains, lakes, forests, rivers, rolling green meadows spotted with grazing cattle. When he passes farms, children wave cheerful greetings. This is the country at its peaceful best.

Yet to speak only of bus transportation in the 1980s is to ignore all other aspects of The Greyhound Corporation. For example, one of its major subsidiaries owns and leases everything from trucks to jet planes, from railroad cars to computers. Other subsidiaries offer widespread financial services that range from the issuance of money orders to residential mortgage insurance. Still other subsidiaries offer a wide range of services including duty-free shops at major international airports, ground-handling and fueling services for airlines, a temporary help service, and convention and exhibitors services.

Even after selling its Armour Foods operation in 1983, the company still maintains a significant presence in the manufacture and distribution of consumer products including a broad line of shelf-stable canned meats and a wide variety of personal care and household products. Its food service companies not only operate a successful chain of fast food restaurants in bus terminals and office buildings, but also provide food service for industry, military installations, schools, and other commercial establishments as well as logistical support services at remote construction sites around the world.

Today Greyhound not only *runs* buses; it *manufactures* them. Three huge plants are devoted to this part of the business—in Roswell, New Mexico, in Pembina, North Dakota, and in Winnipeg, Canada.

One could go on listing the company's diversified activities here and abroad. One security analyst said, "You really can't call the Greyhound company a conglomerate. You need a stronger word that hasn't yet been invented."

Disparate as some of these operations may seem, they represent a logical growth pattern. For instance, it was natural and practical to establish a package express service. This began as a favor to people who asked a friendly bus driver to drop off a parcel at a nearby town. When such requests multiplied, the rapidly increasing demands upon time justified—in fact, necessitated—making a charge for deliveries. Thus Greyhound Package Express was inaugurated. Within a decade it grew to handle millions of shipments a year.

Similarly, where passengers alighted at bus stops it was as natural to open lunch counters as to provide comfort stations, and this eventually resulted in the successful chain of Post House restaurants, now mostly converted to fast-food operations.

In short, The Greyhound Corporation of today must be regarded as a monument to people who recognized many industrial opportunities. Moreover—and this is amazing—Greyhound built its vast multi-billion dollar business within the lifetime of its former chairman, Gerald H. Trautman. He has seen it grow to a company with some 150,000 stockholders, almost 34,000 employees, and subsidiary operations in scores of other nations.

Incredible as it seems, all this evolved from the fact that a man in Hibbing, Minnesota, found it impossible to sell his automobile.

Part One

THE BUS YEARS

1

The man with the unsalable car was Carl Eric Wickman . . .

Nothing in his early life indicated that he was capable of becoming an outstanding American financier. At the age of seventeen he emigrated from Sweden, leaving school in the eighth grade. A friend of the family had urged him to come to Arizona. He used all his money to pay for the train fare from New York, and when he stepped down to the Tucson platform, there was nobody to meet him. He stood stranded, abandoned, unable to speak a word of English.

But he had a compact, sturdy body, and he somehow found a job carrying logs at a sawmill. It was there that he heard of the many Swedish immigrants who had settled in Hibbing, Minnesota, in the rugged region of the Mesaba iron mines.

So, as soon as he had saved enough to make the journey, Wickman went to Hibbing. There his Americanization was accomplished among miners for whom fistfights and profanity were normal means of expression. Wickman, "built like a block of granite," could match any of them with fists and expletives and frequently proved his ability. It was the only way to hold the respect of one's peers. His new friend, Ralph A. L. Bogan, once remarked, "Never saw him duck a fight or lose one."

In this environment Carl Wickman worked in the mines as a diamond drill operator until he discovered that frequent lay-offs made it impossible to earn a steady living. Without regular wages, how could a man look forward to a normal life of marrying and raising a family? And he very much wanted to marry Olga Rodin, the daughter of another drill operator.

So Wickman left the mines. Seeking what he hoped would be a more reliable and more lucrative career, he acquired, in 1913, the local dealership for Hupmobile cars and Goodyear tires. It was a mistake. For months he demonstrated the big car to anyone who stopped to look at it, but no one offered to buy the thing. He became so frustrated that even kicking the vehicle in disgust could not ease his feelings.

But one day frustration miraculously changed to inspiration. He thought of a novel way of putting the seven-passenger Hupmobile to use. Unlike Ralph Bogan who drove a local taxi, he would transport people to other towns. Nobody else was doing such a thing.

So Wickman made the inspired move of buying the car for himself with $600 he had saved. He announced to everybody he knew that he was ready to drive miners to nearby Alice which had a popular saloon and a few other exotic attractions. With gasoline selling at four cents a gallon in 1914, he could profitably charge fifteen cents for a one-way ride, twenty-five cents for a round trip.

Carl Eric Wickman, a young Swedish immigrant, starting with one Hupmobile carrying miners from Hibbing to Alice, Minnesota, turned a dream into a transcontinental transportation empire.

The response was so good that before long he established a regular daily schedule. Though he was not aware of it, he was launching a new American industry—intercity motor transportation; and he was planting the seed of The Greyhound Corporation which he was destined to head.

(The only challenge to Wickman's being the first to inaugurate intercity bus service has come from defenders of A. L. Hayes who, at the same time, was forming the Imperial Valley Auto Stages in California. Hayes' Locomobile was scheduled to carry people between San Diego and El Centro, 125 miles apart.)

In Hibbing the Hupmobile often had so many customers that miners jumped onto the running boards, clinging to whatever they could grasp. As for Wickman himself, he soon found it was no easy job he had created. On winter days he froze at the wheel despite the flapping isinglass curtains.

Time after time, even in blizzards, a flat tire compelled him to order his passengers out of the car while he jacked it up, patched the tire, and inflated it with a hand pump. And all this time he heard the curses of those who shivered in the icy storm as they watched him. Worst of all, he had to fight miners who refused to pay their fares. He had just decided that he'd had enough of all this when the mines called him back.

It happened because of the war spreading throughout Europe. After the assassination in Sarajevo, Yugoslavia, of the Austrian Archduke Ferdinand, it seemed that Germany's Kaiser Wilhelm was determined to prove that Deutschland could reign *über alles*. True, President Wilson vehemently proclaimed America's neutrality. But the managers of the Mesaba iron mines astutely foresaw that any large-scale war, even if limited to Europe, would demand more and more of the world's steel to be squandered on armament. In anticipation of such needs work at the iron mines increased. Wickman's old job was waiting for him.

And so, when two other Swedish immigrants, Andy Anderson and Charles Wenberg, offered to buy his business,

Wickman gladly sold it to them, car and all, for $1200.

No doubt he thought he had finished with hauling people from town to town. The truth was he had just begun.

•   •   •   •   •

What went wrong—or in the long view what went right— was that Swedish-born Charles Wenberg had never learned to drive a car. Obviously he was not ideally equipped to transport passengers by automobile. The burden fell wholly on Andy Anderson who soon found it as exhausting as had Wickman. One day, waiting for Wickman to emerge from the mine, Anderson walked home with him and begged him to rejoin the bus business.

"You and I could drive on alternate days," he argued. "That should make it easy for both of us."

After long thought Wickman may have felt morally obligated to help his friend. Whatever the reason, he bought back Wenberg's share in the business, refunding $600 of the money he had originally received.

With more and more miners going to work by bus, the venture began to thrive. In their first full year of working together Wickman and Anderson earned $8,000. In 1916 the figure leaped to $16,000. As might be expected, this kind of income gave Wickman the courage at last to marry the patient Olga Rodin. But also, it roused local competition.

Ralph Bogan, a tall, muscular man who could almost equal Wickman's strength and fiery use of invective, had been running a Hibbing taxicab. Now he ambitiously extended his service to driving people to Duluth, ninety miles away. It was a long trip on a narrow, rutted road. In winter Bogan had to supply riders with blankets and hot-brick foot warmers. Fortunately the miners were a hardy lot for whom the attractions of Duluth outweighed the rigors of long hours on the road. So Bogan prospered.

At the same time Wickman and Anderson, unable to accommodate increasing traffic, decided to buy a second car and

ALICE TO
HIBBING 15¢

American bus transportation began with an automobile like this.

build a larger body for it. This, however, would require more capital than they could manage, and that raised a problem. Borrow from a bank? Banks might gladly finance the automotive plans of White, Ford, or General Motors, but would they finance a couple of neophytes in the business like Wickman and Anderson? It was doubtful. Wickman had a better idea.

He went to see competitor Ralph Bogan. By consolidating their capital and forming a partnership, he pointed out, they would be able to buy the additional car, build a larger body for it, and in general expand their business.

Not only did Bogan himself accept the plan, two other friends of Wickman, Arvid Heed and Dominic Bretto who owned cars, also invested in the business. By 1915 they had formally incorporated the firm as the Mesaba Transportation Company, with five cars and five drivers. Wickman headed the project. It marked the beginning of his metamorphosis from bus driver to industrial executive.

The first winter blizzard completely stopped the business.

Every car was either mired in snowdrifts or moved only under hazardous conditions.

Wickman called in his partners. "Can't run a bus line without plows," he said. "Got to buy plows."

Nobody liked the idea, but the expenditure was inevitable. So was the difficult task of clearing roads. It was their first lesson in corporate responsibility: A considerable part of income ought to be set aside for emergencies.

But now came a crisis far greater than that created by snow. In 1915, a German submarine sank the *Lusitania,* killing 128 American citizens.

In Washington, President Wilson, always the apostle of peace, sent protest after protest to the Kaiser. Secretary of State William Jennings Bryan, calling the protest "too severe," resigned. The exchange of notes continued until, without warning in 1917, German submarines began to sink American merchant and passenger ships.

At that President Wilson's devotion to peace finally collapsed. The United States was sucked into the European war, and the mining of iron ore became an essential industry in support of more than a million American troops on their way overseas.

Among the first volunteers to leave Hibbing was big Ralph Bogan, bequeathing all his bus responsibilities to the other members of the Mesaba Transportation Company.

And the company found itself serving a war-pressured region. More miners than ever were using buses to ride to and from their jobs. Wickman's group had to buy additional cars and train additional drivers. Some of the early ones—men like Clifford E. Graves and S. R. Sundstrom—remained with the company all their working lives, eventually becoming top executives.

By 1918 Mesaba Transportation had eighteen cars rolling over the narrow dirt roads of northern Minnesota. It showed a healthy income of $40,000.

2

A proliferation of bus lines was beginning in other parts of the country, too. Automobile manufacturers like White and General Motors were designing vehicles meant specifically for bus use. The White car, for one, described itself as "able to seat eleven passengers with adequate luggage space on the fenders and in the rear boot." A thousand miles away, in Oakland, California, the Fageol brothers, together with the Hall-Scott Motor Company of Berkeley, produced their own elongated bus. Named the "Safety Coach," it could carry twenty-eight people seated four abreast in seven rows, each row having its own exit door.

Exactly how, when, and why these vehicles were compared to greyhounds has been related in many ways. According to the recollections of Clifford Graves, "One of the early bus operators was having lunch in a Duluth restaurant with a friend. Through the window they saw a Fageol bus speed by, and one of them exclaimed, 'Look at that thing! Fast as a greyhound!' " In any event, the descriptive word was gladly used by the bus manufacturers.

With eighteen cars under his supervision in Hibbing, Carl Wickman himself no longer had to drive. During the war and for the next four years he presided over the Mesaba Transportation Company from an office desk.

Of course, at the war's end he was among those who tendered a rousing hero's welcome to returning Ralph Bogan. The big blond man had served in balloon surveillance. Now that Bogan was ready to resume driving a bus, Wickman decided it was time he himself went on to other things.

He yearned to broaden his interests. In 1922, aged 35 and the father of two children, he yielded to the urge. With World War I ended, the world outside of Hibbing was too enticing to be ignored.

Wickman sold his share of the Mesaba Transportation Company to his associates for a gratifying $60,000. With this amount in the bank, he bid farewell to Hibbing and moved his family to Duluth. The city, he probably felt, offered not only broader business opportunities and challenges, but better community facilities for his wife and children. For himself, he was eager to start life anew.

•   •   •   •   •

It is almost axiomatic that great and enduring corporations are built by the vision, the energy, even the occasional recklessness of their founders. Unquestionably the characters of men like Rockefeller, Harriman, Ford, and other pioneer businessmen shaped their companies. Similarly, the character of Carl Eric Wickman was important to the development of The Greyhound Corporation. Vision, energy, and a touch of recklessness were assuredly in his blood.

The limitless potentialities of a bus industry still excited him, even drove him. He went from Duluth to nearby towns to explore possibilities with owners of local bus lines. Most had very short routes. Using his stake of $60,000, he bought shares of those lines that struck him as having the greatest promise for expansion. One of the first, in Superior, was the Superior White Company owned by Orville Swan Caesar.

Wickman could not have made a better alliance. Orville Caesar, a former mechanic with an inventive mind, had as deep an interest in the bus business as had Wickman himself. *Fortune* magazine later referred to him quite aptly as "Wickman's right-hand man." Not only were both pioneers in their industry but they were both also physically handsome, impressively built, with personalities that won confidence and cooperation. Where Wickman was tough and hard-driving, however, Caesar was soft-spoken and more tactful. As a team they complemented each other perfectly. Moreover, both were ambitious. Together they quickly acquired several local lines, uniting them under the name of the Motor Transit Corporation. What they established was in effect a holding corporation. And a vision.

It was clear to both of them that passengers who wished to travel from city to city found it a nuisance to transfer from one local bus line to another. They had to change vehicles, pay additional fares, remove their luggage, and wait for the next scheduled conveyance to carry them onward. The concept of a unified network of lines selling one through ticket became a brilliant goal that animated both men.

But to provide continuity of travel to distant cities on a single ticket meant adding more lines to a network. This in turn required additional capital. Again, getting it was a problem. Money would have to come from someone who shared their confidence in the future of bus travel. But who? Who was rich enough to help?

After days of mulling, Wickman picked up a telephone and called his former partner in Hibbing, Ralph Bogan. The call resulted in Bogan's joining the company (not suspecting that one day his son would marry Wickman's daughter, thereby turning a business relationship into a family affair). In any case, the gathering of these men was a long step toward the creation of their corporation. They bought some lines outright, invested in others.

As their business grew it required not only additional buses but also additional drivers. Finding drivers capable of handling a bus presented a problem. One of the first, Clifford Graves—now retired and living in Sun City, Arizona—grinned as he recalled his own experience.

"What helped me get the job was the fact that my father, a storekeeper, had bought a delivery truck. He wouldn't let me or anybody else touch it. But I'd sit next to him and watch what he did when he drove. One day, when I was sure he wouldn't be around, I cranked up the truck and did what I'd

Winter bus travel in Minnesota was rugged before the 1920s. But as the Mesaba Transportation Company grew the "stages" became larger, roomier, and more comfortable. By the end of World War I the company operated a fleet of 18 motor coaches. Clifford E. Graves, top right, started as a driver and rose to an executive position.

seen him do a hundred times. Then I drove from our door to the corner. There I put it into reverse and backed up to our place. Everything went without a hitch. When I applied for a bus driver's job I could honestly say I had driven a truck. Luckily, they didn't hire me immediately. That gave me a chance to do some practicing, this time with my father's knowledge and help. By the time Wickman did take me on I could drive pretty well.

"But if I'd had any sense," Graves added, "I'd have quit the day they put me on the ninety-mile run from Hibbing to Duluth—a terrible stretch of road that became absolutely impassable in the kind of blizzards we'd get. Just to show you what the early drivers had to contend with, one day I ran into a snowbank that left my bus stalled. Couldn't back up or move ahead. I had five passengers who'd probably have frozen to death if they had to stay in that bus. But I knew we were only a quarter mile or so from a farm, so I got them all out of the bus, and we hunched against the wind-driven snow. I got them to the farm all right, and then I did a pretty dumb thing. I started walking to Duluth for help, and Duluth was twenty-five miles away.

"I repeat, it was a crazy thing to do. I didn't even have boots—just ordinary shoes. And every step made my legs sink deep into the snow. Don't ask how I made it to Duluth. All I know is it took maybe fifteen-sixteen hours, and I was fit to collapse when I finally got to a place where I could ask that a snowplow be sent to rescue those five passengers at the farm and to get my bus running again. I went back with the plow, and that was when I really understood that driving a bus was one of the most responsible jobs in the world. And in those days we worked for two-and-one-half cents a mile!"

Despite its toughness, to be one of the early drivers like Clifford Graves and S. R. Sundstrom had unique long-term advantages. As the company grew it needed experienced people to supervise new areas of operation. Who was better qualified than those who had learned all there was to know from the start? It was men like Graves, Sundstrom, and a few others

HIBBING - DULUTH fare 2 75

By the 1920s drivers were wearing uniforms, the line had expanded its routes, raised its prices, and the buses were commodious.

who bolstered the company's expansion by lending it their experience. Through the years they rose to the executive posts—in fact, to the presidencies of affiliated lines.

E. C. Eckstrom, another early figure in the Wickman venture, had founded a bus line that ran out of Chicago to various towns in Michigan. He, too, had visions of future expansion, and these made him a welcome partner of Wickman, Caesar, and Bogan. Their new coalition was renamed the Northland Transportation Company, with lines running through Michigan, Wisconsin, Minnesota, and prodding ever-deeper into surrounding regions. Its plans were extensive.

But other lines were in trouble. Too many were competing among themselves. In an abortive effort to reduce costs they were curtailing services. Between 1926 and 1930 the total number of their coaches throughout the nation dropped from 22,800 to 14,090. A proportionate number of drivers and maintenance men lost their jobs. The industry seemed to be struggling to survive.

Still, there was a saving grace. Something unexpected was happening in the United States.

Wickman, Bogan, and Caesar held many a concerned conference over the news. According to all accounts, railroads were claiming that buses were sapping passengers away from their lines. To cope with the loss (or to adapt to it) one railroad, the New York, New Haven, and Hartford, was buying its competition. Each bus line it acquired thereupon became a "feeder" to the railroad. The practice was spreading to other railroads as far as the Missouri Pacific on the West Coast. It was bound soon to reach Duluth.

It did. On an historic day in 1928 Wickman and his associates were visited by Ralph Budd, president of the Great Northern Railroad. Budd, accompanied by other officers of his company and its attorneys, announced they were ready to buy all the local lines of the Northland Transportation Company.

Wickman's group did not leap at the proposal. They, who had themselves been buying bus routes, were being asked to sell—an odd, almost disconcerting, reversal. How could their Northland Transportation be benefited by such a move?

Budd had the answers, in terms of dollars and further expansion. The accord finally reached ceded 80 percent of Northland Transportation's stock to the railroad, but it did not abridge Northland's right to expand independently elsewhere. The pact brought Wickman's company the substantial sum of $240,000.

With this fresh capital the excited men from Hibbing were ready to expand on a hitherto unthinkable scale.

3

At the outset one important thing was in their favor. With World War I no longer absorbing the country's energy and production, and President Hoover optimistically proclaiming a state of "normalcy," the country could concentrate on peacetime needs. Among these were the needs of long-neglected roads. Now they were being improved with almost feverish speed. Historian Henry Bamford Parkes wrote, "Federal and state governments cooperated by spending vast sums, in excess of $1,000,000,000 a year, on hard-surfaced highways."

These had to be built if only to keep pace with the millions of cars Ford, General Motors, Chrysler, and others were producing. One Washington journalist said, "The automobile is the greatest road builder in history."

For the time—at least until the next American disaster—people could again think of pleasures. No longer were they singing "Over There" and "There's A Long, Long Trail A-Winding." Now it was "Tea For Two" and "California, Here I Come!" In their happier spirits Americans were traveling to see their country, marveling at its scenic wonders. Wickman's group, backed by the $240,000 received from the Great Northern Railroad, went to work with renewed vigor.

Their goal was to gather as many bus lines as possible into a cohesive system that would encompass a large part of the country, perhaps all of it. In the case of these men, so vast an objective was regarded as fantastic, even ridiculous. The *Saturday Evening Post* said, "None of the Mesaba group could be called wise in geography. Wickman had only the scantiest acquaintance with the shape and extent of the United States.

None of the group had finished more than high school, and some fell short of that."

But what if their dreams did exceed their knowledge? Men with knowledge lacked their dreams.

Besides, if ignorance of geography did exist in the formative years of the project, it was not a permanent condition. Like Caesar, Wickman and Bogan were insatiable readers. They read every book and every magazine article of importance that came their way. "These were self-educated men in the fullest sense of the term," said Ralph Bogan, Jr., with pardonable pride. "They became as knowledgeable as any men I ever met. What's more, they developed a talent for picking the right people to work with them—people with the ability, the education, and the determination to help reach company goals."

Another thing they developed was the self-confidence to approach any banker in the country, whether in Minneapolis, Chicago, San Francisco, or New York, with a request for a sizable loan. What had once, in Hibbing, been hesitation in seeking even a small amount to buy one extra car became the courage to ask for millions.

"As their business grew they simply didn't know the meaning of timidity," Ralph Bogan's son added. "I believe that if they had needed help from the President of the United States they would have found a way to walk right into the Oval Office for a man-to-man talk. And if you ask me where that kind of courage came from, my guess is that it originated in the Mesaba iron mines where a man had to show the courage to face up to every other man in the world."

At the start it may well have been their very haziness of geography that made the imagination of Wickman's group so daring that they confidently set out to develop a transportation pattern that would reach from border to border and coast to coast.

One may raise skeptical brows at the report that in their zeal they actually acquired sixty bus lines in less than six weeks.

Yet it was true. Closer inquiry discloses the fact that, according to law, anyone with even two vehicles running from one town to another could call his venture "an intercity line." On that basis, to quote federal figures, "more than 6,500 intercity bus companies existed in the United States." Most of them, of course, were small, independent wildcatters.

Could they be laughed off as unimportant because of their size? Not at all. The newly formed National Motor Bus Association pointed out: "A diminutive bus line can often be found holding the exclusive right on an arterial highway, and no plea that bigger and better service is needed can take it away. The franchise has to be bought if it is to go to a new owner; and thus it tends to be a property far surpassing in value the physical equipment that a small line may possess. In its early days what is now Greyhound frequently won franchises without great cost. In the latter days one of them might have cost as much as $100,000."

The West Coast Pioneer Stages line in 1923. The Company eventually merged with Wickman's expanding corporation.

(For tax purposes the overvaluation of such purchases was reported as payment for intangible property. This was a legal tax deduction until the late 1930s. Then the Interstate Commerce Commission (ICC) refused to recognize intangible property as a valid claim. It ceased to be tax-deductible. How costly this change was is best illustrated by the fact that in a single year, 1941, Greyhound had to write off $1,074,160 of its investment in intangible property.)

Pragmatically, the targets of Wickman's group were the larger companies. As they were assimilated he must have been disturbed by the appearance of many of their drivers. "We usually wore our worst clothes to work," one of them admitted. Wickman brought an air of distinction to the operation by having all drivers furnished with handsome, military-type uniforms that included Sam Browne belts and leather puttees. Now everybody could recognize the company's drivers— though the men had to pay thirty-five dollars for their outfits.

As the campaign for acquisitions continued, reports of the manner in which proposals for mergers were made were generally the same:

> This man Wickman would come to our town—or maybe it would be Caesar or Bogan or Eckstrom—and we'd sit down to talk. They had written or telephoned us in advance, so we knew what they wanted. They said we could continue to run our business locally even after we'd merged with them. The idea was that travelers could ride across the country from state to state on a single ticket, and we'd get our share of the total business. What it amounted to was that we'd become part of a big, interlocking system.

Was this considered an attractive offer?

> For most of us, absolutely yes. Why not? It didn't take anything away from our local business. If anything, it added to our income. Besides, the parent company would take on the cost of bus maintenance, garages, advertising, wages, insurance, and the rest, including taxes and the cost of new buses. This last could be quite an item as we grew and found it necessary to replace old vehicles. General Motors was

Wickman brought dash to his bus service by ordering military type uniforms for his drivers, including jaunty hats. Sam Browne belts, and leather puttees.

charging $13,500 for its buses at the time. It seems Ralph Bogan went to Detroit and made a deal to buy GM buses for the next few years at a price of $10,000 each. That was an immediate saving of $3,500 on every new coach.

Wickman and his people also saved a considerable amount of money on deals with the Goodyear and Firestone tire people. They'd rent tires instead of buying them. They'd pay a few mills per mile, and the original agreement was that they could exchange every old set for new tires at the end of 25,000 miles. That was really a tremendous achievement. It made it unnecessary for the company to invest heavily in maintaining its own inventory of tires.

Bogan or Caesar also made a price deal for gasoline with Texaco and Standard Oil. When they offered us all that, plus money or stock in exchange for joining them, there weren't many of us, believe me, who could turn away. The deal made so much sense that you just couldn't say no. But the most important thing, I'd say, was the enthusiasm of the men who talked to us. That was catching.

And, for a time, it was incredibly successful. For a time.

•   •   •   •   •

The Northland Transportation Company was not the only one trying to establish a far-reaching, interlocking bus system. Among their most successful early competitors were two on the West Coast, Charles Wren's Pickwick System and a dynamic group headed by Wesley Elgin (Buck) Travis and his accountant, Frederick W. Ackerman of San Francisco.

Travis and Ackerman had organized a network of lines that was already reaching far across the nation. In order to demonstrate the unity of their system they had persuaded all its member lines to copy the yellow color of their buses. As a result they called their project the Pioneer Yelloway System.

In some ways early Yelloway buses actually outdid Wickman's. In 1927 one of theirs, with Travis aboard, was the first to make a coast-to-coast trip. It sped from San Francisco to New York in five days and fourteen hours, a journey terminated with a procession on Broadway in New York, with appropriate speeches, flag waving, and the clicking of newspaper cameras. Not that it was as earthshaking an event as Charles Lindbergh's transoceanic flight shortly thereafter, but nevertheless Yelloway won its share of national publicity.

Meanwhile Wickman continued to be extremely busy in Minnesota, while Bogan, Caesar, and Eckstrom traveled elsewhere, all seeking ways to extend their system.

Through 1928 and into 1929 they added to their network a number of the larger firms that had already adopted the "Greyhound" label for their vehicles. Among them were the

The Northland Transportation Company absorbed several other lines in the late 1920s to become the Greyhound Corporation.

Northland Greyhound Lines, Southland Greyhound Lines, Pickwick-Greyhound Lines, and the Richmond Greyhound Corporation.

At least two of these presented problems in pride. Wickman might go to California with a merger plan; but which corporate name would survive to indicate top management? Would Greyhound absorb Pickwick, or would Pickwick annex Greyhound? Negotiations were sometimes difficult, for strong men do not easily yield prestige. In the end the two companies met in St. Louis, reaching an agreement that Pickwick Lines announced as "making 1928 the big year in motor coach industry." Pickwick became part of Greyhound, and Wickman was able to tell his stockholders, "We now serve practically every city of importance in the territory between Chicago and St. Louis and New York."

So a Hibbing dream was being realized. But nobody in Hibbing would have foreseen that within fifteen years Wickman would be saying, "Our gross earnings increased from $5,741,-103 in 1928 to $7,610,216 in 1929." The increase was stimulated, he added, by a nationwide advertising campaign, in magazines and on radio, by the company's first advertising agency, Beaumont and Hohman of Chicago.

The radio broadcasts in particular were describing the beauty of scenic and historic spots on the Greyhound trail. Usually the commercials came between the musical numbers of the Ozark Ramblers, the Music Box, the Dream Boat Orchestra, the Columbia Grenadiers, and other popular dispensers of song.

One result of acquiring so many affiliates that bore the Greyhound name was that the parent organization changed its own name in 1930 to The Greyhound Corporation. This was more sensible than altering the names of the other companies to indicate their unification. The Greyhound Corporation it has remained ever since.

It was in the course of these activities that the company decided to move its headquarters from Duluth to Chicago. This alarmed some of the bus drivers. A delegation of them crowded into Wickman's office. "Our homes are here," they protested. "Our children go to school here. Are we supposed to uproot everything and go to Chicago to keep our jobs?"

Wickman, facing his first labor problem, rose from his desk and told them flatly that they didn't know what they were talking about. "None of you is being asked to move," he said. "You'll go right on doing your job here. Your bus line will operate where it has always operated. What's moving to Chicago is headquarters—supervisory management only. Now go back to work and quit worrying."

This was in effect laying the foundation of Greyhound staff operations. Chicago was the logical, centralized location from which to manage ever-widening interstate holdings.

There Carl Eric Wickman, well dressed, seated at an impressive presidential desk, could smile over recollections of driving people from Hibbing to Alice, through freezing gales, for fifteen cents a ride. That had been only fifteen years ago. Now a number of publications were describing his career as "a Horatio Alger rise from jitney to giant."

Despite his increasing eminence in the industrial world, some things about him never changed. In meetings he remained the rough, tough product of the Mesaba iron mines. So, for that matter, did Ralph Bogan.

Clifford Graves, himself a muscular, six-foot-four-inch figure, has memories of the day he and Bogan were in a hotel room, awaiting a meeting scheduled for the following morning. They had enjoyed a drink or two when Bogan critically appraised Graves' big figure. "You know, Cliff," he said, "big as you are, I think I could take you in a fight."

"I doubt it," Graves said.

"Let's give it a go and see," Bogan suggested. "But no hitting in the face."

Without awaiting a reply he rose and pushed back bed, chairs, and tables to make room for the bout. Then he rolled up his shirt-sleeves.

"Ready?"

Graves remembers the fight. They pounded each other. They sweated and groaned and gasped for breath. The sounds of combat must have been heard outside the room. Soon there were bangings on the locked door and cries of "What's going on in there? Open up!"

They gave the shouts no attention. The fight continued until Ralph Bogan, recoiling from a terrific blow to the chest, staggered back and fell across the bed. There he lay gasping, staring up in surprise at Clifford Graves. When at last he was able to rise, panting, Bogan conceded defeat with a handshake.

"You're a lot better than I thought, Cliff," he said. "You're okay."

The fight in no way affected their friendship. An amicable

bout, it was forgotten as easily as it began.

"Typical of life among friends in old Hibbing," Graves said with a shrug. "A tough bunch."

Tough indeed. One of their newest employees, Frank L. Nageotte who could write in shorthand, was often called in to take notes at executive sessions. This was done on the theory that feminine ears were too chaste and delicate to be assaulted by some of the blistering language evoked from both Wickman and Ralph Bogan in business arguments.

As more and more lines, large and small, joined the Greyhound network, only one purchase in 1929 did not add to the fleet of buses. This occurred when Bogan, returning from a trip to California, reported that a moving van firm in San Francisco was for sale.

"As long as we're operating buses from city to city," he reasoned, "why not moving vans? It's a natural addition to intercity transportation. And maybe some of our old buses can be converted to vans instead of being scrapped and wasted. I hear about 14 million families move every year. Not a bad market."

It all sounded logical. The purchase was made, and the company organized Greyhound Van Lines, only to discover the penalty for inadequate research and study. Household moving, it quickly became evident, was in general a seasonal business. Mid-spring and mid-fall kept the vans busy. At other times they were apt to stand idle day after day. It took several years of patience, widespread advertising, and skillful salesmanship to lift the van venture out of the loss columns.

The most startling of acquisitions during the late 1920s, however, was the great Yelloway system itself. To buy it with all its far-flung routes cost The Greyhound Corporation a whopping $6.4 million. The purchase commanded headlines on every financial page. Expensive as it was, it brought into the company the experience and executive skills of W. E. Travis and Frederick Ackerman.

Where did so many millions of dollars come from?

There were several sources. First, with some 1,800 Greyhound buses traveling over the country's highways, earnings had been greater than ever. Second, every new acquisition created additional leverage as it increased corporate assets; and this in turn increased lines of credit.

The largest source of capital, however, came into being when a Minneapolis investment banker, Glenn Wood Traer of Lane, Piper, and Jaffray, joined The Greyhound Corporation. A plump, round-faced man, Traer had "the innocent smile of a happy, well-fed monk." Behind that expression lay the keen, imaginative brain of a successful financier.

Traer had previously worked with the Minneapolis bus line that had joined the Wickman network. There he had functioned closely with its auditor, Adam P. Sledz, who had developed "the most accurate and efficient accounting system to be found in any bus line operation." (In fact, on a trip to Minneapolis Wickman was so impressed by the accuracy and reliability of the Sledz records that he asked Sledz to apply his methods to the entire spectrum of Greyhound financial operations. It was the beginning of an association that eventually made Sledz comptroller of The Greyhound Corporation.)

Under Traer's financial direction, the company issued stocks whose principal purchasers were, surprisingly, the company's arch rivals in the business of transportation—the railroads. These included the Southern Pacific, the Pennsylvania, and the New York Central. It was a situation that induced odd questions among financial observers. Were the railroads resorting to the old maxim, "If you can't beat 'em, buy 'em"? Or was this symptomatic of future tight alliances?

In either case, the railroads were investing in bus lines nearest their tracks. They created separate corporations as the nominal owners of bus line securities. This was the simplest way of avoiding the charge that the railroads were tending to monopolize all methods of travel.

The remarkable thing was that Traer was actually able to sell Greyhound stocks. One brokerage firm, Wellington & Company, later told its customers that in 1928:

> The intercity bus business lacked useful background information and statistics. Consequently the few securities of its companies that were available for investment were considered speculative and unseasoned. And because capital entry requirements were low, the industry was characterized by intense competition among many small companies. Also, profits were low and threatened by rising costs.

Despite all such negative factors, Glenn Traer, young, intelligent, and creative, found a way of lending bus securities an aura of importance. He established a Minneapolis company called Automotive Investments. Its purpose was to deal exclusively in motor transport stocks, a fact which in itself tended to lend dignity and strength to such securities.

Soon others besides the railroads began buying them. On Wall Street the Goldman Sachs Trading Corporation invested $2.5 million in the company's securities. It was an eloquent show of faith in Greyhound's future. It was also a show of respect for the considerable cash flow generated by bus fares.

"Wickman's baby," as some were calling it, indeed appeared to be on its way to becoming the strongest intercity bus system in the world. With sublime confidence its subdivisions were ordering hundreds of new coaches and scrapping many of the old. In Chicago, Detroit, and elsewhere they were investing heavily in new garages and maintenance equipment. On all levels the company seemed destined to enjoy prosperous years.

And then it suffered a staggering setback. It was something it could neither avoid nor control—the nation's economic crash of 1929.

4

With banks closing in city after city, with business failures mounting into the thousands, Greyhound could not remain immune to the country's catastrophe. Its revenues were suddenly slashed by more than 50 percent.

Men like Wickman, Caesar, and Bogan, in spite of having risen from bus drivers to executives, still had scant experience outside the field of transportation. Until now their vigor and determination had borne them to success after success. Now, abruptly, vigor and determination were of little use in coping with a national panic. Even Glenn Traer, with all his financial wit and expertise, and Frederick Ackerman, with his accounting background, knew of no way to avoid the day-after-day losses of income. How could you persuade a terrified public to spend its money on bus fares?

There were office meetings that actually seethed. In one officer's words, "Everybody was angry. We all felt we'd been victimized by circumstances we had not brought about, and no amount of fury or profanity could change them."

Even before this crisis a newspaper columnist wrote, "Wickman's financial problems had been fairly simple. He bought new buses and new lines as funds became available out of earnings, and he had not concerned himself with the intricacies of corporate finance." Now, suddenly, he was plunged into a financial predicament that threatened the very existence of the company. He was stunned.

By this time the Goldman Sachs Trading Corporation was the principal owner of Greyhound securities. It held 70,000 shares of common stock, 18,000 shares of participating pre-ferred, and 1,200 shares of preferred. It probably considered itself lucky when, by previous arrangement, its holdings were purchased by the Atlas Corporation in a transaction that in-cluded a portfolio of many other securities.

Atlas, however, did not feel lucky. Greyhound shares were at their lowest. Its common stock had never yet paid a divi-dend for the simple reason that earnings, like borrowings, had been used to acquire additional bus lines. In good times share-holders had not complained about this; their company was steadily growing. But now one Atlas executive referred to his Greyhound holding as "a bitch." And Atlas rushed one of its financial experts, Mathew Robinson, to Chicago to find some way of rescuing Greyhound from its mess.

So, in emergency meetings, there were critical problems to solve. To help solve them, Mathew Robinson was given a seat on the board of directors in 1930. Appraising the others as they gathered around their conference table, he must have re-alized that, in spite of all their troubles, these men represented some of the best brains in the bus industry: Wickman, Caesar, Bogan, Traer, Travis, and Ackerman. One could not ask for a finer array of experience, judgment, and success. Yet despite them the Greyhound company was in serious straits.

The immediate crisis was inability to meet current obliga-tions. In the headlong speed of building their network these men had overextended their credit as well as their optimism. "Their financing," the *Wall Street Journal* said, "had stood on the assumption that boom times were normal times."

As one example of overconfidence, in 1928 there had been a $2.5 million sale of Greyhound one-year notes. When these came due in 1929 they could not be honored. Instead they were refunded by a $4 million issue of three-year notes. In the continuing national frenzy following the 1929 crash it soon became clear that even this second debt would not be paid on time. Nor were the holders of 8 percent preferred stock being sent their dividends. There simply wasn't enough cash on hand. By 1930 the company's net income dropped to $296,794. And according to the *Saturday Evening Post,* "Any creditor could have thrown the company into bankruptcy."

In a desperate attempt to extricate Atlas from all this, Mathew Robinson sat down with Glenn Traer to analyze figures. Starting with basics, they calculated the cost of operating one bus for a single day's run of 250 miles. They computed expenditures for wages, maintenance, gasoline, insurance, taxes, depreciation, and every other item. Next they studied the amount of fares collected on a typical 250-mile run. Since not every passenger traveled the entire daily distance—the average rider went eighty miles—and since a number of seats were usually empty, Robinson reached an appalling conclusion that Traer could not deny.

The net profit from one complete bus run on a normal day was only $4.50!

Robinson stared at Traer in dismay. How could a company hope to survive on so slim a profit margin?

"If we were operating only one bus, it would be hopeless," Traer acknowledged. "But this year we have 1,800 buses on the roads every day. Multiply $4.50 by 1,800 and you have a daily profit of $8,100. Then multiply that by 365 days a year, and you'll find our buses net the company an annual profit of $2,956,500. We're obviously not operating at an overall loss."

Viewing things that way, Robinson was mollified. He had to concede that the situation was not as hopeless as it had seemed. Clearly, Greyhound, with profits of almost $3 million a year, was worth saving. So he and Traer, working together, devised a plan for rescuing the company from its morass of problems.

It comprised a bewildering series of emergency actions. First, the parent corporation sold its partially owned subsidiaries to its wholly owned affiliates. On the parent corporation's books such sales increased the assets (though there was no increased income from fares). With these preliminary arrangements completed, shareholders were informed that "the wholly owned bus affiliates of The Greyhound Corporation now consist of only three comparatively small companies: Illinois Greyhound Lines, Central Greyhound Lines, and Southeastern Greyhound Lines."

Nonetheless, through Greyhound Management Company—the overall staff organization—Wickman's colleagues within the parent company continued to manage all its affiliates.

Traer's most startling coup was the agreement he negotiated after rushing to Detroit to talk to General Motors. There is no record of the persuasive eloquence he used; it must have been historic. For General Motors (no doubt to preserve the life of one of its major bus customers) assumed $1 million of Greyhound's indebtedness, a sum to be repaid on a long-term basis.

Not that this ended all of the corporation's financial difficulties. There were still the claims of preferred stockholders to be satisfied. How this was accomplished was reported by a business commentator in ironic terms just short of being malicious:

> The holders of the participating preferred got a letter which said to them in effect: "If you know what's good for you, you will exchange each share of your stock, and claims on all accrued dividends, for five shares of the common stock." And they said the same thing to holders of the old common, except that they gave them the privilege of trading in twenty shares of their old common for one share of the new, par value $5. The stockholders saw the inevitable; they approved the change.

And so, the column concluded, "Greyhound became a much healthier animal."

Healthier, perhaps, but not altogether cured. Financial difficulties were bound to persist as long as the nation's economic illness continued.

How trying these few years were could be measured not only in the decline in revenues but also in the number of passenger miles traveled. (A passenger mile is, in industry parlance, the distance covered in carrying one person one mile. If a bus contains forty passengers, a single mile driven will account for forty passenger miles.) On this basis of calculation all of the nation's intercity buses, including Greyhound's, covered 7.1 billion passenger miles in 1930. For the following two years the figure dropped to 6.3 billion.

The best way to counteract such bad times, apart from curtailing services on many routes, was through greater emphasis on advertising. Wickman's many consultations with advertising experts centered on one salient point: "The basic thing Greyhound has to sell is travel. Remember that—travel, travel, travel!"

The agency did remember. In 1931 national magazines carried beautifully illustrated pages that urged:

> While you are planning a spring or summer outing, make this practical test: Take the next business or weekend trip by Greyhound bus. Mark the savings in dollars—the unusual comfort—the thrill of new scenes that unfold only along the great highways. Then you'll decide on Greyhound for the vacation trip too! These blue and white coaches reach every desirable playground in this nation. . . . National Parks, North Woods, Great Lakes, Pacific Coast, the Rockies, Atlantic beaches.
>
> The Greyhound agent in your city will gladly give you full information about vacation trips, low fares, frequent schedules, and our many stopover privileges.
>
> There is no better way to see America than the Greyhound way.
>
> Write the nearest Greyhound office for a Scenic Highway folder and any desired information.

Results, unfortunately, were hardly spectacular. The fundamental trouble was that neither advertising, managerial skills, nor optimism could counteract the effects of the Depression. In the tortuous months preceding the Roosevelt "bank holiday" all of American industry was struggling to survive. And Greyhound took a step that apparently had occurred to no other firm.

Easter
Travel savings

MAKE the Easter trip by Greyhound Bus. Spring-time highways invite you to go this modern way —to find more pleasure in each mile of budding country-side, while saving dollars for the new Easter ward-robe. Deep-cushioned reclining chairs relax and rest you. Many daily schedules save hours for Easter enjoy-ment. One high standard of courtesy and service—to the next town or across the continent.

Dollars Ahead When You Go Greyhound!

DETROIT	$ 3.50	ST. LOUIS	$ 12.00
CHICAGO	8.00	DENVER	29.50
PITTSBURGH	3.25	LOS ANGELES	46.70
BUFFALO	4.50	OMAHA	19.00
ERIE	2.75	JACKSONVILLE	24.50
NEW YORK	12.50	NEW ORLEANS	27.00
PHILADELPHIA	10.50	FLINT, MICH.	5.50
WASHINGTON, D. C.	10.25	ROCHESTER	6.50
ALBANY	12.00	SCRANTON	9.50
ATLANTA	17.50	SYRACUSE	8.75
BOSTON	14.50	TORONTO	7.40

UNION MOTOR COACH TERMINAL
2133 E. 9th Street
Phone: MAin 8737

Other Offices: W. Third and Superior—1378 Sloan Avenue—
10516 Euclid—5310 Euclid—1903 E. Ninth Street

GREYHOUND
Lines

A 1931 advertisement.

In Minneapolis Adam Sledz was serving as auditor for the entire Greyhound organization. He experienced what he called "a sixth sense premonition" of what would happen when Franklin Roosevelt took office in Washington.

"The possibility of his closing all banks for a period struck me as very likely" he said, recalling those fateful days as he gazed out of the sixty-ninth-floor window of his Chicago apartment. "If the banks did close we'd all be financially stymied. There would be no way of paying current salaries to our employees. So I sent a telegram to the office of every Greyhound line across the United States. I instructed them all to deposit no funds in their banks. Instead, I asked them to go to their post offices and use the money on hand to buy money orders. These money orders were to be mailed to us at corporate headquarters. When they arrived we kept them uncashed.

"Well, the banks were closed during Roosevelt's 'bank holiday.' And the normal channels for paying our employees were blocked. So we took our money orders to the post office and used them to buy other money orders for the payment of wages. These were mailed to our employees. They had no problem in cashing them at their own post office windows. Thus the bank holiday did not deprive our people of their salaries."

Depression or not, Wickman and his associates could not be dissuaded from the effort to encompass the entire United States with their network. Their newest target was the Atlantic Greyhound Lines.

Based in the south, it had grown under the strong leadership of Arthur M. Hill to blanket the South Atlantic states. This was a geographic area Wickman's forces still had to enter. Wickman went to work. He traveled south to see Hill.

He did not have an easy time. Arthur Hill was not an easy man to buy, nor was he disposed to give up control of what he had so painstakingly built. Even when he finally saw the advantage of joining a nationwide organization, he demanded

The late 1920s and early 30s saw a variety of innovations in motor coach styles and accommodations including double deckers and a bus with sleeping accommodations on the transcontinental line, above.

As the bus lines expanded in the 1930s the style and comfort of the coaches attracted growing numbers of passengers.

so high a price for his business—a price to be paid largely in stocks—that the 1932 culmination of the deal made him one of The Greyhound Corporation's largest individual shareholders. It also won him a seat on the board of directors. The general consensus of press reports was that Greyhound was lucky to get him.

In many ways that was true. In his own right Arthur Hill was an outstanding figure in the world of bus transportation. Elected president of the National Association of Motor Bus Operators, which he had helped to organize, he had become the official Washington spokesman for the industry. His lobbying position was now considerably strengthened by his affiliation with Wickman's organization. When he appeared before a Congressional committee, he could speak for virtually every part of the nation.

"It would be hard to imagine two men more dissimilar in personality and outlook than Hill and Wickman," many who knew them have said. "Hill, the smooth, handsome, soft-spoken Southern gentleman; Wickman, the hard-driving Minnesota Swede. Culturally they were on different levels. They were bound to clash. But in one thing they were united—the need to strengthen the position of bus travel in the United States."

Despite all their efforts, including the well-illustrated and enticing advertising campaigns, bus receipts remained far below their pre-1929 levels, until, almost miraculously, two unrelated and wholly unexpected events came to the company's rescue. One, of all things, was a 1934 motion picture. Starring Clark Gable and Claudette Colbert, *It Happened One Night* romanticized bus travel by having some of the action occur on a Greyhound bus. Immediately Greyhound's business increased. It was a boon nobody had anticipated. Even Arthur Hill, the only director who had opposed lending the motion picture producers a bus, now felt it had been a good idea. He shook Wickman's hand as if to say, "In this case your judgment was better than mine."

In 1933 Greyhound brought Americans to the Chicago World's Fair and gave them tours of the fairgrounds (above). The next year a Hollywood movie, It Happened One Night, starring Clark Gable and Claudette Colbert (below) gave the depression-burdened Greyhound Company a welcome boost.

Yet more important for Greyhound's emergence from financial doldrums was a deal Wickman and his associates were able to make with the Chicago Century of Progress Exposition of 1933. They won the exclusive right for sixty Greyhound buses to provide transportation within the fairgrounds. If there were competing bids, no other line could match the kind of service Greyhound was geared to offer. Wickman promptly organized World's Fair Greyhound Lines to handle the project.

Then came a masterstroke. John B. Walker, who had long been advertising manager for several of the corporation's affiliates, hurried into Wickman's office with a plan so reckless, so optimistic, so undreamed of by anybody else, that it promptly won the support of reckless, optimistic dreamers like Wickman and Bogan and Caesar.

What Walker proposed, despite its financial hazards, was to reserve 2,000 hotel rooms for the duration of the fair.

Expensive? Of course. Risky? Certainly. But the outcome was that The Greyhound Corporation could advertise all-expense bus tours to the Chicago Fair from every state in the Union. Together with transportation it could provide admission to the fair and guaranteed hotel rooms at a time when hotel rooms were almost impossible to reserve.

Thereafter transportation within the fair netted Greyhound over $500,000; transportation to the fair brought in millions.

One can understand why the rejuvenated directors refused to concede that American prosperity had been permanently crippled. With new enthusiasm they continued the quest for additional lines. John Maynard Keynes might be saying, "The last depression of this kind was called The Dark Ages and it lasted four hundred years." President Franklin D. Roosevelt might declare a "holiday" that closed all American banks. When Wickman or any other Greyhound official switched on a radio, the song they might most frequently hear was "Brother, Can You Spare A Dime?" Yes, times in general were bad. But nothing dissuaded the company from seeking new acquisitions.

Before the nation's dark days ended, the Greyhound roster of affiliates and subsidiaries included Blue Goose Lines, Sunny South Lines, Royal Rapid Lines, Cardinal Stages, Purple Swan Lines, Great Lakes Stages—all in addition to the major affiliates. The nation might still be struggling to rise out of the depths, but Greyhound buses, like the mighty Mississippi, just kept rolling along.

Note:

In 1933 The Greyhound Corporation included fourteen major companies that controlled its various subsidiaries. Some were completely owned by the parent corporation; others were affiliates. They were:

COMPLETELY OWNED

1. Central Greyhound Lines
2. Illinois Greyhound Lines
3. Eastern Greyhound Lines (New England)

AFFILIATED COMPANIES

4. Pennsylvania Greyhound Lines
5. Eastern Greyhound (Delaware)
6. Pacific Greyhound Lines
7. Northland Greyhound Lines
8. Richmond Greyhound Lines
9. Dixie Greyhound Lines
10. Atlantic Greyhound Lines
11. Capitol Greyhound Lines
12. Teche Lines
13. Southland Greyhound Lines
14. Western Greyhound Lines

Note: The last two were being liquidated, their routes transferred to the Southwestern Greyhound Lines.

5

Today the company's magazine, *Go Greyhound,* is distributed to its affiliates throughout the nation. Over the years, however, some of the bus lines published their own periodicals. Pickwick-Greyhound, for one, had its *Highway Log;* and if *Highway Log* did nothing else, it dissolved the tedium of long stretches of duty for its drivers by challenging them to report—or invent—their experiences. Some responded with assertions worthy of Baron Münchhausen. One driver declared that on the way to Des Moines "he came upon one of those muddy places in the road. There he saw a man buried almost head and shoulders in the black ooze. The driver asked the man if he needed help, and the fellow replied, 'No, not unless my horse gives out.' "

Another driver declared that, just outside San Francisco, he saw two hitchhikers. He stopped his bus, talked to them awhile, and on the spot sold them through tickets to Flint, Michigan, three-quarters of the way across the United States.

Yes, the business had its light moments and its times for rejoicing.

Certainly, after the bonanza at the fair, Wickman, Caesar, Bogan, and their colleagues were entitled to relax with a sense of gratification. But circumstances denied them that pleasure. Almost immediately they were forced to contend with another threat to solvency.

This one rose out of a fierce price-cutting war among competing bus lines, most of them owned by independent operators. They wrought chaos throughout the industry. At a busy bus stop, there might be half a dozen touts shouting like circus barkers to attract customers to their vehicles. An unwary traveler might find his luggage seized by an overzealous driver crying, "This way! Bus ready to leave!" As he followed in bewilderment the traveler would pass others who assailed him with "Right here! Cheapest, fastest way to———"

On the New York-to-Boston route operators were slashing the regular four-dollar rate to one dollar and fifty cents. Worse things happened on the New York-to-Chicago route. To remain in contention here Greyhound had "practically to give its tickets away for eight dollars." The nadir of undercutting occurred when one small entrepreneur—probably intent on making customers for the future rather than profits for the present—offered the 900-mile trip from New York-to-Chicago for one dollar. Meanwhile the buses themselves were racing each other on highways in order to be first to reach the next pickup spot.

In the face of keen competition and the hard times of the 1930s, Greyhound upgraded its service.

This kind of ruinous competition, becoming more and more prevalent throughout the country, caused the federal coordinator of transportation, Joseph B. Eastman, to urge that the bus industry, like the railroads, be placed under the "regulatory authority" of the federal government. (Historically, of course, American corporations have opposed the stringent regulation of free enterprise. In this case, however, Greyhound's people heartily approved rule by government as the best way to end the suicidal, price-cutting competition.)

Most major companies did not idly await federal rescue. Acting under the National Industrial Recovery Act, Wickman and Caesar, like a number of others, signed a Code of Fair Competition. Its aim was to restore sanity to the industry. Wickman wrote to shareholders, "The code provides an instrument for self-regulation, and we hope that it will be the means of correcting competitive abuses."

Unfortunately the very people responsible for price cutting did not sign the code. And self-destructive competition continued.

The result was that the government, through the Interstate Commerce Commission (ICC), finally had to intervene to bring order out of chaos. The situation was so new and without precedent that the commission needed indoctrination from experienced bus people. Adam Sledz of Greyhound, called upon to offer counsel, became chairman of the advisory committee that met with the lawmakers. Their objective was, of course, to serve the public interest as well as the bus industry itself. Sledz attended all hearings, helped formulate regulations, and of even greater importance, he prevented the inclusion of some onerous provisions in the final draft of the bill.

Not that his advice prevailed in every instance. When at last the Motor Carrier's Act was adopted in 1935, it contained stipulations both good and bad as far as Greyhound was concerned.

On the good side it provided stringent requirements for the adequacy of service and for passenger safety. It imposed limits on mergers that might lead to monopolies. It demanded uniformity in keeping accounts, the establishment of "just and reasonable rates," and insisted on "certificates of public necessity and convenience" before any new line could operate.

And there was more to the legislation. Admittedly it rescued Greyhound and other established carriers from destruction by unfair, price-cutting competition, but it also created restrictions of a drastic nature. No longer could Greyhound buy another carrier at its own discretion. Henceforth any offer Greyhound might want to make for another company had first to be approved by the ICC. So would the means of raising funds for the purchase.

"Case of having to take the bad with the good," said Adam Sledz.

By this time, in 1936, Carl Eric Wickman was approaching his fiftieth birthday. As robust as ever, still "built like a block of granite," he had nevertheless been softened by circumstance and experience. His language was more moderate, his manner more relaxed. He had learned that personal success carried its obligations, and he had long since begun to send funds to the Swedish village in which he had been born.

To keep pace with other business executives, he joined one golf club near Chicago and another in Florida, where he bought a home. Though he never became an outstanding golfer, one of his efforts won national attention through a Ripley's "Believe It Or Not" cartoon. This showed Wickman's tee shot slicing off toward an "out-of-bounds" sign; but the ball struck a telephone pole that diverted it to another telephone pole. This second hit again diverted its course, and the ball dropped onto the green. Howard H. Morgan, then general manager of the Pickwick-Greyhound Lines, who was playing with Wickman, asserted that the cartoon was accurate in every detail.

"He might have been a genius in building a bus system," another golf partner said, "but a golfer he was not."

After the company's annual report for 1935 was issued, rep-

Now a successful American business executive, the former immigrant miner Carl Eric Wickman took his wife to his homeland Sweden in style in the 1930s.

resentatives of the *Wall Street Journal, Barron's,* and other financial publications came to interview Wickman. He sat behind his enormous polished desk, facing reporters. Every year he indoctrinated himself for these sessions. This year, as always, he had his facts and figures ready. The questions, if not his answers, were fairly routine:

Can you tell us if and to what extent Greyhound's condition improved last year?

In 1935 we were operating 1,726 buses and running them over 46,249 miles of route. We employed 6,364 people. Our net profit was $7,949,799 as compared with $6,055,648 the previous year. So, all things considered, I'd say there was satisfactory improvement.

Did the passage of the Motor Carrier Act change the corporation's internal organization?

To some extent, yes. Until now our parent company, The Greyhound Corporation, did not engage directly, in its own right, in interstate bus operation. We left that to our affiliates. But since the ICC wants to deal only with operating companies, we've made arrangements to take over the operations of our Eastern Greyhound Lines.

Is that the only line you will be operating directly from staff headquarters?

Yes. We'd like to do it throughout our entire system, but we are stopped by the laws of states which require bus franchises to be granted to their own in-state operators only.

Companies like yours have been accused, especially by some railroads, of paying inadequate taxes for the use of the nation's highways. How do you answer that charge?

Very simply. Last year thirteen cents out of every dollar of our revenues went to taxes. Our total tax bill amounted to $4,904,922. I hope you realize that proportionally the bus industry is probably the highest taxpayer of all American industries. We pay taxes to every state our buses cross—this in addition to our federal income taxes. If you divide the total tax figure by the number of our buses, you'll find we pay $2,500 in taxes for every bus on the road.

Why is it that the railroads own so much Greyhound stock?
Because it makes sense. We are all interested in developing coordinated passenger service. Ever since we reached an agreement with the Great Northern Railroad years ago we've been encouraging and inviting railway participation in serving the public. We'd all save money by the use of joint facilities; we'd substitute bus service for unprofitable train runs, and we could bring passengers to railways from distant points. We now enjoy that kind of cooperation—joint ownership—with seven major railroads: the Great Northern, the New York Central, the Pennsylvania, the Richmond, Fredericksburg and Potomac, the St. Louis Southwestern, and the Southern Pacific.

So the interview went, with Carl Eric Wickman, the quiet, self-assured corporate president, handling the press in a calm, self-assured manner. But once the interview ended and the reporters were gone, he would rise—according to those who remember—and deliver himself of some blistering invective. It was his way of easing tension. Under the guise of the self-controlled corporate president there were still vestiges, never to be lost, of the tough Mesaba miner.

•　•　•　•　•

From the very beginning of intercity travel it was obvious that to attract passengers bus transportation had to be recognized as safe. To ensure such recognition as far as possible the Pickwick-Greyhound Lines had, as early as September 1931, retained the services of Marcus Dow, a renowned safety expert. Dow had been president of the National Safety Council as well as a safety consultant to major railroads and to the police department of New York City. Though he began his connection with buses at Pickwick-Greyhound, he was soon serving the entire Greyhound network, working with experienced drivers as well as with applicants for jobs.

"The man was a genius," said Clifford Graves. "He knew everything there was to know about every kind of accident imaginable and its causes. When he told you the things that could happen to you while you sat at the wheel of a bus, you felt chills go up and down your spine. Your palms began to sweat. He was a dynamo as he lectured, striding back and forth while he talked, suddenly pointing an accusing finger at you as if you yourself were responsible—or could be responsible—for everything from a simple sideswipe to a fatal smashup. Believe me, after you'd spent some time listening to Marcus Dow you became a different, more alert, more cautious driver. You appreciated what he meant when he said it was more important to get to your destination safely than to get there on time."

Year after year Dow supervised the company's campaign for safety. No prospective driver could take out a bus before he had been thoroughly indoctrinated in safety rules and before he had served an apprenticeship with an experienced driver. Before long one of the Greyhound affiliates published a description of the kind of driver it did not want. This went beyond safety regulations; it touched on personal conduct, declaring *We Can't Use A Driver Who:*

- Snaps short reply to passengers who want information, or throws baggage around carelessly.

- Delays at rest stops to use slot machine or to kid the waitress, irritating his passengers—then goes whooping down the highway at sixty miles an hour to make up time, scaring passengers speechless.

- Turns head while driving to carry on snappy conversation with girl in nearest seat; takes hands off wheel and eyes off the road to demonstrate what a good driver he is.

- Lights a cigarette and smokes while driving.

- Tells about accidents he has seen—and soon has the whole coach in near panic.

- At the journey's end his passengers swear that they will never again ride another motor coach.

- Can you blame them?

What the company was trying to do, clearly, was to stress

courtesy and common sense, as well as safety, as the concomitants of good driving.

(Since the engagement of Marcus Dow emphasis on safety has never been relaxed. Today every prospective driver must take a six-week course at one of the training stations the company maintains in various parts of the country. Nor is such indoctrination enough. An applicant must be between the ages of twenty-four and thirty-five; he must undergo physical tests that apply to everything from vision to speed of reaction under stress. He must ride buses as an observer. The result of it all has been a safety record that sets The Greyhound Corporation's accident rate far below that of railroads or private cars. Dow actually went so far as to organize a private motorcycle corps that patrolled the roads like policemen to make sure that bus drivers violated no laws or precepts of safety!)

•   •   •   •   •

As expansion through the acquisition of other bus lines progressed, one might have foreseen that bringing so many bus pioneers together—men from every part of the country, men of differing backgrounds and characteristics—would cause some personality clashes. In time they did. But ignoring such possibilities, Wickman's team resolutely drove ahead. The astonishing thing was that at the outset there were so few personality difficulties. Whatever happened during arguments in closed committee rooms or in private discussions was never revealed—even when Fred Ackerman emerged from one such encounter with a blackened eye that kept him at home for three weeks.

To read the names on Greyhound's board of directors in the mid-1930s may well puzzle some modern officers of the corporation. In the cases of I. B. Babcocks of Pontiac, Richard L. Griggs of Duluth, R. F. Pack and D. R. West of Minneapolis, C. S. Sheedy of Los Angeles, C. A. Steen of Chicago, what had they done to earn directorships?

One thing is certain: they were not mere figureheads. Nor were they there to enhance the voting power of Wickman,

Caesar, or anyone else. In most cases they had been the chief executive officers of the bus lines The Greyhound Corporation had acquired. Others were bankers or large holders of Greyhound securities.

This was the board which once decided that the company's chief officers were being underpaid. They devised what was termed *A Plan for Compensation of Management,* approved by shareholders at the company's 1933 annual meeting. The plan provided a 10 percent bonus to management, paid in stock after preferred dividends had been paid and after one dollar per share had been earned on common stock.

At the time the officers might immediately have received 9,000 shares of common stock, except for the sudden decision of the directors to amend their own resolution. That second thought held the plan in abeyance for more than two years, with the result that the ICC eventually studied it and forced a drastic diminution of the amounts to be distributed. In the end Greyhound officers received only 20 percent of the original amount planned for them.

In other words, neither officers nor directors always had their way at Greyhound. Even founders like Wickman, Bogan, and Caesar had to relinquish some degree of authority to the government. "It's the American way" was one editorial comment.

Nor did new acquisitions always support the hopes of the founders. Had some bus lines been absorbed too quickly, too rashly, without sufficient study? Apparently this was so. In one communication to stockholders Wickman was forced to confess, "The two weakest operating companies in the Greyhound system have been Southland Greyhound Lines and Western Greyhound Lines." Both were incurring losses for a reason that should have been discerned before the purchase: both were serving the most thinly populated areas in the Southwest. With too few passengers, both were showing discouraging losses. So was a competing line that had been established by the St. Louis, Southwestern Railway Company.

What should be done? Sell the companies? Who would buy them? Nobody.

At this point Wickman, Caesar, Bogan, and the other directors found a simple way of turning losses into profits. They formed a single new corporation named Southwestern Greyhound Lines. Into it the former three companies were merged in 1933. Thus one budget for the three entities eliminated a triplication of overhead expenses, and the new company showed a modest profit from the start.

In another region a different kind of obstacle impeded profitable operations. This threatened to undermine one of the primary reasons for traveling by bus: its reasonable cost compared with railroad fares. In most cases bus fares were deliberately kept at a price of 10 to 20 percent lower than train fares. It was a satisfactory ratio if it lasted. But if the railroads were to lower their fares, compelling the buses to cut theirs even below their present low rates, such cuts could well be ruinous.

In New Orleans there had long been an agreement between trains and buses to preserve the railroad's fare at two cents a mile. When the railway suddenly announced that it intended to cut fares to one-and-three-quarters cents a mile, the bus line angrily protested. This was more than the abandonment of an agreement. It could mean the destruction of the bus line.

The ICC quickly intervened to study the situation, then issued a verdict in favor of the railroads.

A dismayed yet helpless Greyhound staff found itself owning a bus line that faced an unenviable future. Could it survive a drastic lowering of fares? There was little choice of action except to give it a chance to improve its position. In the present circumstances nobody would want to buy it, and it would be folly to close it at a heavy immediate loss. Luckily the parent organization could now afford to wait for a change. Throughout the United States it owned 1,692 buses that were rolling over 43,000 miles of highways and an encouraging amount of cash was flowing into Greyhound's coffers.

This was not the only instance of such fare regulation by the ICC. In New England, Greyhound's "Eastern District," the commission ordered the railroads to reduce passenger fares to two cents per passenger mile. This instantly compelled Greyhound's fares to be lowered proportionately if it hoped to retain a competitive position. The outcome, as announced by the company, was inescapable:

> Our lower fares attracted more passengers, but not enough of them to prevent a decline in gross revenues. Also, the amount of service had to be increased in order to handle the larger volume of traffic, with a corresponding addition in operating expense. Between reduced revenues and increased expense the net profit of the eastern lines naturally suffered a shrinkage.

In the Eastern District that shrinkage cost the company over 10 percent of previous revenues. But when a reporter for *Collier's* magazine asked Wickman if he was satisfied with Greyhound's general situation, Wickman smiled and jocularly reverted to his old Swedish accent as he said, "Yah. Is okay."

Why not? That year, 1936, his dream of an ever-widening network of bus lines was yielding a profit of $4,239,000. The stockholders received not only dividend checks but also a four for one split of their shares.

The largest beneficiaries of this financial progress, however, were the state and federal treasuries. That year they collected total taxes in excess of $5,623,000.

Success invariably engenders competition, and in the 1930s the Greyhound system was by no means the only one striving to achieve a wider geographic range of service. Its most formidable competitor was an association of some forty independent bus lines operating as National Trailways.

Trailways differed from Greyhound primarily in the way it was organized. Each of its components retained its individual ownership while joining the others in a partnership. As *Fortune* magazine observed:

Getting forty independent bus operators to work together has not been one of the world's easy tasks. Each acts like a king in his own domain and tends to resist coordinating measures. Some Trailways people talk today of transforming their association into a real corporation with central management. Until this is done, Greyhound should have no uneasy moments about Trailways.

Of course, National Trailways became stronger and more cohesive as it spread across the nation, but in its formative years it caused neither Wickman nor any of his group real concern. On the contrary, they felt it was healthy to have at least one powerful competitor in the field. There could be no such thing as a charge of monopolizing the highways.

•   •   •   •   •

When W. C. Will, president of the Greyhound Motor Bus Company—a manufacturing concern—joined the Wickman group, he brought with him his outstanding mechanic, William A. Duvall.

Greyhound's San Francisco maintenance shops in 1941.

As long ago as 1926 Duvall recognized the importance of vigilant maintenance. Though the company had comparatively few buses at the time, those vehicles had to be kept running smoothly. "A bus that's out of order, standing idle at the roadside or in a garage, is a dead heap, a wasted investment, and a terrible advertisement for the company."

When Duvall organized Greyhound's maintenance department, he started with himself as its sole mechanic, but within a year he had added four employees.

Today Greyhound's maintenance crews chuckle over those manpower figures while some 2,000 people keep the thousands of buses running smoothly. Throughout the country they work in eighty-six garages and maintenance centers.

No coach is permitted to move over highways until something goes wrong. The primary task of the mechanics is one of prevention. Any abnormal hum, any suspicion of a click, any flickering of lights has to be immediately investigated and corrected. The reward for such vigilance, in the words of the publication *Bus Ride,* is:

> More than 97 percent of the entire Greyhound fleet is kept running efficiently every day of the year. This is the equivalent of having 168 additional buses on the road full time.

W. A. Duvall, retired now and living in St. Paul, must smile with gratification when he reads the achievements of the maintenance department he founded.

6

On the evening of November 23, 1936, Carl Wickman slammed down his telephone in an explosion of anger. The news that infuriated him was utterly unexpected: "Without notice to the management and without even holding a strike vote, the Brotherhood of Railroad Trainmen has called a strike of Greyhound drivers in the company's Eastern District, the strike to become effective at midnight tomorrow."

Though it was almost midnight, Wickman immediately telephoned Caesar and Bogan as well as Robert Driscoll, the Chicago lawyer who had become the company's general counsel. Using some of his choicest expletives, Wickman ordered an emergency meeting of Greyhound officers for early morning. Since the strike threatened to cripple all operations on the eastern seaboard, from Delaware up through New England, it demanded instant action.

Nobody should have been surprised by the blow. Through the years, in the rush to acquire one bus line after another, concern about future labor relations had not risen to deter the company's efforts toward expansion. Some of the acquired lines had already made agreements with their own unions; others were in the process of negotiating contracts. On the West Coast Greyhound itself had signed pacts with the Amalgamated Association of Street, Electric Railway, and Motor Coach Employees of America. In the East, however, where the company had taken no action, it had been notified by the Labor Relations Board that the Brotherhood of Railroad Trainmen had been designated to represent Greyhound employees.

The unexpected strike interrupted seven weeks of patient negotiations. What most enraged Wickman now was the

The chief executive officers of the Greyhound Corporation and its
affiliates circa 1940.

Orville S. Caesar
Greyhound Corporation

Carl E. Wickman
Greyhound Corporation

G. W. Traer, Jr.
Greyhound Corporation

W. J. Kay
Northland Greyhound

S. R. Sundstrom
Pennsylvania Greyhound

W. E. Travis
Pacific Greyhound

O. W. Townsend
Teche Greyhound

C. E. Graves
Capitol Greyhound

R. W. Budd
Central Greyhound

Frederick Smith
Dixie Greyhound

Manferd Burleigh
Ohio Greyhound

A. M. Hill
Atlantic Greyhound

Guy Huguelet
Southeastern Greyhound

W. R. Woollatt
Canadian Greyhound

P. W. Tibbetts
Southwestern Greyhound

union's demand for a 40 percent increase in wages as well as a closed shop. When a newspaper telephoned Wickman for a comment on this, he angrily declared, "The wages we have been paying our drivers are the highest in our industry, and higher than any wages paid by those bus lines owned by railroads—the very lines with which the Brotherhood has already signed contracts. Our immediate response? We're instituting damage suits against the Brotherhood and its officers."

He need not have been so outraged. A gratifying number of Greyhound drivers refused to go on strike. Despite the jeers and catcalls of others, they climbed into their buses and drove out of their garages; and Greyhound service continued, though on a reduced scale.

Within a week the strike ended. The terms of the new contract brought a sense of relief to Greyhound executives. The Brotherhood of Trainmen accepted a wage increase of one-fourth cent per mile—which was a 7 percent rise instead of 40 percent. For its part, the company thereupon withdrew its damage suit against the union, and Wickman was able to inform stockholders:

> With the exception of this strike and a few minor differences elsewhere, relations between management and employees are and have been cordial. All problems have been approached in a cooperative spirit with a view to improving service and treating all interests fairly.

What the strike had interrupted among other things was the corporation's attempt to consolidate its holdings. Such consolidation had long been needed. The ICC had realized this when it had tried to deal with Greyhound's twenty-nine affiliates. In its discouragement the ICC had urged a plan to merge all Greyhound affiliates into seven major operating divisions. The National Motor Bus Association, too, endorsed the wisdom of such a move, saying, "It does much to eliminate confusion among the many Greyhound companies, and it has its good effects on clearing up Greyhound's corporate structure."

[It also had the effect of driving Wall Street brokers to distraction as they tried to keep pace with Greyhound consolidations. When the National Motor Bus Association published a résumé of the company's 1936 changes in organization, there were those in financial circles who laughed aloud and challenged anyone to understand what Greyhound was doing. As listed by the Association, the changes were these:

1. Atlantic Greyhound Corporation merged into itself the Atlantic Greyhound Lines, East Coast Stages, and Safeway Transit Lines.

2. Capitol Greyhound Lines was permitted to merge the Capitol Greyhound of Virginia into itself.

3. Central Greyhound Lines merged into itself the Central Greyhound Lines of Michigan. Its former parent, Eastern Greyhound Lines of Delaware was also merged.

4. Northland Greyhound Lines merged itself with the Northland Greyhound Lines of Illinois, a subsidiary.

5. The Golden Eagle Southern Lines was brought into the Southwestern Greyhound Lines.

6. Eight companies were merged into Pacific Greyhound Lines. These were Golden Gates Stages, Kern County Transportation Corporation, Peninsula Rapid Transit Company, Union Auto Stages Company, Pacific Auto Stage, Pickwick Stages, Southern Pacific Motor Transportation Company, and Pacific Greyhound Lines.

7. The last of the mergers affected the Pennsylvania Greyhound Lines into which was merged the Buffalo Interurban Bus Lines, Montgomery Bus Company, People's Rapid Transit, Pennsylvania Virginia General Transit Company, and the Pennsylvania General Transit Company.]

An outsider could hardly be blamed for being confused (or amused) by all these ramifications. But within the corporation the consolidations brought cohesion and strength. It was easier and more intelligent for staff officers to deal with seven divisions than with twenty-nine. By 1939 all these changes had been completed and the entire parent organization was running smoothly.

In preparation for the annual stockholders' meeting that year Comptroller W. S. Moore and Assistant Comptroller Adam Sledz placed several documents on the desks of Wickman, Caesar, and Bogan. One paper showed the year's operating revenues, principally from fares and package deliveries, to be a healthy $55,989,765, an increase of 12.4 percent over the preceding year; and net income was $6,562,802.

As always Wickman asked for the latest statistics to describe the company's geographic expansion and the increase of its transportation services. These came on a single sheet provided by Sledz:

Bus miles operated	201,558,145
Buses owned.	2,525
Average miles per bus.	79,632
Miles of routes	54,992
Number of stations	4,750
Number of employees.	9,552

For a company that had not been even a dream twenty-five years earlier, it was an impressive record. That day Carl Eric Wickman may well have leaned back from his desk to ponder what might have happened if in 1914 he had become a successful Hupmobile dealer.

•   •   •   •   •

During the 1930s, when Orville Caesar was not traveling here and there in search of additional lines, one interest above all others—some called it a passion—seemed to dominate his thoughts. This was a determination to improve the quality of Greyhound buses. "Comforts and conveniences offered by buses," he maintained, "should at the very least match those offered by trains." This conviction, sharpened by his background as a mechanic, stimulated endless ideas. One of his goals was to create greater seating capacity in coaches.

He had long been hampered by state laws that limited the length of buses to thirty-three feet. But now, in the 1930s, such regulations were being relaxed so that thirty-five-foot coaches were permitted. This allowed space for another row

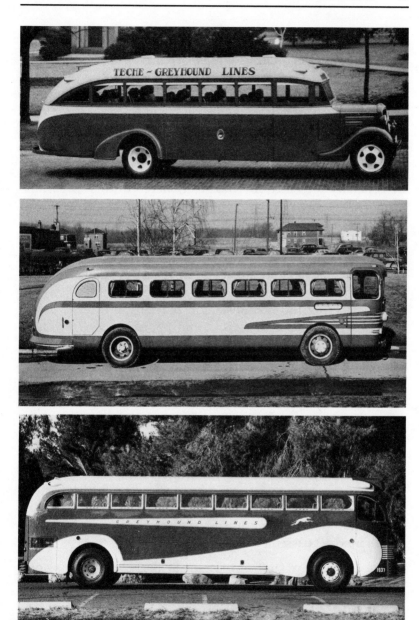

Streamlining was the dominant style design of the late 1930s and early 1940s.

of seats and also for the wider play of Caesar's ingenuity.

At that time The Greyhound Corporation had not yet in-augurated formal research facilities of its own. The one occa-sion on which the company's people had attempted to develop a steam engine, it had exploded in their faces. Nobody was killed, but several employees were burned. Thereafter nobody else tried to build such an engine.

Having no research and development staff of his own, Cae-sar generally presented his ideas to General Motors' engineers. After all, it was from General Motors that Greyhound was buying its buses. Though some of the innovations he sug-gested resulted in failures, others were remarkably successful. As one example, by moving the engine from the front to the back of the bus, he found space to increase the number of seats to more than forty. Another of his ideas brought Tropic-Aire air-conditioning (both cooling and heating) into the coaches. This proved to be so successful and popular that Greyhound built its own manufacturing plant to produce air-conditioning equipment. Nobody considered this Chicago factory as a step in diversification; it was simply another source of supply for Greyhound coaches.

Then, at Caesar's urging, came the experiments with diesel engines. Again and again the fumes they exuded were unbear-able. More than one engineer told Caesar, "It just isn't going to work. Sorry." But Caesar persisted. He persuaded his own company to continue financing research. And finally General Motors' engineers did solve the problem of noxious exhausts. Quite triumphantly they introduced diesel engines that saved Greyhound 40 percent in fuel costs.

But Caesar was far from satisfied. There was a day—per-haps an inspired day—when he telephoned New York's distin-guished industrial engineer, Raymond Loewe.

"We know," he said in effect, "that you've designed every-thing from cardboard boxes to office equipment and trade-marks. But do you think you can design a new type of motor coach?"

"Depends on what you want it to do."

"I know what I want it to do," Caesar said. "Can you come out and talk it over?"

Raymond Loewe did come. The trip, in 1935, launched a long association with Greyhound. Its first result was the appearance of what an automobile publication called "the most beautiful and spacious motor coach yet conceived." Substituting aluminum for steel wherever possible, this Supercoach, as it was named, was lighter than other buses and therefore consumed less fuel. Being larger than its predecessors, it had greater seating capacity. Its engineers, eager to demonstrate it to company executives, invited them to assemble for an inaugural ride.

Famed designer Raymond Loewe was asked by Greyhound executives to provide a new bus design for their company. The result was called "the most beautiful and spacious motor coach yet conceived."

When officers and directors arrived, they constituted the very top echelons of Greyhound dignitaries. The first to enter the new coach were Wickman, Bogan, Caesar, Hill, Travis, and Traer, followed by Counsel Robert Driscoll, Comptroller Moore, and Assistant Comptroller Sledz. After them came twelve others, the principal executives of affiliated lines.

First all of them were shown the interior comforts of the new bus—the more spacious dimensions of the seats, the air-conditioning, the enlarged baggage compartment, all the rest. Then, with everyone seated, the model took off on its demonstration run, followed by a parade of cars that included engineers, mechanics, advertising men, newspaper reporters, and others.

For a mile all went smoothly; then the bus stalled.

It was perhaps the most horrifying and embarrassing occurrence in the Greyhound history.

The mechanics, jumping out of their cars, ran to the bus. They uncovered its engine and quickly found what was wrong—a simple disconnection that was easily fixed. Thereafter the demonstration continued without further setbacks.

In fact, the Supercoach soon proved itself an outstanding achievement. Within months Wickman was able to announce:

> Both mechanically and in public appeal the Supercoach is a marked success. As of January 1 of this year [1940], 350 units were on order, and we are planning to place orders for 526 additional coaches. Once they are in production we should be receiving them at the rate of one a day. They will help solve a problem that has troubled us for too long a time.

The problem of which he spoke was this: Over the years Greyhound acquisitions had been made so quickly and so often that little attention had been given to the fact that each affiliate used its own favorite make of coach. As a result the need of storing spare parts required an enormous, expensive, and self-duplicating inventory. So Wickman was aiming toward having one type of coach used by the entire Greyhound network. And he had supported every idea Caesar had of producing a bus superior to all others. This Supercoach appeared to be the one.

Yet Raymond Loewe, working with Caesar, already had a few revolutionary ideas for improving the Supercoach. They were on the drawing board, but Wickman had not seen them.

He was too busy with another problem.

On several inspection trips he had been distressed to the point of groaning by the poor condition of toilets at many rest stops. Also, he found the quality of food and service far from satisfactory at many of the bus stations where passengers might want refreshments.

"We've got to get those toilets cleaned and we've got to provide better food," he declared, "or people will laugh at everything we advertise about bus travel."

It was easy enough to order a cleanup of rest rooms. The managers of bus stops knew they would either comply or lose their jobs. But providing better food in more attractive quarters was a more complicated task. The lunchrooms were being operated by independent concessionaires. Could their standards be controlled? Wickman's answer was brusque: "They can't stand a court case charging their food is rotten. They either clean up or get out. From now on we operate our own restaurants."

In a number of cities (Atlanta, Dayton, Spartanburg, and others) beautiful and costly new bus terminals were being built. Into some of them the company was pouring as much as $700,000. In these it was feasible enough to install company-owned restaurants. When they were opened under Greyhound's own management, they were the first of Greyhound's chain of Post Houses. Eight were completed by 1940. Some served 100 busloads of passengers a day, or about 2,500 meals. And they were soon listed in *Best Places To Eat*.

If no one carped about the expenses for all of these changes, one reason was that the company was doing well. Even a West

In 1939 Greyhound promoted bus travel to the New York World's Fair and the Golden Gate Exposition in San Francisco.

Coast strike by Pacific Greyhound drivers, though it lasted from May to September 1940, was not a crippling blow. As in the East, the loyalty of many employees enabled the company to continue services on a reduced scale.

(This strike made no monetary demands on Greyhound. It was a jurisdictional dispute between two unions—the Brotherhood of Railroad Trainmen and the Amalgamated Association of Street, Electric Railway and Motor Coach Employees of America. Its purpose was to determine which would represent the Greyhound employees in negotiations. The Brotherhood finally withdrew from contention.)

In the area of labor relations there were, however, other things to consider. One of the most urgent was the retention of experienced employees. To train replacements for bus drivers and maintenance people was expensive and time-consuming. How, then, could they best be persuaded to remain with the company?

To discuss this specific problem the directors met in March 1941. There was no opposition to what Wickman and Caesar proposed. What they described as Greyhound's first Retirement Annuity Plan, providing for a generous pension, was unanimously adopted. By its terms an employee would contribute only 2 percent of his compensation to the fund; the rest would be paid by the company.

The response fulfilled all of Wickman's hopes. By the time he made his first report to stockholders 67 percent of Greyhound employees had become what one of them termed "life members of the company."

•　　•　　•　　•　　•

In fact, all the early months of 1941 must have delighted the Greyhound founders. Business was good. Back in 1939 their buses had become the official carriers within the grounds of New York's World's Fair, and the company had also won the right to open restaurants throughout the grounds, an offshoot of its broadening experience in establishing Post Houses. So there was a healthy amount of cash flow with which to satisfy current plans.

Month after month the company announced achievements that had won the approval of the ICC. The list was awesome:

• On April 1, 1941 the corporation acquired all the capital stock of Eastern Michigan Motorbuses and changed its name to Great Lakes Greyhound Lines. These routes ran through lower Michigan.

• On July 1 the company acquired, through its Richmond-Greyhound subsidiary, all the properties of the Peninsula Transit Corporation, covering routes from Baltimore and Washington to Richmond and Norfolk.

• In December Greyhound bought 50 percent of all the outstanding stock of Pennsylvania Greyhound Lines.

• Also in early December it acquired 99.7 percent of the Greyhound Motors and Supply Company, a manufacturing firm.

• Teche Lines, operating in the South, was merged into the corporation—one of the year's most important deals.

• An 80 percent interest in Western Canadian Greyhound Lines, though negotiated earlier, became confirmed.

In addition to all these transactions the corporation made one agreement it was later to regret. It undertook to provide suburban bus service from San Francisco across the Golden Gate Bridge to Marin County, thereby replacing ferry and rail transportation. But there was little time to foresee the disadvantages of this move. For suddenly, tragically, all of American business, all of American life was disrupted. The bombs that fell on Pearl Harbor on December 7, 1941, exploded plans and activities throughout the country.

7

Never in the nation's history had the people of the United States been so outraged as on this "day of infamy." With the country declaring instant war on Japan, all other considerations for American industry gave way to the one question: How can we help?

Wickman at once communicated with the War Department. He offered to put Greyhound's fleet of almost 3,000 buses at the government's immediate disposal. The shocking reply he received must have made him feel as if he had been slapped. Greyhound's help was not needed! The fact that the message came from some bureaucratic underling did not lessen its sting.

Wickman was furious. Stockholders would soon be asking what Greyhound was doing to further the war effort. Anyone who knew Wickman would have realized that his instinctive answer would be to unleash a flood of invective as he paced his office. But a few days later an explanation of the government's message arrived from a more responsible source. It calmed Wickman, and he composed a quiet announcement:

> Because of the previous existence of Joint Military-Passenger Agreements between the War and Navy Departments on the one hand, and the railroad passenger associations on the other, the bus lines have experienced difficulty in participating in the movement of military personnel, even where bus service is superior to rail service.

His was not the only bus company to have its offer declined. The National Association of Motor Bus Operators, receiving many similar complaints, indignantly intervened.

Dealing directly with the Quartermaster General's office, the association arranged for the transportation of draftees to and from induction centers, especially in communities where there was no railroad.

Of course, Greyhound participated in this service. But its major wartime contribution began after July 1, 1942. That was when the government's agreement with the railroad associations expired. Thereafter Greyhound put its buses more fully into war service. In the words of a *Fortune* reporter:

> Not only did they haul millions of rural selectees to induction centers, they serviced training camps and Army and Navy bases where no railroads ran. They transported millions of war workers to huge new factories that necessarily had to be built at a distance from metropolitan railroad terminals; and when such plants were far from housing facilities, the busmen set up regular commuting schedules. Still another part of their wartime traffic consisted of carrying visitors—usually family members—to distantly stationed servicemen and war workers.

When the Pacific Greyhound Line was asked to operate a service for the Navy Yard at Mare Island, California, it lacked enough buses for the task. So the Navy, exercising its priorities, promptly bought 300 coaches for the line to run.

Simultaneously Greyhound began a wholly different type of operation, disassociated with transportation. In Chicago its Tropic-Aire plant, manufacturing air-conditioners for buses, was visited by Army personnel. To the surprise of everyone except Tropic-Aire's own engineers, it became evident that the factory, with few changes, could produce proximity fuses for armament.

"We went into production as fast as we could convert equipment," Adam Sledz said. "During the rest of the war years that was the plant's primary job. It won a Navy E for its efforts."

From the start there was unanimous agreement on one point

among Greyhound officers and directors: There would be no profiteering on war contracts. All services, whether on buses or in the manufacture of proximity fuses, would be rendered on a reasonable cost-plus basis. This stricture was never violated.

One retired engineer who had worked on proximity fuses recalled, "Back in that Chicago plant we'd hear all about the Battle of Midway in 1942, when our Navy destroyed the Japanese fleet. And we'd hear the radio report that our Marines had landed on Guadalcanal. We'd keep telling one another that our fuses were in those battles. Made us feel we were part of it all, as if we were there. The same feeling gripped us when ur troops invaded Italy in 1943 and Normandy in 1944. We 'ere among their primary suppliers."

Back in Chicago the comptroller and his staff studied every nancial statement, poring over them to make sure that the)st-plus agreement was scrupulously maintained. Yet in spite ¯ all good intentions Greyhound coaches were soon reaping venues from an unexpected source. Despite the government's pleas to avoid unnecessary travel, despite its exhortations to conserve gasoline, despite Greyhound's own advertisements asking people to make only essential trips, the civilian population was traveling—and traveling for pleasure.

"There was a simple reason," said former bus line president Clifford Graves. "With millions of young people going into the armed forces, civilian jobs were plentiful. Wages were high. Many civilians were earning more than enough to pay for weekend trips, and they were making the most of the opportunity."

Thus, with both civilian and military demands to meet, Greyhound buses covered a record 206.5 million miles in that first war year. The load factor on each bus (that is, the ratio of occupied seats to the full number of seats on a bus during a trip of many stops) normally ran between 50 and 70 percent. With troops cramming a bus to capacity, military runs often achieved a load factor of 100 percent.

During World War II every branch of the service traveled by Greyhound as buses were pressed into troop transport duties in the United States.

Yet, paradoxically, revenues decreased. Troops were riding at rates far below the one-and-one-half cents per mile paid by civilians. Simultaneously the company had to increase the wages of its employees to meet wartime conditions. Also, Greyhound was paying more for gasoline, spare parts, supplies, and services.

Still another shrinkage of revenues occurred at the New York World's Fair. The Fair's dedication to world peace was being mocked by world events, and attendance figures shriveled. That Greyhound's enterprises at the exposition continued to show even a moderate profit was remarkable. "All things considered," said Sledz who was assistant comptroller at the time, "we managed to get along without undue losses or undue profits.

"Our biggest problem, of course," he went on, "was the scarcity of materials during the war. We could not get the parts we needed, which meant a good many buses were laid up for repairs. As for the delivery of new coaches on order, they were so badly delayed that in some civilian areas we had to curtail schedules.

"Worst of all was the manpower problem. More than 4,000 of our drivers, maintenance men, and other employees went into the armed forces. It was no easy task to replace them. When we managed to find recruits for our driver staff, for instance, we had to take experienced drivers off their jobs and turn them into trainers of newcomers. Women? Today we have almost 600 driving buses. But in those days you might see WACs driving ambulances or the cars of generals, but very few women thought of driving big, intercity buses."

Out of all these shortage problems, however, grew at least one constructive and permanent innovation. This began with the difficulty of finding spare parts for buses in need of repair.

The mechanical interests of Orville Caesar led the company into seeking ways of reconstructing old bus parts. Little by little this process was mastered in the Chicago plant. It could be described as Greyhound's first long step into its own re-

The shortage of male drivers during World War II gave women a chance to enter the ranks of an exclusively male domain.

search and development operation. Over the years this ability to repair old parts has saved the company untold time and funds.

"But in looking back over the war years," Adam Sledz once said, "I feel one of our most important contributions to the war effort was a highly personal one. It lay in releasing Ralph Bogan to serve the armed forces in Alaska."

• • • • •

With some 1,600 miles of the new Alcan Highway in use in Alaska, Army matériel and manpower had to be transported north and south. Neither summer heat nor winter blizzards could be allowed to block military movements. Bogan's long experience with bus traffic made him the perfect choice to supervise traffic on the Alcan Highway. Commissioned a colonel, he served as aide to the commanding general; Bogan was the one Greyhound founder to serve in two world wars.

His son, Ralph Bogan, Jr., said, "There was a time when my father, talking to us at the dinner table, used to describe the road between Hibbing and Duluth as a rough place to drive in a snowstorm. That must have been a joy ride compared to pushing through Alaska's blizzards."

Others remember seeing Bogan on the highway in freezing weather, his breath spurting in cloudlets as he ran back and forth, yelling, gesturing as he told drivers which way to turn to avoid being stalled in snowdrifts. He was never an office-desk supervisor; you could count on him to be wherever there was trouble in every kind of weather. He was a familiar figure all the way down the line from Dawson Creek and Whitehorse to Fairbanks.

When Western Canadian Greyhound Lines (a recent acquisition of The Greyhound Corporation) was put under contract by the War Department, Bogan called on it to send its fleet of coaches to transport troops. The man to whom he spoke sounded dismayed. What was to happen to civilian traffic?

"Remind me to discuss that," Bogan said, "after we win this war."

On the home front, and of a more peaceful nature, one thing that pleased everyone at Greyhound headquarters was that more than 95 percent of the company's employees enrolled in its retirement annuity program. That signified their desire to retain a permanent relationship. "I think the only ones who didn't take advantage of the fund," said one officer, "were those war workers, mostly women, who planned to leave their jobs once the conflict ended and devote themselves to raising families. Call it a choice between having a child or a pension. In their case the mother-urge won."

8

Many a Greyhound bus driver, hearing a sudden overhead roar as he approached a military base, glanced up to see a helicopter race past, leaving his bus far behind. The copters were transporting everything from personnel to hospital supplies at speeds unattainable on the ground.

Did that mean there was a chance they might one day supplant buses as the automobile had supplanted the horse?

The question roused a few worrisome thoughts at meetings of Greyhound executives. Manferd Burleigh in particular, president of Great Lakes Greyhound Lines, urged serious consideration of the helicopter's challenge. But the others were inclined to shrug the matter off. In fact, when Wickman was invited to inspect a Sikorsky helicopter at work, someone asked him what he thought of its potential usefulness to Greyhound. Wickman scratched his jaw as he watched the copter rise, then said, "When that thing can pick up one of my buses and deliver it safely to the next bus stop, I'll give it serious thought."

Such skepticism was undermined, however, by the endless newspaper stories people brought to Wickman's desk: In England helicopters were rushing victims of the blitz to hospitals; they were lifting shot-down aviators out of the North Sea; they were speeding plasma to save human lives. Here in the United States their missions were equally dramatic. One of the latest involved two mountain climbers seriously injured in a bone-breaking fall. They had just been lifted off an 8,000-foot-high crag by helicopter. Nothing else could have saved their lives.

Eventually Manferd Burleigh suggested, "Why don't we buy a couple of helicopters, experiment on our own, and make decisions based on our experience, not on reports?"

It was a sound idea. The helicopters were bought and immediately raised a plethora of new questions: Where and how do you pick up passengers in a convenient part of a large city? You certainly won't be permitted to land and take off in, say, New York's Times Square. How much baggage can a helicopter carry with its passengers, and where can it be stowed? What kind of training will a pilot need? How much must passengers be charged to make helicopter transportation profitable? At this stage of their development, are copters safe?

Despite all such questions—and there were many more—the prospect of adopting helicopter transportation as an adjunct to bus travel became very real. By early 1944 Greyhound shareholders were startled by a novel announcement:

> Greyhound has made a preliminary survey of the possibilities of operating helicopters over nationwide routes at the conclusion of the war. A hearing has been held before the Examiners appointed by the Civil Aeronautics Board.

But shortly thereafter came a second announcement:

> The Examiners recently handed down a report recommending that surface transportation companies should not be permitted to operate air service, and that application for such service involving helicopters should not be heard until such time as this type of unit has proven itself practical for commercial air transportation.

In spite of the adverse decision, Robert Driscoll, the company's general counsel at the time, did apply for the right to "operate civil aircraft service for the carrying of persons, mail, baggage, and light express routes now being operated by the Greyhound bus companies."

If air transportation was indeed to be the way of the future, Greyhound proposed to be ready for it. The company went so far as to create a new subsidiary, Greyhound Skyways. Driscoll continued to argue its case before federal authorities. He

In 1944 Greyhound executives decided to enter the air transportation field with the introduction of Greyhound Skyways helicopter service. The plan was soon abandoned.

pressed these efforts without success until, by 1947, the company had to concede:

> It now appears that it will be some years before the development of a helicopter of sufficient capacity for commercial operation in regular intercity transportation service can be expected. Greyhound has therefore abandoned its efforts to obtain authority to establish such service, without prejudice to its right to revive the program if it seems advisable at a later date.

Was this to be regarded as a defeat? As one Greyhound officer pointed out, "It had its bright side. It meant that we wouldn't have to write off as obsolete millions upon millions of dollars sunk in buses, garages, equipment, terminals, trained personnel, and so on. Much of this would have been made obsolete if we had turned full-tilt to helicopter transportation. Maybe we will do it some day. But for the present let's just count our blessings and go on running our buses."

•   •   •   •   •

The company did just that. In every state from Texas to Alaska it carried troops and war-plant workers wherever they were needed. Overseas, the Philippines were lost and rewon; Guadalcanal became the scene of some of the war's most brutal encounters; North Africa was invaded; Italy was invaded. In the Pacific, the Japanese fleet was finally decimated at Coral Sea and at Midway. And while America's forces fought in every area of the world, there could be no diminution of effort within the United States. As far as Greyhound was concerned, its Chicago plant continued to pour out proximity fuses, and some of its buses kept rolling twenty-four hours a day with relays of drivers.

William Cruselle of Jacksonville, Florida, was one of the wartime drivers. "What do I remember most about those days?" he said. "I guess it's the feelings I had when I watched my busload of young recruits—just a bunch of kids—pile out of the coach at the Army camp. I'd look at every face, wondering which of them would never return. I knew that in every busload there were a few who would soon be dead. And always, always, deep in my heart, lay the pain of saying an unspoken good-bye."

There were other difficult experiences for drivers like Cruselle: Having to put on a burst of speed to rush a pregnant passenger to the nearest hospital when she began to moan with labor pains; actually having to stop the bus on another occasion to help deliver a child on the coach floor. But for sheer poignancy nothing equalled the memory of watching doomed young men scramble out of the bus.

Far less emotional, yet constantly disturbing, was the realization that the buses were deteriorating. The replacement of worn-out parts became more difficult day by day. Only the salvaging ability developed by Greyhound's engineers kept many a coach rolling. General Motors tried to ease the situation by producing a few "Victory buses." These were little more than the stripped-down shells of peacetime coaches. They were uncomfortable, uneconomical, and unpredictable in their life-span. Still, they had to suffice as did many other emergency products.

As the war went from crisis to crisis, a different kind of problem arose for The Greyhound Corporation: What happens with money that cannot be spent?

Revenues from bus transportation, all in cash, continued to flow to the company. They piled up in millions. For the year 1943 Greyhound showed a net income of $10,762,469. This was an increase of $2,334,488 over the previous year's earnings. It represented what remained in bank deposits even after the huge sum of $40,245,869 had been set aside for federal taxes. Yet it was impossible to use the money for the purchase of equipment that was either nonexistent or preempted by the armed forces.

So what do you do with funds you cannot spend on necessities? Do you put them aside, in escrow as it were, awaiting the day when essential materials will once more become available?

This was what several directors advocated. Wickman granted the wisdom of their counsel, but only to a degree. He had other plans. First, as a practical matter, he ordered that $1,225,981 of 1943 income and $1,217,750 of 1942 revenues be segregated for future purchases. As to the rest of the available money, he knew exactly what he wanted to do with it.

His thoughts went back to the times when the company had so desperately needed funds for expansion that it had gladly (and perhaps recklessly) sold its stock to railroads. That had been an essential course to take to finance growth.

But now new considerations had arisen. The ICC was beginning to suggest that the union of railroads and bus lines might lead to monopolistic control of American travel. The commission preferred to see each group, railroads and bus lines, independent of the other.

Wickman felt the same way, though not for the same reasons. He urged using at least part of the dormant funds to buy back Greyhound stock owned by railroads.

"I suspect," said Frank Nageotte, now chairman of the vast network of Greyhound bus lines, "that, apart from its intrinsic wisdom, buying back the railroads' interests was secretly a matter of pride with Wickman. He had seen his vision of a coast-to-coast bus service realized. There it was, a map on his wall he could survey with pride as he leaned back from his desk. Yet much of what he had helped to create was owned by the railroads. One can understand his desire to bring full ownership home where it belonged."

It was not accomplished overnight. With the help of Driscoll's legal staff and the financial acumen of Glenn Traer, negotiations consumed many months; in fact, they ran into 1946. But Wickman achieved his purpose. With the exception of the concurrence of the Pennsylvania Railroad, for which he had to wait several years, he acquired control of all those lines formerly shared with the railroads. In some cases he had to buy only 50 percent of outstanding voting stock because, as he explained, "In these companies The Greyhound Corporation already has voting control through ownership of additional

Early badges of Greyhound and associated bus lines were works of art.

stock by certain of the Associated Greyhound Bus Companies."

Greyhound's directors were practical men. They could not permit these expenditures to leave the corporation's treasury too depleted to deal with future needs. They therefore applied for the right to sell $10 million of fifteen-year, 3 percent sinking fund debentures and $5 million in 4.5 percent cumulative preferred stock.

These funds were to be used, in the legal department's words, "to finance the retirement by subsidiaries of preferred stocks having dividend rates generally higher than currently prevailing rates; to augment the working capital of the company and its subsidiaries; to finance payments on the purchase of new equipment (when available); to finance the acquisition, improvement, and expansion of terminals, garages, offices, and other facilities of the company and its subsidiaries; to purchase the stock of Penn-Ohio Coach Lines Company, subject to the approval of the ICC; and to purchase stock of the company's subsidiaries held by others."

All this made one thing clear: While Wickman, Bogan, Caesar, and their associates devoted themselves to the war effort, they never neglected preparations for the rigorous demands of peace.

Investments in Stocks of Associated Companies, December 31, 1946

ASSOCIATED GREYHOUND BUS COMPANIES:	Class	Number of Shares	Percent of Outstanding Securities
Atlantic Greyhound Corporation	Common*	. . . 27,977	79.74
Capitol Greyhound Lines . .	Common*	. . . 1,432	50.00(a)
	Preferred	. . . 11,600	100.00
Central Greyhound Lines, Inc.	Common A	. . 200,000	100.00
	Common B*	. . 145,468	72.73
Cincinnati & Lake Erie Transportation Company . .	Common*	. . . 32,512-31/32	99.23
Dixie Greyhound Lines, Inc.	Common*	. . . 14,700	100.00
Eastern Canadian Greyhound Lines, Limited	Common*	. . . 1,250	100.00
Florida Greyhound Lines, Inc.	Common*	. . 135,920	99.47
Great Lakes Greyhound Lines, Inc.	Common*	. . 400,000	100.00
Great Lakes Greyhound Lines, Inc. of Indiana	Common*	. . . 5,247	100.00
Illinois Greyhound Lines, Inc.	Common*	. . . 3,105	100.00
New England Greyhound Lines, Incorporated	Preferred	. . . 2,320	50.00
	Common*	. . . 10,000	50.00(b)
Northland Greyhound Lines, Inc.	Common*	. . . 77,147	51.20
Ohio Greyhound Lines, Inc.	Common*	. . . 5,000	100.00
Pacific Greyhound Lines . .	Common*	. . 297,000	61.05
Pennsylvania Greyhound Lines, Inc.	Preferred	. . . 4,000	50.00
	Common*	. . . 77,000	50.00
Richmond-Greyhound Lines, Incorporated	Common*	. . . 25,500	51.00
Southwestern Greyhound Lines, Inc.	Common A*	. . . 4,800	100.00
	Common B	. . 16,234	82.83
Valley Greyhound Lines, Inc.	Preferred	. . 500	100.00
	Common*	. . . 1,000	100.00
Western Canadian Greyhound Lines, Ltd	Common*	. . . 15,000	100.00
West Ridge Transportation Company	Common*	. . . 1,423	100.00

OTHER ASSOCIATED COMPANIES:

Greyhound Motors & Supply Co	Common*	. . . 2,760	5.14(a)
Greyhound Post Houses, Inc.	Common*	. . . 4,950	100.00
Greyhound Terminal of Boston, Inc.	Common*	. . . 500	100.00
Greyhound Highway Tours, Inc.	Common*	. . . 5	100.00
Greyvan Lines, Inc.	Preferred	. . . 510	51.00
	Common*	. . . 516	51.60
Greyhound Skyways, Inc. . .	Common*	. . . 1,000	100.00
Michigan Greyhound Skyways, Inc.	Common*	. . . 10,000	100.00
Greyhound Oil Company . .	Common*	. . . 3,000	60.00

(a) The Greyhound Corporation has voting control through ownership of additional stock by certain of the Associated Greyhound Bus Companies.

(b) The remaining common stock may not vote, except in certain circumstances, because of restrictions imposed by the Interstate Commerce Commission.

*Denotes voting stock.

9

Any attempt to chart the ups and downs of a company like Greyhound must of course be based on the ups and downs of the nation itself. Thus, in the 1940s, Greyhound's activities were largely dictated by the demands of war. So, for that matter, were the emotions of everyone who worked for the company, from bus drivers to executives. And those emotions were never more searing than on the day of Franklin Delano Roosevelt's death.

The loss to the nation—indeed, to the world—wrought not only grief but confusion, uncertainty, even fear. Could anyone, including Harry Truman, hope to take the place of a man who, in the words of one editorial writer, "towered above all others"? Could an untested vice president lead the country through this period of strife? Would he be dominated by giants like Churchill and Stalin?

Yet Harry Truman, on less than an hour's notice after the President's death at 5:00 P.M. on April 12, 1945, not only took Roosevelt's place but instantly made a place of his own. Had Wickman, Bogan, and Caesar been in Washington that day, they would have recognized in this new president a man of their own kind—forthright, simple in rhetoric, candid to the point of bluntness, absolutely fearless in following his own judgment of right and wrong.

Truman was scheduled to address the nation at eight o'clock, some two hours after his inauguration. The purpose of the talk was to reassure the world. The staff at the White House, knowing he would have no time to prepare a speech, hurriedly called on a speechwriter to draft an appropriate message. The speechwriter was stunned. What could one say at a time like this? Nonetheless he managed to produce two pages of appropriate thoughts. Shortly after seven o'clock a liaison officer carried the document to the Truman apartment on Connecticut Avenue.

How did the new president react?

"He refused even to look at the speech," the emissary reported. "He said that on a night like this he could not parrot words somebody else had prepared for him. If he could not say what was in his heart he would not talk at all."

That was the measure of the man, revealed in his first act as president.

At eight o'clock that evening he did speak to the nation. In his own words he assured the country that the war would be

A classic Greyhound terminal of the 1930s and 40s in Evansville, Indiana.

prosecuted with every bit of energy at the country's command. It was the kind of straightforward statement that imbued his listeners with confidence and trust.

"Hearing that broadcast," one Greyhound veteran recalled, "made us go back to our jobs with renewed faith and determination. It was clear even then that our new president was every inch a leader."

After the final victory of World War II, after the cessation of all hostilities, Greyhound's wartime responsibilities were not ended. As Orville Caesar explained in 1946, "At the beginning of the war soldiers, sailors, workmen and all other classes of people were moving in unprecedented numbers about the country in an effort to find their respective places in the great struggle. After the war the same people were again on the move to relocate themselves. And there were homecoming troops, too. Our buses continued to be crowded with standees filling the aisles. Traffic was of such proportions as to cause real discomfort, but passengers accepted it, knowing its cause."

For almost five years nothing had been able to stop the steady deterioration of equipment. Now at last, in 1946, Orville Caesar was able to report, "The first of a fleet of some 1,200 cruiser-type Silversides coaches that have been on order during the war are now being delivered to Greyhound operating companies."

Before long, he predicted, these would be arriving at the rate of one a day. Meanwhile engineers were developing a new fifty-passenger coach that would embody many improvements.

"All in all," Caesar concluded, "there are 1,562 new buses on order for delivery in 1947 and 1948 at a total cost of approximately $39 million."

The fact that financing of such proportions was readily available offered impressive testimony of the company's reputation among individual investors and banks.

And there were other significant developments in this first postwar year. In Chicago the Tropic-Aire plant, relieved of the production of military matériel, was "resuming its normal peacetime production of automotive units." This, too, promised a substantial increase in revenues.

Some of the most important of early postwar changes, however, had nothing to do with buses, or with the availability of spare parts, or with the number of passengers traveling on Greyhound coaches. These were personal matters.

For one, the company's future chairman, Gerald Trautman, returned from war service as a Navy lieutenant to rejoin the San Francisco law firm of McCutchen, Doyle, Brown, Trautman, and Enerson. This partnership had in 1946 begun handling the legal affairs of Western Greyhound Lines, owned by Wesley Elgin Travis and Frederick Ackerman. Trautman, back at his desk, quickly became immersed in Greyhound operations.

One troublesome challenge soon confronted him. It might be said that he inherited it because the senior partner of the law firm (the one nominally in charge of this case) had gone to Hawaii.

The problem stemmed from the efforts of the American Bus Lines first to win interstate transportation rights from the Mexican border to Canada along routes already served by Greyhound lines; and now (a more immediate demand) to obtain intrastate rights within the state of Oregon. This too would be in direct competition with Greyhound lines.

Trautman at once sped up to the Oregon hearings.

He entered a room crowded with witnesses the American Bus Lines had brought to support its case. On tables lay piles of documents ready to supply all the data anyone could ask for.

Listening to witness after witness, Trautman knew that to lose this case would involve a real loss to Greyhound transportation. But how could one prevent the granting of a license to American Bus against the weight of all these witnesses and their formidable array of documents?

He had a sudden idea. Believing that American Bus could hardly supply efficient service to Oregon unless it could drive people into and out of the state, he rose to put a blunt question: How could American Bus operate effectively in Oregon unless it had interstate rights? Would passengers bound for cities outside the state be forced to leave their bus at the state lines?

With complete confidence the opposing lawyer said, "We expect to get interstate rights."

Trautman promptly moved for a dismissal of the petition. "When they have their interstate licenses," he maintained, "that will be the proper time to consider intrastate operations in Oregon."

This was so logical that he saw sage nods of agreement among those who considered the case. The right to operate in Oregon was denied to the American Bus Lines, and Gerald Trautman went home with his victory—thereby winning the attention, and no doubt the admiration, of Frederick Ackerman.

•   •   •   •   •

Another development of a personal nature concerned Carl Eric Wickman, and this one brought no pleasure to any of his associates. At the age of fifty-nine Wickman had been supervising Greyhound's growth for thirty-two years. Was he tiring? Was he ill? Did he feel his dream had been realized, his mission in life fulfilled? Or was he simply frustrated?

Ever since the enactment of the Motor Carrier Act he had lost much of his executive freedom. Every undertaking he suggested had to be tempered with the phrase, "Subject to the approval of the Interstate Commerce Commission." And the commission said no as often as it said yes. It was discouraging. Since ultimate decisions of the presidency were no longer his to make, why hold the office?

This was not a sudden feeling. A year earlier he had tried to have Bogan named chief executive officer in his place, but some of the directors had demurred. Possibly they had found Bogan too aggressive. In any case, Wickman persisted in his decision to retire. He had even bought a home in Florida where he hoped to relax in the sun and become a better golfer.

Finally—on May 25, 1946, at a conference of directors that followed the annual stockholders' meeting—he succeeded, as the minutes put it, "in being relieved of his duties and responsibilities as president. He was thereupon elected chairman of the board of directors. In this capacity he will continue to give The Greyhound Corporation the benefit of his experience in the intercity motor bus industry."

Orville Caesar became president while Ralph Bogan was named executive vice president.

And there were other personnel changes; so many, in truth, as to constitute a management upheaval. Arthur Hill assumed the influential post of chairman of the executive committee; Adam Sledz succeeded W. S. Moore as comptroller; Clifford Graves, one of the earliest bus drivers, went to Seattle as president of Northwest Greyhound Lines; and Frederick Ackerman became president of Pacific Greyhound Lines.

Yet these and other management changes did not stop Greyhound's growth, especially in subsidiary activities. For example, the development of Post House restaurants had been entrusted to an experienced restaurant manager, S. B. Browne. Under Browne's direction the eating places increased at a remarkable rate. By the end of 1947 there were ninety-eight of them in twenty-four states and Canada, and sixteen more were being built. They were serving some 25 million meals a year; and though they were intended primarily to be an accommodation to travelers, they were yielding a very satisfactory profit. Even in retirement Wickman must have observed these figures with a contented smile.

"You pick good men and you get good results," he always maintained.

Whether he was happy no one really knew. In his Florida home he cherished the privacy he shared with his wife, his daughter, and his son—a privacy reduced to a home for two when both children married and left for homes of their own.

Even with close friends Wickman seldom discussed his non-business interests. Few people knew anything about the philanthropic sums he sent to Sweden, there to be disbursed by a cousin. Back in 1940, when the king of Sweden conferred on him the Royal Order of Vasa, it was assumed that the decoration came only in recognition of Wickman's leadership in the field of transportation. He never corrected that impression.

One thing in his family life must have hurt and disappointed him. His son, together with Bogan's son and the sons of four other Greyhound executives, were given a thorough two-year training course in all aspects of bus transportation. These young men, back from military service, were being groomed for high-management positions. Yet after their period of training every one of them left Greyhound employment.

No one ever knew why. Bogan's son said, "I simply felt I'd be happier in another line of work," and eventually became chairman of a large Chicago bank. Wickman's son, curiously enough, established two Florida bus lines of his own, which he operated independently. The other trainees likewise departed for jobs of their own choosing.

"So you see," Adam Sledz once philosophically remarked, "there was no nepotism in the Greyhound organization. The sons wouldn't let it happen."

One cannot help wondering about the effects of Wickman's departure on Greyhound's policies. In the single year after his retirement the company's net income dropped from $19,934,935 to $17,243,563. The following year, 1948, it fell to $16,127,253, and by 1949 it was down to $11,593,280.

It was hardly surprising that some of the directors, especially the more conservative men like Hill, Ackerman, and Herbert G. Wellington, became uneasy. Though they blamed

As travel expanded and passenger loads grew, Greyhound became a major operator of restaurants in its innovative Post Houses.

Food services in terminals provided a significant part of Greyhound's annual revenue.

no one at this point, not knowing whom to blame, they no doubt felt something had to be done. But what? How could they stem the steady decrease in earnings?

As president, Orville Caesar tried pragmatically to explain what was happening. He acknowledged, "The year 1949 presented Greyhound with unusual problems and difficulties." And he outlined several of them:

Travel in general had been reduced by prolonged strikes in two major industries, coal and steel.

Greyhound itself had been forced to contend with difficult labor problems. Two strikes among its subsidiaries, one of 105 days' duration at North Coast Greyhound Lines, had reduced the earnings of these companies by about two million dollars.

Tropic-Aire and the Greyhound Motor and Supply Company had fallen approximately a million dollars below their 1948 earnings.

And there were other factors that Caesar enumerated. For instance, supplementary pension benefits had gone into effect on July 1, 1949, and wages had risen, as had fuel prices and other costs. There had been no compensating increase in bus fares. All such explanations were valid, yet they did not wholly overcome every director's uneasiness. Investors, they knew, demand profits not explanations.

Astonishing as it was, Wall Street did not seem to share such misgivings. One brokerage firm, Thomson & Mc-Kinnon, made an exhaustive study of Greyhound's prospects, then issued an extraordinary report:

> Bus travel has become so much a part of the nation's basic transportation system that songs have been written about it, motion pictures have been based on it, and radio has used it as a theme for many programs and stories. This outstanding acceptance of a relatively new mode of transportation is indicated by the rate of growth in the use of this service. For example, in 1939 gross revenues of The Greyhound Corporation were $56 million. Nine years later, in 1948, they were

more than $192 million and this year, 1949, they are expected to be well over $200 million.

The report all but ignored the company's recent decline in net earnings. Instead it pointed out that bus travel was bound to increase because of many social changes. "These," it said, "were evidenced in such things as paid vacations, shorter workweeks giving more leisure time, and the steady rise in consumer purchasing power which has brought the opportunity for travel to a larger number of people. It has been said with considerable truth that America is a nation on wheels. The Greyhound Corporation has played its part in this respect by bringing low-cost bus service to millions of Americans."

Then, addressing investors directly, the brokerage firm said, "Selling at approximately twelve dollars a share and paying a dividend at the rate of one dollar annually, to yield 8.3 percent, the common stock of Greyhound affords investors an unusually attractive opportunity to participate in the future gains of this industry."

Such optimism certainly was not quixotic. It was founded on sound developments. For example, in intensive national and local advertising campaigns—covering newspapers, magazines, and broadcasts—the company was promoting "Amazing America Tours." Through its specially formed Highway Tours it offered sight-seeing trips that varied in length from days to months, trips that covered virtually all the country's scenic and historical attractions. These all-expense tours proved to be remarkably popular. Their revenues soared from $635,196 in 1946 to $3,161,915 in 1948.

At the same time, according to Thomas & McKinnon, "The company now has the largest and best fleet of buses in its history (5,837 coaches) and experimental road tests are continuing with a new fifty-passenger bus called the Highway Traveler."

The company did indeed expect a great deal from this Highway Traveler. It was powered by two air-cooled motors—an innovation Greyhound's own engineers had developed. The coach itself, built on two levels, contained three air-conditioned compartments, a lavatory, a refrigerated cabinet for refreshments, much larger luggage space, individual radio receivers built into the headrests, and two-way shortwave radio communication. Air and rubber, replacing metal-coiled springs, added immeasurably to riding comfort. According to all predictions, the Highway Traveler was sure to attract record numbers of passengers.

And since outsiders like the brokerage house envisioned a glowing future for The Greyhound Corporation, was there really any reason for insiders to feel distressed over a temporary decrease in net income?

Some company officers—primarily those who had hoped to see Ralph Bogan succeed Wickman as president—began to mutter doubts about Caesar's ability. Others vigorously defended him. It was the beginning of the first personality schism in the corporation's history—a schism that was to lead to increasing bitterness. And to increasing trouble.

Orville D. Caesar started as a mechanic in the early days of bus transportation and rose to become Greyhound's chairman of the board.

10

If there was one enduring principle Carl Wickman had established during his years of Greyhound leadership, it was insistence on constant growth. In good times or bad, the company had never been static. Nor was it now, even while the pain of divisiveness was beginning to gnaw at Greyhound executives.

Though the company's bus routes already extended from coast to coast and from Canada to the Mexican border, local lines were constantly being bought and added to the major network; many of them served as "feeder" lines to transcontinental runs. At least one, the North Coast Transportation Company, ran from Portland, Oregon, to Vancouver in British Columbia, improving international travel between the United States and Canada.

No one ever accused Ralph Bogan of hiding his feelings. When he was angered, this tall, commanding man could slam a fist on his desk and "cuss loud enough to be heard from Hibbing to Tijuana." During these years of his return from war service, he had ample reason to vent his fury against "blundering bureaucrats." There were actions he wished the company to take that were bluntly stopped by the ICC. Moreover, the commission repeatedly ordered Greyhound to sell its holdings in some lines it had previously bought. Thus Greyhound had to dispose of a 40 percent interest in the Southern Limited, in Southern Stages, and other lines. It had to enter into a consent decree requiring first the sale of Dollar Lines, then the withdrawal by the Southern Pacific Company of all representation on the board of directors and executive committee of Pacific Greyhound Lines. And there were other stip-

The Greyhound name and symbol became a familiar and traditional part of the American urban scene in cities and towns.

Shown here are terminals in (opposite page) Providence, Rhode Island, top, and Los Angeles, bottom; Cincinnati, top, and Cleveland, bottom.

ulations, all of which must have infuriated Bogan when he felt what some of his colleagues called "the government's stranglehold on our freedom of action."

Fortunately, however, the ICC approved as many plans as it opposed, and so Greyhound acquisitions never ceased. Where it did not buy new lines, the corporation increased its stock ownership in affiliates. As a matter of record, it consummated at least six such transactions every year in the late 1940s.

One of these, in January 1948, was quite different from all the rest. It occurred when the Great Lakes Greyhound Lines purchased the Airlines Passenger and Transfer Company that serviced the Willow Run Airport near Detroit. "This," said Caesar, "will permit Greyhound to furnish the service, to the advantage of the company as well as the public and the airlines." (Its long-range importance was that it set a model for eventual Greyhound services at airports in New York and Miami.)

One thing the ICC did not oppose or even challenge was the construction of garages and terminals. These were urgently needed. During the war years and immediately afterward few such facilities had been built; the scarcity of materials had made the cost of construction prohibitive. But now, with many adjustments to a peacetime economy achieved, the building program was resumed on a hitherto unmatched scale.

During the twelve months of 1949 twenty-one major terminals, ten garages, and seven combinations of the two were completed.

And that was only the beginning. Fully fifty such structures were planned for the future. They represented total outlays of more than $17 million.

Today, if one wishes to assess the progress of Greyhound's architecture in terminals, as well as the constant improvement of its bus designs, there is no better "museum" in which to view them than the office of Fred Dunikoski, president and chief operating officer of all affiliated Greyhound bus lines. His enthusiasm as a collector of Greyhound memorabilia is evident not only on his office walls but in all nearby corridors. Everywhere one sees models and pictures of buses and terminals.

On this occasion he discussed the huge installation in Chicago, from a picture taken the day it was completed. "The cost ran to about $11 million," he said, "and it has been regarded as a model for other terminals. All its loading facilities for passengers and luggage are underground. Escalators carry people to and from the upper waiting rooms. Actually, the maintenance of such a building, big as it is, costs very little. Practically every part of the street floor is occupied by rent-paying stores. And some day, if we utilize the air rights above the terminal by erecting a skyscraper over it, the place may bring in a fortune."

The contemporary Greyhound logo is displayed on the brick walls of a new terminal.

Dallas, Cleveland, Cincinnati, and many other cities now have architecturally impressive terminals. Once he has shown their pictures, Dunikoski delights in concentrating on the models and photographs of Greyhound buses. They range from the earliest Hibbing vehicles, almost ludicrous today, to resplendent modern Americruisers, each emblazoned with its running greyhound.

"These buses of ours," Dunikoski said, "have set standards for the entire industry. For years, under the supervision of W. A. Duvall, long head of maintenance, the innovations created by our engineers have been adopted by other bus lines. We're very proud of the contributions we've made to the industry."

Those contributions have been listed with similar pride by two veteran Greyhound engineers, G. A. Hunt and R. N. Pawlisz. In their words Greyhound was:

- First to install diesel engines, creating a 100 percent diesel fleet.

- First to operate buses with engines in rear.

- First to operate buses with air suspension (on air cushions instead of springs).

- First to install air-conditioning in intercity buses.

- First with a central heating system.

- First major fleet to specify power steering (introduced in experimental coach GX-1 in 1946).

- First to specify lavatories on all new coaches.

- First to power its fleet of intercity buses with turbocharged engines.

- First to specify automatic transmissions as standard on all new coaches.

What made these and other research-and-development innovations extraordinary was that Greyhound had no central research laboratories. Its engineers were scattered throughout the nationwide system of maintenance stations. That so much was accomplished in spite of their widely separated bases has been a source of astonishment to all other engineers.

"At intervals our men would meet to discuss what they were doing and to exchange ideas," Dunikoski said. "If what they achieved surprised and puzzled many of their colleagues in technological laboratories, I must confess it also surprised and puzzled many of us at Greyhound." He grinned and added, "It still does."

•　•　•　•　•

At the 1950 annual meeting of Greyhound stockholders, Orville Caesar stepped to the lectern—a handsome, well-dressed figure exuding all the confidence of the president of a great corporation. He had much to report. To begin, he spoke of what he termed "one of the most important acquisitions in the history of the Greyhound company."

This referred to Southern Greyhound Lines.

"It is an acquisition for which we finally received the approval of the Interstate Commerce Commission," he said, "and it will greatly strengthen our network of routes. Southern Greyhound operates over 7,517 route miles in nine southern states. It has 629 buses that run some 50 million bus miles annually, and it has 1,946 employees. It should raise Greyhound's total revenues to well over $200 million a year."

Of course, this brought a hum of interest from the audience. Caesar glanced down at his notes for the next item.

The government's enactment of draft legislation for the "Defense of Peace," he went on, once more resulted in thousands of selectees being transported to Army camps. Greyhound buses were again performing this service, to the considerable enhancement of their revenues. And an additional source of income, Caesar told his audience, lay in the newly introduced Express or Limited runs. In this arrangement buses traveled to major long-distance destinations without making intermediate stops. Saving passengers' time, they were proving to be excitingly popular.

Still another item of 1950 good news concerned the chain of Post House restaurants. During the year twenty-four had been opened for a total of 139; they had fed 40 million patrons!

Perhaps most reassuring of all, however, was the report that the downward trend of the corporation's net income had at last been reversed, despite a 1950 expenditure of $20 million for new coaches. The figure was $256,574 better than that of the preceding year; not much, admittedly, but an indication that better days were on the way.

With so many positive points to make, Caesar should have roused a good deal of stockholder enthusiasm. There he stood on the stage, flanked by the corporation's senior officers—Arthur Hill, chairman of the executive committee; Ralph Bogan, executive vice president; Robert Driscoll, general counsel; Ivan Bowen, vice president; G. A. Stevens, treasurer; Adam Sledz, comptroller; Merrill Buffington, secretary; only Carl Eric Wickman was missing, illness having kept him in his Florida home.

Was the audience silent because all these men sat expressionless, seemingly unmoved by the recital of good news? Or did the stockholders already know, as did the executives on the platform, that the rift between Caesar and Bogan was steadily becoming more embittered, a management split that harbingered bad days ahead?

•   •   •   •   •

The threat did not materialize that year or even in the following year. After all, 1951 marked a time to recognize achievement, not dissension. It was the twenty-fifth anniversary of the corporation's inception in its modern form—a holding company with many far-flung, nationwide affiliates.

At this quarter-century point the certified public accounting firm of Touche, Niven, Bailey & Smart provided financial statistics that were as startling as they were heartening. For 1951 Greyhound had record operating revenues of $226,597,000 and a net income of more than $13,713,000. Bad times seemed a thing of the past. The Greyhound Corporation now employed 26,416 people and owned 6,280 buses that covered 89,585 miles of the nation's highways. Perhaps best of all was the confidence shown by the investing public. The company now had 55,716 stockholders, a number that was growing every day of the year.

So supporters of Orville Caesar had good reason to acclaim his leadership. Bogan's partisans, on the other hand, could attribute the company's gains to the general improvement of the nation's economy. In retrospect both opinions were valid.

A typical Greyhound advertisement from the 1950s.

For American business was indeed showing an upward trend in spite of the possibility of another devastating world war. More than 100,000 United States troops, under the command of General of the Army Douglas MacArthur, were fighting Chinese communist forces in South Korea. Though President Truman called their presence there a "police action" in support of the United Nation's demand for peace, the situation could at any moment explode into widespread conflict involving all of America's fighting power. And Greyhound buses continued to carry thousands of young selectees to Army camps.

"The difference was," said a former bus driver, "that this time the bewildered kids didn't know what they were fighting for."

In the midst of all this The Greyhound Corporation was jolted, shocked, and suddenly sobered by internal tragedy. On January 24, 1952, one of its earliest leaders, Wesley Travis, died in his San Francisco home.

To many in the organization it was a frightening reminder that all of the founders had reached an age at which they were approaching the end of their careers. Who and where were their replacements? Certainly there were many able and experienced candidates among the younger officers at corporate headquarters and in the subsidiary operations. But would the adherents of Orville Caesar endorse a Bogan choice, and would Bogan's friends support a Caesar man?

"What we sorely missed," said one company executive, "was the firm, unchallenged, determined leadership of a Carl Eric Wickman. Before his retirement we had no such problems. It would have been good to bring him back into service. But he was ill, and we would have to seek solutions elsewhere."

Part Two

YEARS OF TRANSITION

11

Wickman was indeed ill—so ill that he could do nothing for the company he had founded and nurtured through its earliest years. This sense of helplessness must have tormented him, especially when he was forced to forego every meeting of directors.

Weakened by diabetes and a complication of other ailments, he spent most of his time on a small yacht he had bought. There, in the harbor of Fort Lauderdale, Florida, he lay back in a deck chair, his eyes closed against the glare of the sun. That robust figure of his, no longer "like a block of granite," became lax, almost flaccid, and the once powerful jaw began to droop.

He did, nonetheless, thoughtfully study all Greyhound reports that came to him by mail. He must have been fascinated to read how far coach development had progressed since he drove his seven-passenger Hupmobile to Alice. According to the communication:

> Scheduled for construction and delivery in 1954 is the Scenicruiser, a dramatically new type of motor coach, the product of many years' research and testing. This greatly advanced model will not only incorporate the air suspension principle, but because of its new design will provide the smoothest and quietest ride of any bus equipment yet developed. There will be additional room for passengers, more spacious seats, an observation deck for greater scenic enjoyment, washroom facilities, and other new and attractive appointments.

What pleased him most, according to his family, were reports of company innovations like Through Bus Schedules or

The classic Greyhound Scenicruiser was introduced in 1954.

Express Services. "This extra fare service," he read, "provides reserved seats, a steward on each bus, toilet facilities, and free pillows. It is now possible to make trips by Greyhound between numerous cities and towns—some of these trips upwards of 2,300 miles—without change of bus or transfer of baggage."

Items like these made him smile and nod approval. This was progress. And since he himself had long ago, far back in 1931, retained Marcus Dow to train Greyhound drivers in safety, he was inordinately gratified to learn, year after year, that "Greyhound has led all other forms of domestic transportation in passenger safety."

But sitting there in the sun on the deck of his boat, Wickman could only grieve in silence when he learned that S. B. Browne, whom he had made president of Post Houses, had died. Browne, who had spent the past fifteen years in developing the Post House chain, had been more than a business associate; he had been a friend. Now his vice president, J. F. Edwards, was taking Browne's place. Edwards was inheriting 149 restaurants on Greyhound's routes—a business that had earned revenues of $16.4 million by feeding more than 62 million patrons. One can only guess how Wickman felt when he recalled that he himself had launched this chain of eating places because he found the original counters unsanitary and unappetizing.

Even as his strength ebbed away, he invariably mumbled approval of new Greyhound acquisitions and of the repurchase of bus stocks held by railroads. These actions reflected and continued his own ways of doing business. He was still pleased by them when, quietly and alone on February 5, 1954, dozing in the Florida sunshine, Carl Eric Wickman died.

In Mora, Sweden, his 1887 birthplace, and in the many American cities where he had lived, church services, philanthropic organizations, and newspaper obituaries joined in expressing admiration for the career of Carl Wickman. Yet no such expression was simpler or more moving than the resolution adopted by Greyhound's board of directors. Among its statements were these:

> Eric Wickman was a man of great vision. He saw far beyond the confines of the community and state in which he lived. He looked far into the future in his conception of a motor bus system. . . . From the humble beginning in Hibbing grew the present Greyhound Lines, comprising the nation's largest intercity passenger transportation system. With great skill and with the help of a team of able men in whom he instilled a spirit of loyalty and devotion, he developed a constantly improving vehicle, worked out methods of management, and consolidated and coordinated the early bus lines into a great integrated system of transportation. . . .
>
> He was always a man with a hand on the other fellow's shoulder. He was a friend of the bus driver, the bus mechanic, and of countless others in all departments of the organization. He was generous to a fault, ever ready to help his friend. These great human characteristics helped him to attract able men. He imparted much to his friends and, in turn, received much from them. He inspired men to do their best and rewarded them with the fruits of their success. He had a clear mind, sound judgment, and an uncanny ability to arrive at the right decision in solving the problems faced by the new intercity bus business. He had the confidence that was based on ability, simplicity, sincerity, and integrity. . . .
>
> The Greyhound Lines will always serve as a living memorial to his brilliant career in the transportation field. He

will stand high on the list of immortals in the history of transportation in America.

• • • • •

In a sense the death of Carl Eric Wickman left the company without its father figure. Active or retired, he had been a living force who held the respect of every man working for Greyhound. Now leadership was divided to such an extent as to be not only tragic but almost childish in its petty jealousies. When the company issued a special annual report for its employees, Orville Caesar had his picture and the president's message inside the front cover of the booklet; Ralph Bogan had his picture and message inside the back cover.

Those most annoyed by this managerial rivalry were, understandably, those members of the board of directors who were not company officers—"outsiders" like Richard Griggs of Duluth; C. G. Schultz of Jacksonville; Herbert Wellington of New York. Others within the organization, especially Arthur Hill and Frederick Ackerman, shared the outsiders' concern.

All of them knew that something had to be done to mend the internal rift. A company divided could anticipate nothing but trouble. In fact, trouble was already evident. Earnings were once more decreasing.

Those veteran executives who had been bus drivers in the Hibbing days—men like Sundstrom, Graves, and their generation—were loyal to their Hibbing compatriot, Ralph Bogan. Yet they all agreed on what was necessary to ease internal tensions:

> There could be no peace within the company until it had leadership that wasn't partisan. No matter which Greyhound executive might succeed Caesar, he would be regarded as either a Caesar man or a Bogan man. He would be distrusted by half the organization. The only cure for this stand-off situation, the only way to end this corporate infighting, was to bring in impartial outside leadership. A chief executive who was neither a Caesar man nor a Bogan man was

the only kind who could reunite Greyhound, the only kind who could concentrate its energies on growth instead of on haggling.

Quietly at first, then more overtly, the search for such a man was undertaken by the directors.

There was nothing unusual in a corporation's seeking fresh, outside leadership. Many of America's outstanding companies were doing it to bring in new ideas, new thinking. They were doing it almost as readily as they sought fresh sales inspiration by changing advertising agencies. In most cases it was done at a time of sagging business "to turn the company around."

Greyhound's search for the right man was not easy, though many names were discussed in private among directors. Eventually one man emerged as best equipped by background and experience to head a transportation company like Greyhound. This was Arthur S. Genet.

A brief biographical sketch distributed at headquarters reported, "Mr. Genet, now 47 years of age, has a background of wide experience in both transportation and financial management. He has held important positions in banking and in the coal and railroad industries. Most recently Mr. Genet has been serving as vice president for traffic of the Chesapeake and Ohio Railway Company, a position he assumed in 1947. Previously he held executive positions with the Bank of Manhattan, the Central Coal Company of New York, the Metropolitan Coal Company of Boston, and the National Car Loading Company of New York."

Several directors met privately with Genet to form their own impressions of the man. They found him to be a brisk, efficient, no-nonsense individual. He had the reputation of refusing to tolerate laxity.

In any case, Arthur Genet became the board's choice to rescue The Greyhound Corporation from divisiveness, to set it on the road to renewed growth and prosperity.

On November 22, 1955, Genet was elected to the board of directors. Five weeks later, on January 1, 1956, he became president and chief executive—the only Greyhound leader who had not risen through the ranks from the days when management had lain in the hands of former bus drivers.

Genet was given full authority and a salary of $90,000 a year. At the same time Orville Caesar, after serving ten years as president, was "elevated" to the position of chairman of the board of directors. He replaced Arthur Hill who became chairman of the executive committee.

As for Ralph Bogan, considering his explosive temperament he remained strangely quiet, simply retaining the title of executive vice president.

And so, with a new chief executive in command, the directors of The Greyhound Corporation waited to see what would happen.

•   •   •   •   •

They realized that many things were beyond Genet's immediate control. As an example, bus revenues were increasing because the ICC had granted a 6 percent rise in fares and because more and more people were patronizing the widely advertised Expense Paid Tours and Package Express. Yet these facts had little effect on the company's net income.

The reason for the discrepancy lay first in higher labor costs. American unions were fighting for and winning pay increases everywhere, and Greyhound was not exempt from the trend. Many of its affiliates had accepted new pay levels. Almost 50 percent of income went to wages.

Maintenance costs too had risen, as had the price of constructing everything from a repair shop to a big-city bus terminal. As for buses, which had once been available for $10,000 per unit, the figure was now closer to $50,000.

So no one expected immediate wonders from the new president. There was general approval when he decided to familiarize himself with the organization by visiting offices of the affiliated lines. What prompted some uneasiness, however, was his decision to emulate certain railroad tycoons. These men traveled luxuriously in specially built private railroad cars. Genet ordered a Greyhound bus to be transformed into a combination office and drawing room. The result rivaled the splendor of any private car on railway tracks. Its interior was photographed and reproduced in a number of publications.

He may have been told or perhaps he sensed that some people considered his private bus a needless extravagance. They even questioned its taste. Certainly Carl Wickman, who had traveled far and wide, had built a solid business without resorting to such a show. But criticism did not deter Genet. He felt he could justify his idea by explaining it to stockholders in the company's annual report. There, under the heading, *The President's Trip*, he wrote:

> No executive can operate from an ivory tower, so, to get more firsthand information on our operations as well as to add momentum to our public relations, I boarded a standard Scenicruiser, which has been converted internally to serve as an office on wheels, and took a three-month tour of all our facilities. It was a rewarding and reassuring inspection trip. . . .
>
> It was a point of great pleasure to observe, throughout the entire journey, that the Scenicruiser in which I traveled, known as "G.C.13," became a focal point for the general public. It was inspected and commented on at every stop we made. Civic and business officials, as well as representatives of the press, radio, and television, rode into cities with me, along with the presidents of our operating subsidiaries who came aboard as I entered their respective territories.
>
> These thought leaders generated a flood of highly favorable comment about Greyhound and its services in all the mass communications media—newspapers, magazines, radio, and TV.

Thus Genet described his bus as a publicity asset. But the doubters continued to doubt. Others shrugged and said, "He's boss now. He's entitled to his way of running the company."

One thing augured well for Greyhound's future. This was what one historian described as President Eisenhower's contribution to the American landscape. His interstate highway system was just getting under way; it would provide 41,000 miles of new roads—the biggest public works project in the nation's history (ultimately at a cost of $76 billion).

Genet promised that the Greyhound system would inaugurate new routes as quickly as the new highways were opened. In preparation for such expansion he announced, "We have placed an order for 500 intercity Highway Traveler buses, in the amount of approximately $20 million, with the GMC Truck and Coach Division."

This plan evoked little comment; it sounded routine. But soon the Genet administration resorted to some dramatic innovations.

First it invited several New York advertising agencies to submit programs that would supplant the campaigns heretofore managed by Beaumont and Hohman. A number of agencies responded. David Ogilvie of Ogilvie and Mather arrived in Chicago at the same time as did Arthur Fatt of Grey Advertising. The two men, old friends, chatted in an anteroom while waiting to be interviewed by Genet. If they frankly discussed the contents of their presentations, it was because they knew neither would copy from the other.

Finally Genet came out of his office to shake hands. He invited Ogilvie to join him first. To Genet's astonishment—and to Arthur Fatt's utter amazement—Ogilvie said, "I've just heard the Grey program. It's so much better than ours that I'm withdrawing our proposal. I strongly urge you to take on Grey. Their plans are excellent." In the entire history of agency competition, Arthur Fatt later said, he knew of no similar act.

The Greyhound Corporation did retain Grey. The agency's presentation included a plan to use the phrase "It's such a comfort to go by bus—and leave the driving to us." Over the years the various mutations of this finally resulted in one of

Workers putting final brush strokes to a famous dog high on a terminal wall. "Go Greyhound—and leave the driving to us" became the company's slogan in the 1950s.

the most effective slogans in advertising annals: "Go Greyhound—and leave the driving to us."

Genet did not entrust all of Greyhound's advertising to a single agency. To develop Greyvan Lines, the moving van operation that had at last begun to show profits, he retained Maxon & Company of Chicago in 1957–58. A year later, when he established Greyhound Rent-A-Car Service, he appointed Robert Conahay, Inc., of New York to handle that account.

His most unexpected managerial change, however—one which was to lead to widespread consternation, even to stupefaction—rose out of what Genet termed "personnel development." No doubt some self-styled efficiency expert had imbued him with the idea. Whatever its source, in 1956 Genet announced:

> We are inaugurating an extensive personnel development program throughout the Greyhound system. It will go from the executive and management level through the ranks of the entire staff ranging from supervisors to sales agents, from maintenance managers to safety directors.

Millions of words have been written about placing the right man in the right job. We are directing our major attention to match individual qualifications to the right jobs, and vice versa. Until this is done it will be impossible for us to have an effective and efficient operation.

Could this be interpreted—as did some shocked and incredulous employees—as inferring that the company was being managed by *in*effective and *in*efficient people? Could men with the long experience of Bogan, Caesar, Sledz, Sundstrom, Graves, and others who had helped build The Greyhound Corporation be required to prove they were in "the right jobs"? It was too grotesque an idea to be believable. One might as well question the late Carl Wickman's fitness to head the company he had created.

Besides, employees were asking, just how did Genet propose to fit the right man into the right job? When the answer came from the president's office, it baffled some people and brought jeers from others. The plan sounded ridiculous.

According to Genet's orders every Greyhound employee throughout the United States and Canada would be subjected to psychological tests, educational tests, physical fitness tests, and other tests to ascertain his capabilities. No one (except Arthur Genet himself) would be excused from submitting to the examinations. They would be conducted by an outside agency experienced in making personnel surveys.

Clearly, even able supervisors with twenty-five and thirty years of experience would have to prove their right to hold their jobs. Resistance among them was inevitable.

As for Ralph Bogan, he wanted no part of Genet's program. He even refused to give any indication that he was willing to countenance it. Certainly he could not submit—or see his lifetime associates submit—to the indignity of being judged by "some young eggheads who never worked in this or any other business." Bogan resigned as executive vice president and as a director of the company. After forty-two years of helping to make bus travel part of American life, he was finished.

12

Genet's testing team pervaded Chicago headquarters like Internal Revenue auditors. They gave employees oral tests and written tests. They touched on subjects from philosophy to mathematics which, for most people, had no perceptible connection with bus operations. When questioned they explained, "The idea is to get a measure of a person's total intellectual capacity and of his personality as well as of his vocational aptitudes."

To many an automobile mechanic this was sheer gibberish. At the terminal of one midwestern city the Greyhound maintenance supervisor, an engineer who had been servicing the company's buses for twenty-three years, found it impossible to answer questions that required a cultural background wholly different from his own. After an hour of frustrating failure he lost patience.

"Look," he said to his questioner, a spectacled man young enough to be his son. "You went to college, right?"

"Of course."

"Got a degree?"

"Certainly. Master's. In psychology."

"Great. Master's in psychology. So let me ask you this: If a diesel goes blooey on a bus, what do you do?"

The examiner laughed. "No idea."

"How would you describe a turbocharged engine?"

"Can't say. Why do you ask?"

"To show you that you don't have to know everything to be good at your job. This is an age of specialization. Should I say you don't know anything about psychology because you don't know anything about diesels? Of course not. And there's no reason you should say I'm not a good mechanic because I don't know much about your specialty. I'm a damned good engineer, see? So why don't we quit this stupid nonsense? You go back to studying psychology and I'll go back to repairing buses."

"You miss the point," the tester said. "The company is planning to give people advanced training in areas where they're proficient. Fit them for bigger jobs."

"I've been giving my men advanced training for years."

It was a futile argument. This engineer did not measure up to the young psychologist's standards of general knowledge. After twenty-three years of service with the company he was asked to resign—one of 258 Greyhound employees fired that year because they could not meet the intellectual demands of the test.

"Those examinations," Clifford Graves grimly recalled, "cost the company some of the most experienced people on its payroll. It sent shock waves through the ranks. Nobody knew how safe his job was."

Either Genet was insensitive to the feelings he engendered or he pretended to be unaware of them. In either case he went on to other matters, some of them indisputably constructive.

For instance, he simplified the complicated Greyhound structure by integrating all United States bus lines into six and later four geographic groupings.

He incorporated the Canadian lines into Greyhound of Canada, its management headed by Robert L. Borden of Calgary, Alberta.

In a single year new terminals were opened in Philadelphia, Richmond, San Jose, LaCrosse, and Goldsboro, with three more under construction.

Genet spurred the moving van business with a generous advertising appropriation, and Greyvan Lines produced a 1955 profit of $240,000.

With Package Express he was resourceful and successful. He negotiated contracts with airlines to develop joint air–bus deliveries in distant cities, an imaginative, profitable service.

"No question that many of Genet's projects paid off," Graves granted. "With increased advertising he increased revenues from Highway Tours, from Charter Service, from ordinary business travel."

Yet the corporation's 1955 operating revenues of $225,881,451 were a million dollars below those of the previous year; and net income of $12,923,277 was almost $2 million less than the 1954 figure.

"Several factors accounted for this decline," Genet explained. "A long strike on Atlantic Greyhound Lines considerably affected the revenues and earnings not only of that company but of connecting operations. Also, during the year many Scenicruisers developed mechanical difficulties which caused service failures. They resulted in substantially higher maintenance costs than would ordinarily be expected with new equipment."

He might have added that another million dollars was being spent to renovate an old warehouse in Niles, Illinois. Genet had found it inefficient to have headquarters offices spread through seven floors of the Chicago building. The converted Niles warehouse would allow all offices to be on the street floor. A move to Niles was scheduled for 1957.

"Your company is an ambitious one," Genet told shareholders, "and a healthy one. We are growing. We are keeping pace with the surging expansion of America. We are moving ahead with vision and imagination, but with sound business caution. If in my position as president I may be regarded as being in the driver's seat, I am pleased to report that I can look through the windshield and see we are on the right road—the one marked 'Progress.' "

All might have been well if he had devoted himself to promoting Greyhound's normal ongoing activities—everything from bus travel to building more and more Post House restaurants. But he decided on a wholly new venture.

This was to launch Greyhound Rent-A-Car Service.

There was some irrefutable logic in the plan, even if it involved competition with established firms like Hertz, Avis, and National. As Genet put it, "We deemed ourselves well-qualified to take on this venture because of our vast network of bus operations and the company's unique experience over thirty years with maintenance, safety, and service of transportation and transportation equipment."

It did indeed seem a logical step for a company like Greyhound to take; after all, it was essentially a motorcar organization. And it seemed equally obvious that Genet could not have undertaken this new business without the approval of the directors. So it was reasonable for shareholders to assume the project had been thoroughly analyzed at board meetings and had been found practicable and profitable. No one predicted it could lead to disaster.

• • • • •

In truth, it might have been as successful as Genet hoped if this diversification had been nurtured with patience. As company executives later said, the practical procedure would have been to open two or three geographically scattered offices as pilot plants. There the rent-a-car business could be learned; a cadre of office personnel could be trained. These people could then be used to instruct trainees in additional offices.

Such a procedure might well have succeeded, despite the time needed to test it step by step.

But that was not the method Genet favored. As a start he opened an office in Greyhound's Cleveland terminal. Preceded by a spate of newspaper advertisements, then given an opening day fanfare plus "introductory prices," the office attracted an encouraging number of customers. Genet interpreted this in his own way. "The immediate response," he said, "showed that we had met a real need and that we were supplying a much appreciated convenience."

No doubt he believed the initial Cleveland success would continue endlessly and be duplicated everywhere else, since he immediately plunged into national expansion. He did so with incredible speed. Some called it impossible speed. Genet himself must have been proud of the pace he set, reckless, expensive, and wild though it was. Within a year he informed stockholders in a proud statement:

> During the past twelve months Greyhound rent-a-car stations rose from one to 122. Company-owned vehicles totaled 16,466. . . . It is expected that within another year nearly 400 communities will be served by company-owned or franchised Greyhound stations. Eventually Greyhound should be represented in more than 700 cities.

The 1957 plan was stupendous. But so were the problems.

How do you open 122 efficient branches in a single year—ten every month? Where do you find competent, experienced representatives who can fan out from Chicago headquarters to establish hundreds of offices throughout the country? How do they equip these branches with requisite needs—not only office supplies and cars, but garages and maintenance men? Where do they find employees in city after city who know how to manage a car-rental agency?

To all such questions and many more there was one answer: You don't, you can't, you shouldn't.

Most of the employees in the 122 offices knew nothing of the business. They had to grope their way, and their mistakes were costly. Again and again rented cars failed to be returned, and no provisions had been made to cope with such cases. Years later abandoned Greyhound cars were found in town after town. Adam Sledz, the company's comptroller at the time, still shakes his head over memories of the financial reports he received. "Inexperienced office help cost us millions," he recalls.

One does not demand glowing profits in the first year of a new venture; starting costs can very well consume earnings. But in this case, when the board of directors gathered around their long table to hear the first year results of Arthur Genet's project, they were appalled. Those "outside" directors who were financiers—Richard Griggs of Duluth, and Herbert Wellington and Charles S. Munson of New York—found the figures incredible.

The millions of dollars invested in leases for offices and garages, for wages paid to 475 employees; the price of equipment, of advertising, of insurance—such necessities were but a fraction of the total costs to be considered. There was the price of 16,466 automobiles at an average cost of $4,000 per unit.

The car-rental project had steeped the company into debts beyond anyone's imagination. "Those debts," said Sledz, "were so bad as to threaten the whole Greyhound system."

Genet attempted to ease the fears. "In establishing this business," he said, "we were faced with development charges which we knew were bound to result in losses in 1957. In 1958 these growth and development charges will be behind us, and we have reason to expect substantial earnings from this new subsidiary."

Week after week revenues diminished and indebtedness increased. By July 1958 it was inescapably clear that Genet's predictions had been baseless. Rent-a-car receipts were down by more than 50 percent.

Confronted by this ever-worsening situation, the directors summoned Genet to a special meeting in July. When he came he was tight-lipped. As he glanced from one stern face to another, he had no need to wait for questions. After having served less than three years as Greyhound's president, Arthur Genet resigned.

Despite the frightening debts he had incurred, he had unwittingly achieved one purpose for which he had been hired. He had ended the rift among Greyhound personnel.

13

In addition to having to cope with staggering indebtedness the eight solemn men around the director's table now had to contemplate an empty presidential office.

Who was to fill it? One thing was certain: It should not be another outsider ready to commit corporate funds to reckless experimentation. The board had to find a man whose primary purpose would be to restore sound management principles while finding ways to climb out of debt.

With this in mind, the directors understandably leaned toward conservatism. It would be wise to select someone who understood the spirit, the aims, and the operating procedures of The Greyhound Corporation; someone whose personal experience could help bring back the methods and the wisdom of, say, a Wickman or a Bogan.

But Wickman was dead, and Bogan, since his resignation, had risen swiftly in another world of industry and finance. Apart from serving as chairman of the LaSalle Corporation and chairman of the Chicago North Shore Railroad, he was a director of half a dozen other companies—far too busy and successful an executive to relinquish those positions.

So, of Greyhound's founding group, few were available. Sundstrom had recently died. Orville Caesar, now chairman of the board, had already had ten years of the presidency; he wanted no more of that responsibility. Arthur Hill, chairman of the executive committee, preferred to retain that position. The board considered other surviving veterans of the company's earliest days—Clifford Graves, for instance. Now president of Northwest Greyhound Lines in Seattle, Graves was in the midst of coordinating United States and Canadian operations, an important task it would be unwise to interrupt.

Inevitably attention focused on one of the board's own members, Frederick Ackerman. He had been connected with the bus industry all his adult life, starting as an accountant and partner of Wesley Travis on the West Coast. He had joined Wickman and Bogan in building Greyhound to its present size. No one had stronger ties to the business. No one more clearly understood its problems, its aims, the glowing dreams and ambitions of the founders.

As significant as any other factor was Ackerman's temperament. An accountant by profession, he would analyze the company's indebtedness with cold detachment. His job would be to avoid financial chaos, and nobody could think of a man better qualified to grapple with the challenge of this crisis.

The board unanimously elected him president.

A formal notification to shareholders said simply that in August 1958 he became the fifth president of The Greyhound Corporation, then added:

> Mr. Ackerman has been a Greyhound operating executive for thirty-two years. He has been president of its largest division, Western Greyhound Lines, since 1946, when he also became a director of the National Association of Motor Bus Operators. Two years ago he was elected a director and member of the executive committee of The Greyhound Corporation. Mr. Ackerman therefore brings valuable managerial, financial, and operating experience to the office.
>
> A native of San Francisco, he has achieved eminence in other fields. He is a director and executive committee member of the Crocker-Anglo National Bank of San Francisco and is a director of the Yale & Towne Manufacturing Company, the Seaboard Finance Company, and the Lucky Lager Brewing Company.

•   •   •   •   •

On a hot midsummer day Frederick Ackerman settled behind his desk in the new headquarters Genet had opened in Niles, Illinois.

One thing he soon discovered was that the move to the converted warehouse in Niles had been useless, expensive, and a
nuisance to all those who had to travel out of Chicago to come
to work. To everyone's relief, the new president ordered an
immediate search for quarters that would enable the company
to move back to Chicago. "The first sign," one employee remarked, "of returning sanity and normalcy."

(By 1958 The Greyhound Corporation's headquarters was
indeed back in Chicago, in the Marquette Building at 140
South Dearborn Street.)

Having taken care of the headquarters change, Ackerman
turned to the task of lifting The Greyhound Corporation out
of its morass of debt. One can visualize this imperturbable accountant adjusting his glasses for a dispassionate appraisal of
the assets at his disposal.

Much of Greyhound's strength lay in the fact that, for the
most part, its revenues came in the form of cash. Moreover,
they came the instant service was rendered—from bus fares,
from Post House income, from Package Express charges.
That year, 1958, cash receipts from bus fares alone amounted to $272,075,355. In addition, restaurant services yield-
ed $21,983,190, and the moving van operation brought
$7,353,636. All of these suggested a strong and healthy busi-
ness, an unshakable bulwark against any threat of bankruptcy.

One might say that Ackerman now headed two separate enterprises—the thriving bus business on the one hand, and the
almost bankrupt rent-a-car business on the other. As a parent
keeps a sick child away from his healthy brother to prevent
infection, so it seemed necessary to prevent car-rental debts
from undermining the healthy transportation business.

Could such a thing be done? There were dubious voices in
the company that suggested trying to build the rental business
into a successful operation. Ackerman vetoed this. It would
mean heavy added investment over a period of years, only to
bolster a project that had so far been an utter failure.

"The wisest move we can make," he decided, "is to get rid

of the entire rent-a-car business, to sell off whatever we can, even at a loss. Better to take one loss quickly now than to take year after year of losses by trying to continue the business."

Who would buy an enterprise that was losing so many millions? He did not know. The only logical purchaser, one would have said, would be a company that wanted, for tax purposes, to offset a huge profit by "buying a loss"—something not many companies were doing in the mid-1950s. As for major fleet owners, they would probably turn away from automobiles at least two years old and in questionable condition.

So the next question was: Could the rent-a-car system be sold piecemeal? After all, Rent-A-Car owned more than automobiles.

It had contracted to buy or had taken long-term leases on 122 sites in ninety cities. These were generally in excellent business locations. Maybe a buyer could be found for them. But if such real estate obligations were disposed of separately, what would happen to the 16,466 cars now parked in garages, or behind Greyhound rental offices, or being driven by those who had rented the vehicles? Ackerman was no doubt shocked, as any methodical person would be, to find that records were so inept as to make it impossible to locate thousands of the rented passenger cars or U-Drive trucks.

These were problems that the president took to attorney Gerald H. Trautman in the offices of the corporation's San Francisco law firm. Trautman, as he studied what everyone now termed "the mess," came upon one of its worst features. In Los Angeles, San Francisco, and elsewhere The Greyhound Corporation was committed to paying high rental fees for certain properties "until suitable offices were built on the sites"; then Greyhound would assume ownership. But no construction had been started at any of these places. If the present owners chose to do nothing, Greyhound would be compelled, by its contract, to go on paying high rentals forever while receiving nothing in return.

The attorney seized upon this as a violation of a seldom invoked, often forgotten "rule against perpetuity." The law limited such an agreement to "lives in being and twenty-one years." But Genet's contracts had no such time limitation. It was a technical point on which Trautman promptly took legal action—and won his case. Greyhound was relieved from having to pay perpetual rents on these expensive sites.

The next problem took a good deal longer to solve: How could Greyhound be rid of the entire car-rental organization—offices, equipment, cars, leases, everything? No matter how this was accomplished it would involve heavy losses—this both Trautman and Ackerman knew. The search for a buyer, with the aid of brokers, bankers, and others was often discouraging. But it eventually led to the Commercial Credit Company. And there Greyhound made its initial breakthrough.

"Negotiations for the sale of the Vehicle Leasing division were successfully concluded in February 1958 by selling our long-term leases to the Commercial Credit Company," Ackerman was able to announce. To soften the impact of the sacrificial price the company had been forced to acccept, he added, "For five years Greyhound will share equally in the net profits of these leasing operations. We are confident that this liquidation can be fully completed before the end of 1959. No accurate estimate can be made of what the total losses will be, but it is believed they will be moderate compared to the losses of the past two years."

The prediction was fully justified by results.

• • • • •

As he might have foreseen, while entrusting much of the car-rental case to Trautman, Ackerman was being called upon to fulfill other executive duties in every part of the nation. The more popular bus transportation became, the greater demands there were on his time. And Greyhound bus travel, spurred by nationwide advertising and promotion, expanded every year. In 1959 its revenues rose again to exceed $323 million.

The enormous cash flow enabled the company to meet most obligations with cash payments. In one case it sent General Motors a $13 million check for 300 new Scenicruisers that were being delivered at the rate of four a day.

When the first of these coaches arrived in Chicago, they were greeted with appropriate ceremonies. Ackerman presided. Standing at the door of a bus, surrounded by a number of his vice presidents, he posed for cameramen and reporters and told them, "These buses have brought passengers increased visibility, greater safety, and unmatched comforts which make them a major advance in intercity bus transportation." Of course, he was repeating words his predecessors had spoken again and again as one new bus model after another had appeared.

(There are collectors of miniature coach models, perhaps none more avid than Donald M. Coffin of Montclair, New Jersey, whose miniatures are a year-by-year record of Greyhound's contributions to the improvement of American bus travel.)

At any rate, Ackerman properly extolled the first Scenicruisers when they appeared in Chicago. Attending such ceremonials was a duty he seemed not to relish. "He never looked comfortable," one of his associates remarked. "Yet he realized some were unavoidable, like the one in New York, for instance."

This one was historic. Greyhound had two New York terminals, but they were becoming obsolete in size and location. For years the company sought the right to build a modern terminal in a more convenient location farther east. The city not only objected, it passed a law making it illegal to construct such a building east of 8th Avenue.

Naturally the company contested the ruling. Its New York attorneys fought long and hard, but it was a futile struggle. The city remained obdurate—until the administration of Mayor Robert Wagner confronted the problem of renting space in the projected Port Authority terminal in New York City. That broke the deadlock.

This time the city's lawyers met amicably with those of Greyhound, and the bus company was promised fifteen loading platforms in the new terminal.

These lanes, once they were completed, would be able to accommodate the arrival and departure of 400 Greyhound buses a day. Nor was that all. The company gained the right to build a huge modern garage on West 40th Street between 11th and 12th avenues, just a few blocks from the Port of New York Authority Building. It would then have a new and convenient base of operations in the city.

Naturally the triumphant culmination of this long deferred agreement required the formal presence of Greyhound's president in New York. It also required the formal presence of New York's mayor. The two signed their contract before photographers, reporters, and representatives of radio and television. Someone labeled the ceremony "opening a new gateway to the West."

Within days Ackerman again had to face cameras and reporters. This time it was on the occasion of his presenting the Marcus Dow Safety Award to Greyhound of Canada, an award established in honor of the corporation's first supervisor of safety education.

Yet all such formalities, and they were endless, never curbed Frederick Ackerman's instincts as an accountant. Before all else he remained a guardian of Greyhound's finances. "Day and night," some said, he sought ways of saving the company's funds, and those ways were often unpopular.

"It was as if he judged people solely by what they cost the corporation," one of his colleagues charged.

Clifford Graves illustrated this by his own experience. He had just entered his Seattle office when Ackerman's secretary telephoned to ask him to come to San Francisco. The summons, Graves felt, must concern his efforts to stimulate northwest travel between Seattle and Vancouver. He went to San Francisco, happy with the thought that he would have an opportunity to see his old bus-driving colleague, Bob Budd, who was working in the California office.

Ackerman, behind his desk, rose cordially to shake hands and complimented Graves on his successful efforts in Canada. The conversation was casual enough until Graves asked, "How's Budd? I'd like to say hello."

Ackerman picked up a pencil, frowned at it. "Matter of fact, Cliff, he isn't here," he said. "Last week we had him take early retirement." Ackerman looked up. "That's what I want to talk to you about."

Graves was incredulous. "About early retirement? You want me to quit?"

Ackerman nodded.

Yet it was true. One can only conclude that in seeking ways to balance out company losses incurred in the car-rental sacrifice—the task for which he had originally been made president—Ackerman had decided to eliminate some highly paid executives and replace them with lower salaried people. It was not only high salaries he would thereby reduce. By letting men go a year or two before they would be entitled to full pension benefits he was also saving money for the company's pension fund.

Some of his colleagues angrily charged that Ackerman was more interested in pennies than in people. For his part, he issued a terse year-end statement: "We are carefully studying all areas of dealing with expense and revenues. We are confident that policies for continued growth and successful operation are being followed."

Figures indicated that he was right. There was indeed an upsurge of revenues. But, as many pointed out, these gains could not in every case be attributed to Ackerman's methods. Other people were making their contributions to Greyhound's growth. There was a great deal of ingenuity in Greyhound's ranks, and the innovations with which that ingenuity was demonstrated are worth considering.

14

There were, for example, the extraordinary, widely advertised promotions of Greyhound Highway Tours. Of course, this subsidiary, managed by C. E. Holderby in Evanston, Illinois, had for years been running escorted, all-expense tours to the most popular vacation and scenic areas in the United States. Now it added new horizons by sponsoring travel to foreign lands. Special arrangements with shipping lines and Trans World Airlines enabled Greyhound buses to carry people from their hometowns to international airports, or to the docks beside ocean liners. From there they could go on to Europe, to the islands of the Caribbean, to the South Pacific.

What spurred a swift response was the announcement that henceforth trips could be enjoyed for a 10 percent down payment, the balance to be defrayed in monthly installments. True, this was contrary to the company's pay-as-you-go precedent. Wickman and Bogan—who had begun life by collecting fares as passengers stepped into their cars—might have hesitated over this policy. But in the end they would probably have conceded that in the process of growth a business had to remain competitive and aware of economic changes. One of the current economic changes was a swift, broadening use of credit cards. What Alfred Bloomingdale had started with his Diner's Club was being adopted by many others. In this era of deferred payments Greyhound had to make its competitive response.

It worked. To attract those with limited time to see America's wonders, Highway Tours introduced another novel feature—Bus Out–Buzz-Back. You went to your destination by bus; you returned by plane. As former comptroller Sledz said,

"What those fellows in Evanston were doing brought, in 1962, a 26 percent increase in tour revenues. They were certainly doing a good deal of original thinking."

One significant contribution to the increase was an arrangement with the American Express Company which agreed to advertise and sell Greyhound tours in its hundreds of offices. A similar agreement was made with some of the leading travel bureaus in Europe. (One says that glibly, ignoring the weeks of European travel, conferences, and detailed arrangements Greyhound representatives had to make, including the promise to have bilingual escorts on buses.)

In this connection the company launched its remarkably successful ninety-nine-dollar invitation: The resident of a foreign country—with Canada soon included—could travel by Greyhound coach anywhere in the United States for ninety-nine days, with unlimited mileage privileges. The plan brought to this country thousands of adult tourists and thousands of students.

But the masterpiece of promotional ploys occurred when a colorful, streamlined Scenicruiser was dispatched to travel through seven European nations. Going from city to city, it carried bilingual drivers and attendants, newspaper reporters, and an American jazz band. Wherever it stopped curious crowds were invited to inspect the inside of the coach, to test its comfortable seats. They were given pamphlets that described the scenic beauties of the United States, plus an invitation to "Go Greyhound—and leave the driving to us."

Greyhound Tours were doing so well that they received the government's "E" award for the record number of foreign visitors they brought to this country. Not that special occasions at home were ignored. Two hundred Greyhound buses transported some 50,000 people to the Winter Olympics in Squaw Valley, California. And in preparation for Seattle's World's Fair the company's engineers designed special sightseeing vehicles for use inside the exposition grounds—open Glide-A-Ride cars and the smaller Escorts.

Yet few things inspired the tour-planners as did public events. Greyhound buses carried thousands of people to the inauguration of President John F. Kennedy. They carried thousands to the New Orleans celebration of Mardi Gras. "If you want to see where history is being made," wrote a columnist, "follow a chartered Greyhound bus."

The tours, however, were by no means the only contributors to increasing revenues. Some resulted from savings inspired by individuals. Thus N. L. Maino, vice president for transportation, proposed an ingenious plan to create a bus pool. Somehow, obvious as it seemed, no one had ever before considered this. In its simplest definition it meant maintaining a reserve of vehicles to be used where most needed. Once it had been tried and adopted, Maino explained to reporters:

> Besides giving us more flexibility of assignment, the pool makes possible the actual reduction of our fleet. Service to low-traffic routes can be reduced or abandoned, while the more heavily traveled routes can receive additional schedules. With fewer buses we can increase efficiency. We use buses where they are most needed.
>
> Also, the installation of advanced teletype equipment throughout our offices—something we've just done—has permitted far better coordination throughout our system. "GCS," for Greyhound Communications Service, provides instant pretrip and en route information. It transmits all necessary data on operational orders, weather reports, road and traffic conditions, baggage information, schedule changes, reservations, and anticipated passenger volume. I believe we are the first intercity bus company to install such equipment.

Another form of savings was achieved by veteran William Duvall, vice president for maintenance and equipment. His explanation of how he reduced costs by $1.25 million was startling in its very simplicity.

"It was accomplished," Duvall explained, "through the establishment of four major maintenance centers in Atlanta, Chicago, Washington, D.C., and San Francisco, with a fifth being constructed in Dallas." These centers, strategically lo-

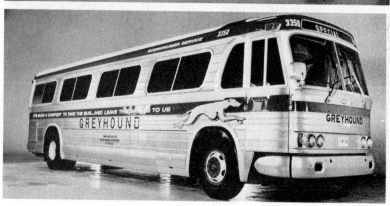

An evolution in design is shown in these buses of the 1950s and 60s.

Frederick Ackerman (center), chief executive officer of the
Greyhound Corporation at a meeting with top executives at the company's
corporate headquarters in Chicago in 1961. Adam Sledz, first row, far right, the
company's long time chief financial officer, attended.

cated, were swiftly and efficiently supplying their regional garages with necessary parts. Inventories no longer had to be
duplicated in scores of repair shops. The annual savings were
enough to pay for twenty-five new buses.

All such sources of better business were undeniably impressive to the company's officers. But if you asked some of its
advertising people to name what made the public most keenly
aware of The Greyhound Corporation, the answer would in
all probability have been, "The dog."

The dog? Twenty-odd years later this requires explanation.

•   •   •   •   •

A beautiful thoroughbred greyhound originally named
Steverino, the dog was introduced to America in 1957 on the
Steve Allen television show. Greyhound at the time sponsored
the program. When the company terminated its sponsorship,
the dog's name was meaningless for any identification with the
corporation. So it was changed to Lady Greyhound.

For years thereafter Lady Greyhound, accompanied by her
trainer, appeared as the company's symbol at countless public
events. For illustration, her 1962 appearances included fifty-
one television shows in forty-three major cities; seventeen radio "interviews"; scores of fashion shows in department stores
where she invariably wore her crown of jewels and a jewelled
necklace; the openings of new bus terminals; entertainments at
orphanages and schools; gatherings at football, baseball, and
basketball games; parades and other events that drew crowds.
The company's advertising staff said:

> This year her activities were topped by her appearance in
> Mason City, Iowa. There she attended the premiere of Mer-
> edith Willson's play, The Music Man. Greyhound buses
> brought fifty busloads of bands to the festivities, and Lady
> Greyhound led the parade of bands before 75,000 onlookers.

The most significant thing about such reports was that the
company's advertising and publicity people were finding every
possible opportunity to exhibit Lady Greyhound. Their vigi-

lance and initiative kept the corporation's name vividly in the public mind wherever the sleek greyhound appeared.

Once, when someone commented that Greyhound's president "worked like a dog," his secretary said, "But not as hard as *the* dog."

In time Lady Greyhound became so popular as the company's symbol that an annual report printed her biography for the benefit of inquiring shareholders. It said:

> In 1957 a spindle-legged Greyhound puppy left Clay Center, Kansas, to step before television cameras and into millions of American homes and hearts. Today she is a star known from coast to coast.
>
> Greyhound's symbol has been talked about on radio and television, written about in magazines and newspapers. Editors like her because she appears everywhere. She opens bank accounts; she has hats designed for her; she goes to swanky night spots to listen to jazz.
>
> As for some of her newsmaking stunts:
>
> • She was crowned Queen of National Dog Week for the second year in a row—no other dog can say that.
>
> • She received the degree of "Associate In Animal Letters" when she was guest of honor at Moravian College in Bethlehem, Pennsylvania, on the occasion of the homecoming of its football team.
>
> • She won the American Humane Association award and was named America's canine symbol for World Day For Animals.
>
> • She helped celebrate the forty-eighth year of American Campfire Girls.
>
> • She aided the March of Dimes and Easter Seal campaigns by attending scores of fund raising affairs.
>
> • She sparked the opening of the Detroit terminal by biting through an official ribbon of dog biscuits.
>
> Through her newsmaking activities Lady Greyhound has helped remind the public by the millions about Greyhound and its services.

Lady Greyhound, the company's mascot, became famous through public appearances.

Eventually Lady Greyhound suffered the same end as do all living creatures. For a time the company substituted another dog, but this one never quite exhibited the flair and the drawing power of the original. Her heart wasn't in it. Nevertheless she managed something her predecessor never accomplished. She delivered herself of six lively puppies.

What can a corporation do with six puppies? By that time Greyhound was sponsoring the Art Linkletter television show. On a memorable day when Linkletter was entertaining a troop of Girl Scout Brownies he made six little girls deliriously happy by presenting each one with a beautiful greyhound puppy.

Thus ended a canine career.

•   •   •   •   •

Despite steadily increasing annual revenues, there were uneasy days when Frederick Ackerman stood at his seventh-floor office window, clasped his hands behind his back, and scowled down at Dearborn Street. He was troubled.

The feeling stemmed largely from his conversations with Gerald Trautman in the law offices of McCutchen, Doyle, Brown, Trautman, and Enerson. As Greyhound's attorney, Trautman had long felt that it was shortsighted for the company to rely wholly on bus operations and bus-related business. The wiser course lay in diversification.

Ackerman agreed. Yet to seek areas for diversification would require more time and concentration than he could give. The duties of the presidency filled his days. Even in the past week he had been unable to give conscientious attention to the fact that the Boothe Leasing Corporation, an extremely successful San Francisco company on whose board he served, might be amenable to a merger proposal. Ackerman simply lacked the time to pursue this avenue of diversification.

What was the wise thing to do? Perhaps the answer lay in passing the day-to-day duties of the presidency to someone else. He himself could become chairman. Freed from the demands on a president, he might find the time to study and consummate opportunities for intelligent diversification.

The longer he considered such a change of office, the wiser it seemed. Still, to take that course meant finding a new president, and that had never been easy. The present board of directors, recently enlarged to sixteen in number, was comprised of experienced businessmen who would demand proven ability before endorsing any presidential candidate.

Considering various possibilities, Ackerman thought first of Gerald Trautman. In his position the attorney was thoroughly familiar with the affairs of the company. Ackerman broached the thought to him, but the lawyer, smiling his thanks, waved a hand to indicate surroundings he had no desire to leave. He enjoyed his work, enjoyed his legal associations, enjoyed life in San Francisco.

Ackerman had to look elsewhere. But first he had to go to Japan. And before he left he asked Trautman to pursue the acquisition of the Boothe Leasing Corporation. This had obviously been gnawing at his mind.

The attorney already knew a great deal about the Boothe firm, and he was not surprised when its president, D. P. Boothe, Jr., readily agreed to meet with him.

Both men understood the value of uniting the companies they represented. Boothe, buying and leasing office equipment, was doing well within its limits, but its opportunities were circumscribed by its modest finances. Given the support of Greyhound's cash flow and credit, its business could rise to unpredictable heights.

Trautman and Boothe reached agreement on merger terms: For approximately $14 million in Greyhound stock, the parent company would buy Boothe's stock. This had to be done within six months—the longest time Boothe was willing to keep its shares on deposit for transfer. It was agreed that if the purchase was not made by then, the plan for acquisition would be abandoned.

Like Ackerman, Trautman anticipated no problems with Greyhound's board of directors. But he was wrong.

One director was furious because he had not been informed earlier of this acquisition plan. Slapping the conference table, he made so vehement a point of it that others suspected he would have liked to buy Boothe stock at a low price, to be sold to Greyhound at a profit once the merger was in process. If that was in his mind he seemed to have little concern about the attitude of the Securities and Exchange Commission toward such activities.

But despite him the motion to acquire the Boothe Leasing Corporation was passed. Now there was a third party to satisfy—the Interstate Commerce Commission.

After the necessary papers of application had been prepared for the commission, they had to be signed by the corporation's head. In Ackerman's absence—he was still in Japan—Trautman asked Greyhound's executive vice president to sign the document.

He refused. "Ackerman's estimated figures are too optimistic," he declared.

This was unbelievable. If there was one thing on which Frederick Ackerman, a former accountant, could be relied on, it was the accuracy of his figures. Yet the executive vice president insisted on changing them before he signed the application. There was no way to dissuade him and the altered estimates—being only estimates—would probably not affect the commission's decisions. So Trautman flew to Washington and filed the application.

When Ackerman returned from the Orient and read a copy of the document, he called in members of his staff. "Who the hell changed my figures?" he demanded. He was told what had happened. Within two days the office of executive vice president was vacant.

Now there was nothing to do but await the commission's decision. The weeks passed, and the months, without word from Washington. Trautman became edgy, then worried. Telephone inquiries brought no answer beyond "still under consideration." With only one week left before the six-month deadline in the agreement with Boothe, Trautman flew back to Washington to investigate.

The official in charge of the three-man finance division, a very dour individual, received him coldly. Trautman did his utmost to explain how valuable this acquisition would be to all concerned, and how urgent a decision was. The only reply he elicited was that he return at three o'clock.

Promptly at three Trautman was back—and learned in amazement that the full eleven-man committee had approved the Boothe acquisition by a vote of 6 to 5. The only dissenting opinion had been written by the official Trautman had seen in the morning.

So Trautman left Washington with the knowledge that Greyhound was entering a new phase of its history, the era of diversification. Not that this was an abrupt decision on the company's part. As long ago as 1960 the board of directors had retained the Stanford University Institute to appraise the company's potentialities for a broad program of diversification. Its chief attributes were a large cash flow, excellent credit rating, and a wide exposure to the public through some 5,000 bus stations and commission agents. Based on these factors, the Institute had pointed to many areas in which diversification would be logical: everything from parking lots behind terminals to selling travel accident insurance and bolstering Post House operations by entering the food business on a large scale. The report had been a road map to the future.

But one thing troubled Trautman, largely as a result of the long delay in winning government approval for the Boothe acquisition. A way had to be found to avoid similar delays in conducting an energetic diversification program. And there was a way.

He recommended it to Ackerman as soon as they met. It was to convert The Greyhound Corporation to a holding company as distinct from a bus-operating company. Whereas a bus operator might have a difficult time with the ICC whenever it contemplated entering a different kind of business, a holding company would not be subject to such tight restrictions. A holding company was recognized as being an umbrella over diversified enterprises.

When Ackerman and the board adopted the recommendation they opened a road to endless future possibilities.

Admittedly it would not be an easy road to take. The change in corporate structure would be one which Trautman characterized as "a job of considerable magnitude," since it would involve winning the consent not only of the ICC itself but of regulatory commissions in every state in which Greyhound operated. This would take time, patience, and vigorous efforts. But in time the change to a holding company was achieved, and the new era had begun.

15

While awaiting the decision of the ICC, Frederick Ackerman had not abandoned the idea of relinquishing the presidency. It was not easy, however, to find an acceptable successor, one the current directors would be likely to accept. The board now included such tough-minded business executives as William R. Adams, president of the St. Regis Paper Company; J. Patrick Lannan, chairman of the Susquehanna Corporation; Paul E. Hoover, chairman of the Crocker-Anglo National Bank; John C. Griswold, executive vice president of W. R. Grace & Company, and others of equal stature.

The problem of finding a suitable presidential choice troubled Ackerman even while he went again to Japan. He had several reasons for returning. He went to discuss the opening of a Far Eastern travel and sales office. Since Japanese were visiting the United States in ever-increasing numbers it was certainly wise to acquaint them with Greyhound tours. He was also planning to investigate the possibilities of a leasing business in Tokyo, and the trip lasted several weeks.

But while he was abroad he found time to think, and on his return to Chicago he finally gave the board his choice for the presidency. This was M. C. Frailey.

Ackerman briefly supplied the candidate's background:

"Frailey joined Greyhound in 1929, more than thirty years ago," he said. "He has served the Western division as auditor, general traffic manager, vice president, executive vice president, and is now its president. He is, as you can see, an experienced transportation executive. I can endorse him heartily."

Some of the directors may have regarded the recommendation as one for an interim appointment, since Frailey was hardly two years from the age of mandatory retirement. But no other candidate was proposed, and he was elected. Frederick Ackerman, as he had requested, became chairman. Both men took their posts on February 1, 1962.

If the new chairman expected the change immediately to give him time to relax, think, and plan for the future, he was disillusioned. The company's major problems still came to his desk. Frailey, a tall, gangling, good-humored midwesterner, needed time to familiarize himself with his new responsibilities. And there were some serious situations to face.

One had its beginnings in Montgomery, Alabama. A lady named Rosa Parks had boarded a local city bus and, being weary, had dropped into the first empty seat she could see. It was a front seat.

Rosa Parks was black. A white passenger angrily told her to go to the rear of the bus "where she belonged." In Alabama, as in some other southern states, the rear was traditionally reserved for black people. Mrs. Parks, however, refused to move. Returning the man's glare with a cold look, she insisted that having paid her fare she was entitled to sit where she pleased. The ensuing argument became loud and profane, but Rosa Parks kept her seat and her dignity.

The incident became historic. The publicity it evoked spurred a demand for complete desegregation in the United States—something it took the Congress several years to legislate. Meanwhile the cries for civil rights rose out of endless demonstrations. Some were led peacefully by Dr. Martin Luther King, Jr., others became riotous and uncontrollable. In one of the latter, two Greyhound buses were stopped by a shouting mob in Montgomery's streets. Passengers were ordered to get out, and the empty buses were set on fire. Within half an hour they were burned-out wrecks, smoldering on the pavement. Their destruction was intended to express the crowd's rebellion against backseat discrimination on buses.

The fact that Greyhound, operating in forty-eight states, was not guilty of such discrimination did not deter the rioters. To them a bus was a bus.

The news stunned everyone at Greyhound's Chicago headquarters. Ackerman flew in from California to call an immediate meeting of top executives.

"We know our company isn't antiblack," he said. "Black people are our customers everywhere, and we employ blacks. What happened in Alabama proves that black people in the South simply don't know us or our attitude toward them. We've got to find a way of making them understand us."

Greyhound's vice president for public relations and advertising urged the creation of a company spokesman whom the black community would respect and believe. "I'm sure Grey Advertising can help us find the right man." Grey had found many effective spokesmen for products, he reasoned; surely they could find an effective spokesman for a cause.

They did. But they knew the man they wanted, Joe Black, would never become the mouthpiece for a cause in which he did not believe. A graduate of Morgan State College, where he had been an outstanding athlete, he gained nationwide fame when he became a pitcher for the Brooklyn Dodgers and a teammate of Jackie Robinson. In a memorable season he was named Rookie of the Year. To that he added the distinction of being the first black pitcher to win a World Series game. This was a man whom the black population of the country idolized as an athlete and admired as a modest but forceful individual.

Aware of Joe Black's personal ethics, however, the advertising agency offered Ackerman some sound advice: "Let's hire him, but not as a company spokesman. Let him go into marketing or transportation—any job that will make him thoroughly familiar with Greyhound. Let's not ask him to speak for the company until he's been fully indoctrinated in its methods, its spirit, its attitude toward all minorities—that is, till he himself jumps up to defend Greyhound against detractors."

The offer was made, and Joe Black accepted it on the condition that he could leave if he disliked the work. Obviously he did not dislike it, for he stayed on for more than twenty years, rising to a vice presidency. In that time he did indeed become a company spokesman among black people, in lectures, on radio and television, and through every medium that offered a chance to spread his message.

• • • • •

The burning of Greyhound buses was not the only thing that sorely disturbed Ackerman. In view of the long association between Greyhound and General Motors in the production and sale of buses, there were rumors of government action against both companies on the charge of monopolistic collusion. Ackerman indignantly asserted that such presumed collusion was nothing but illusion. Though Greyhound ordered 475 new GM vehicles to be delivered in 1964, other transportation firms, too, could place orders with General Motors.

Nevertheless it seemed wise to avoid the expense and bad publicity of legal procedures. The eleven senior officers of the company sat down to decide what to do about the situation.

After listening to a number of proposals Adam Sledz, now assistant to the president, made a suggestion of his own. In Pembina, North Dakota, the corporation had a subsidiary, the Greyhound Motor and Supply Company, engaged in the manufacture of parts and in assembling motors. Some sixty-eight miles north of Pembina, in Winnipeg, Canada, a company named Motor Coach Industries, owned by Harry Zoltok, manufactured bus "shells," or bodies. These had long been used by Greyhound Lines of Canada.

"Seems to me," Sledz said, "that we've become a company big enough to produce our own buses. We're paying others over $20 million a year for coaches. Why not invest that kind of money in plants of our own? If we bought Zoltok's Canadian company we could get coach bodies there, transport them to Pembina where we have the motors, and wind up putting bodies and motors together to manufacture our own buses. Not only would that do away with this charge of a monopoly. We'd probably save a good deal of money that now goes to GM's profits."

"We'd make money," another officer quickly interjected, inspired by the idea. "We'd sell buses to others."

A logical question was, Would the Canadian firm want to cooperate?

"Only way to answer that is to ask them," Sledz said.

Since it was he who had broached the plan, Ackerman asked him to go to Winnipeg for discussions. Sledz went. To his surprise, he met with a hostile, scowling, defiant group of men.

"They thought I was some sort of industrial spy," he said, "there to undermine and destroy their business—a dangerous competitor from over the border. It took me quite awhile to convince them that my intentions were good, and that for them this was a chance to supply the needs of all the Greyhound Lines in the United States. When Zoltok finally saw the opportunity for what it was, he quickly accepted it."

But there were still international problems to solve. Would tariff costs make it unfeasible to trade across the border? This was something that had to be discussed with authorities in both countries. The meetings involved attorneys and government officials. But since all were conferring on a plan that would bring added employment and earnings to both nations, tariff demands were waived, and the merger was consummated.

Actually, Motor Coach Industries of Winnipeg became a subsidiary of Greyhound Lines of Canada (62 percent of whose stock was owned by The Greyhound Corporation in the United States). And Harry Zoltok was elected to the corporation's board of directors.

On that day in 1961 The Greyhound Corporation began

producing its own motor coaches, thereby taking another major step into the future.

•   •   •   •   •

Greyhound buses carrying some 50,000 people to the Seattle World's Fair, and Glide-A-Rides driving them around the exposition grounds, created a steady flow of cash revenues. Yet this did not offset Ackerman's constant insistence on frugality as a means of increasing net earnings. The results were evident in the kind of reports he received.

The maintenance men, for instance, pointed out, "Every additional quarter mile obtained from a gallon of fuel means a saving of more than $1 million a year. Each one-cent-a-mile decrease in maintenance costs means a saving of $5 million a year."

The transportation summary announced that, without raising costs, Greyhound's 5,000 buses had traveled 508 million miles, "the equivalent of well over 20,000 trips around the world in one year's time!"

Others spoke of progress rather than economies. Boothe Leasing, now backed by Greyhound financing, had in this single year more than doubled its earnings, leaping from $427,141 to $863,820. Its most spectacular innovation was the purchase of five Boeing 707 jet airframes (everything except the engines) which it promptly leased to Trans World Airlines.

Package Express still described itself as "the fastest growing phase of the company's business," adding record revenues of $27.6 million to the corporation's income; and even advertising reports reached new high levels of accomplishment.

"Our advertisements," said one such report, "now appear regularly in 300 newspapers and on 158 different weather-news shows on TV. A simplified version of Greyhound's slogan has been officially adopted. It is now 'Go Greyhound—and leave the driving to us.' The slogan appears in all our advertising, in print and on the air. And we've done quite well in the recognition we've received. In addition to other awards, we have received one from the National Safety Council 'for the exceptional contribution to safety made by the Greyhound advertising.' " (This referred to a daylight "Headlights-On" safety campaign the company now adopted for its buses. The nation's 10 percent reduction in daylight accidents was largely attributable to this innovation. The sight of headlights on big approaching coaches seemed to make all other drivers more cautious.)

With so many gratifying developments to contemplate, top management of The Greyhound Corporation should have been quite happy in 1962. Yet, as always, there were things that worried Frederick Ackerman. Because of his age he himself would soon have to consider retirement, and Frailey was hardly a year from that mandatory date. Before long the matter of presidential succession would again become a problem. In addition, another position had to be filled: since the resignation of G. W. Rauch there was no general counsel on Greyhound's staff. All the legal work had gone to Gerald Trautman.

Now once more, in San Francisco, the chairman called Trautman to his office. This time he asked the lawyer to assume the general counsel's post. The position need not involve a move to Chicago, he said; it need not even involve a departure from the law firm of McCutchen, Doyle, Brown, Trautman, and Enerson. Trautman could attend meetings in Chicago only when necessary. "As I do," Ackerman added.

It was too reasonable a request to be refused. They shook hands in agreement, and on the eve of its fiftieth anniversary the company had a new general counsel.

If in the mind of Frederick Ackerman there was a tinge of wily satisfaction in the thought that he had brought Trautman a step closer to the presidency, it was something he never mentioned or even hinted at to any of his associates.

•   •   •   •   •

On a Friday afternoon that year Ralph Bogan and his son, Ralph Bogan, Jr., were in Florida, playing golf in a foursome with old friends. Bogan, senior—big, athletic, prosperous, in fine spirits—played his usual low-handicap game. He and his son won the match, then went on to a few clubhouse drinks and a hearty dinner.

Next morning Ralph Bogan, Jr., left to join his own family—and never again saw his father. Two nights later the heart of Ralph Bogan, Sr., stopped beating while he slept.

Thus the second of Greyhound's three founders was gone. That left only Orville Caesar, now a member of the company's executive committee.

The death of Ralph Bogan was a reminder of the rift that had once existed between him and Caesar. Some veterans no doubt wondered how Caesar reacted to the news of his former associate's death. Had the two men really hated each other so bitterly? Had that hatred persisted through the years?

If it were true, Caesar would not have retained some of the mementos he had of the days when the first bus lines ran out of Hibbing and Duluth. He had photographs of himself with Bogan and Wickman; photographs of Bogan inscribed "to my friend Orville." No one knew of the existence of these pictures, or that Caesar had kept them for almost half a century as one treasures a memory.

A few weeks after Bogan's death Caesar visited Bogan's son in Chicago. He brought the box that contained the photographs. This he placed in the younger Bogan's hands, saying, "Thought you might want them."

It was his only comment as he turned away. Ralph Bogan, Jr., recalled, "I could see tears in his eyes. It was as if part of his own life had died."

16

As The Greyhound Corporation approached its fiftieth anniversary, Orville Caesar, the last of the three founders, must have been touched by countless memories, some melancholy, some inspiring. He was in his seventies now, and though still a member of the executive committee, he had retired to his home in Barrington, Illinois.

It was an appropriate time for him to meditate with pride on the company's history. Greyhound had made outstanding contributions to the nation. In half a century it had linked together thousands of communities, large and small, from coast to coast, from northern to southern borders. In the process it had created jobs for its current 24,000 employees and incomes for its 87,000 shareholders. Wickman's Hupmobile had expanded into a fleet of 5,171 huge buses that moved over 100,302 miles of highways in the United States and Canada.

In the achievement of all this Caesar had actively participated from the very beginning. Now, resting at home after those fifty years of work, he had the satisfaction of reading Frederick Ackerman's announcement: "The company has concluded its first half century of operation on a high note by attaining peaks in virtually all corporate activities."

Ackerman was not exaggerating. The new acquisitions in particular were doing extremely well. With Motor Coach Industries of Winnipeg shipping its shells for assembling in Pembina, completed buses were being produced at a rate that would soon reach one a day. Boothe Leasing, for its part, dramatically widened its scope of operations with the expenditure of some $50 million for jet aircraft—planes immediately leased to TransWorld Airways. Nor was that all. As Ackerman informed the press and shareholders, "During the year Boothe acquired $86,660,000 of property for lease, as against $32,469,000 acquired in 1962. Rental income earned increased to $9,201,000 from $5,296,000." Much of this resulted from the leasing of computers—so much of it, in fact, that Ackerman added, "By year's end Boothe was the largest independent owner of the most advanced types of computer equipment, with the sole exception of the U.S. government."

Such success with the company's first diversified subsidiaries naturally prompted Greyhound's management to consider others. Every day brokers were mailing and telephoning suggestions. They came by the score. Most had to be discarded, but two warranted consideration for the Post House food-dispensing business.

One was the Prophet Company. With headquarters in Detroit, this company served food to more than 650,000 people a day, some in restaurants, others through vending machines. Its customers included the plants and executive dining rooms of many major corporations as well as hospitals, colleges, and other institutions.

The second suggested acquisition was Horne's Enterprises of Bayard, Florida. They operated a chain of fifty-three roadside food stores. In several states it also provided motel and gasoline-station services—and now it became a source of disagreement.

Though Ackerman sought government approval for both food-dispensing purchases, Trautman opposed the acquisition of Horne's. He felt no adequate investigation of the company had been made, and the figures presented by its owner, Robert Horne, struck him as being unrealistic. Moreover, just before the acquisition was to be consummated, Greyhound faced a tax ruling that was not in accordance with the acquisition agreement. "I begged Ackerman not to proceed," Trautman said later, "but he was adamant." And the deal was concluded.

Robert Horne, who was supposed to remain with the company, did not like living in Detroit, now the headquarters of the Greyhound food operation. One morning he failed to appear at his office, and the next day he filed suit against Greyhound in Florida, his home state. The suit claimed all sorts of abuse and became a nuisance rather than a threat. Trautman recalled, "I struggled with this company until we were fortunate enough to find a buyer who would pay us book value, and we sold it."

The experience provided a somber warning that not every acquisition would necessarily yield a bonanza. Nevertheless the basic food business flourished. Ackerman predicted, "Total combined sales of our food dispensing companies should approximate $94 million in 1964." The accuracy of his estimate was uncanny. The actual figure was $94.4 million.

•　　•　　•　　•　　•

The nearer the company came to its fiftieth anniversary year, 1964, the more publicity it generated in the business press. Long articles on Greyhound appeared in the *Wall Street Journal, Forbes, Time,* and *Business Week,* with shorter pieces in newspapers throughout the country. Radio and television commentators delighted in describing the company's birth in Hibbing, treating it as inspiring Americana. *Newsweek* and *Financial World* waited until 1964, then added lengthy accounts of their own to the Greyhound saga.

This was the year when Frailey's mandated time to retire arrived, and he duly resigned. H. Vance Greenslit of Lexington, Kentucky, might ordinarily have replaced him, but he had been elected president of Greyhound Lines, the company's division for transportation. So Frederick Ackerman himself, reluctantly or not, reassumed the presidency while retaining the chairmanship of the parent Greyhound Corporation.

He could hardly have done so at a busier time. The company was gearing itself to serve New York's imminent World's Fair, a task for which it created a separate entity called Greyhound At The World's Fair. In addition to the hundreds of buses that would be bringing visitors to New York, 300

Glide-A-Rides with improved features were being prepared for service. Men and women had to be hired and trained to run the cars, to deliver brief comments on points of interest. In a wholly new development Post Houses would open several eating places at the Fair. These had to be built, equipped, and put into the care of trained personnel. So would information booths the company would man.

Most of these concerns Ackerman could shift to others, but there were some that required his personal attention as well as the legal approach of Gerald Trautman. Prospective acquisitions of considerable size were being discussed, among them the Travelers Express Company, the Yellowstone Park Company, and a possible 20 percent interest in the Railway Express Agency.

Seeking relief from the pressures of so many responsibilities, Ackerman invited Trautman to spend a weekend at the chairman's summer home at Lake Tahoe. There, relaxed, unhurried, surrounded by natural beauty instead of office walls, they could talk hour after hour. This occurred in August 1965; and in his quiet way Ackerman was more intense than ever in urging Trautman to become Greyhound's president and chief executive officer.

This time Trautman, gazing up at summer skies, contemplated his duty to the company, to his family, to his law firm. Again, as before, Ackerman assured him there was no need to leave San Francisco as long as he attended periodic meetings in Chicago. But this was not foremost in Trautman's mind. He reflected on the fact that he himself was, to a great extent, responsible for the corporation's turn to diversification. He had urged it for years. Now that the change was a reality, it offered the promise of industrial growth beyond limits. To how many men is the opportunity given to lead so vital an enterprise? One had to be stirred by the sheer challenge of running a company like Greyhound, with its $115 million in assets and its annual cash income of over $516 million. As a clinching argument Ackerman suggested that there would be no need for the attorney to leave his law firm.

This long, personal, and candid conference came to an historic climax when Gerald Trautman made his decision. He offered the chairman his hand and accepted the presidency.

Of course, all this would have to be ratified by the board of directors at its next meeting. And meanwhile Trautman continued to be steeped in a legal struggle with California's Public Utilities Commission.

This resulted from the circumstance that Greyhound had undertaken, through a Certificate of Public Convenience and Necessity, to operate commuter buses between San Francisco and neighboring counties. Unwise from the start, it was now showing its worst aspects. To accommodate rush-hour traffic mornings and late afternoons required 350 buses and their drivers. Between those two crowded periods, for long hours every day, there was need for only 50 buses and their drivers. The enforced idleness of some 300 coaches and men every day, for most of the day, was a costly drain on the line's finances. Added to that was the rising price of gasoline and labor, plus a one dollar toll on the Golden Gate Bridge every time a bus crossed it. Greyhound was losing $2 million a year on these commuter runs.

Trautman would have liked to be totally released from rendering such service. But the Public Utilities Commission would not tolerate the request. So, at hearing after hearing, Trautman and other officers of Greyhound sought the right to increase fares and to win a reduction of bridge tolls.

M. G. Cragg, Greyhound's traffic manager who appeared at many hearings with Trautman, said, "Little by little we won consideration for moderate fare increases, and we got a better deal on bridge tolls. But years went by—in fact, it was 1971—before we got out of that losing commuter deal."

But now, in 1965, Trautman could only maintain that eventually the suburban counties would have to operate the commuter lines themselves on a subsidized basis. There was nothing more he could do, and he gave his attention to his future duties as president.

A saddening event may have hastened the ultimate action. From Barrington came the news that Orville Caesar, not much older than Ackerman, had died.

It brought a sense of shock and loss to every veteran worker at Chicago headquarters. It caused a feeling of change as irreversible as time itself. Henceforth the destiny of The Greyhound Corporation would be in the hands of a generation which, in all probability, had never known the town of Hibbing, Minnesota.

Nonetheless, and most fortunately, continuity of experienced management was assured. Gerald Trautman had served the company since he had left the Navy in 1946. He had a thorough knowledge of Greyhound. He had helped to shape its modern image and goals.

And so, at the November 1965 meeting of directors, the board unanimously and with confidence elected him president and chief executive officer of the corporation. His new responsibilities, to take effect on January 1, 1966, marked the start of a new Greyhound era.

Part Three

"DIVERSIFICATION WITHIN DIVERSIFICATION"

17

The morning a new corporate president settles into the leather chair behind his desk, it is customary for his associates to come in to shake his hand and wish him well. In some cases, when the chief executive has been hired away from another company, this is also a time for introductions. Gerald Trautman was spared this formality. After his many years of serving the corporation he already knew all its management personnel.

Some of his distinguished legal colleagues at McCutchen, Doyle, Brown, Trautman, and Enerson congratulated him in verse. Still imbued with the spirit of a Christmas just passed, they sent a parody of the "Jingle Bells" lyrics, one chorus of which ran:

> G.H.T., G.H.T.,
> As you jingle on your way
> By plane or train or Jaguar
> Or one-horse open sleigh,
> G.H.T., G.H.T.,
> There's one thing bothers us:
> On your frequent wanderings
> Do you ever ride a bus?

Despite so pleasant a start, it was not an easy first year. On the West Coast a long strike crippled bus transportation. Trautman and Peter K. Nevitt, then vice president for industrial relations, had long, sometimes bitter meetings with union officials while the forced inactivity of buses drained revenues.

Some Greyhound people suspected that the union was testing the mettle of the corporation's new president. On his part, Trautman considered the strikers' demands for higher wages, longer vacations, and many additional benefits excessive and unreasonable. Worse, they were accompanied by threats of "a prolonged strike until the company gives in." Greyhound's president had no intention of allowing threats to dictate the company's policies. He told Nevitt, "Let them strike as long as they like. There will be no more discussions 'til they're ready to negotiate on fair terms and without threats."

The walkout lasted six weeks. When it ended in the signing of a two-year pact, the strikers went back to work—having gained little more, as it turned out, than they could have had without a strike. And the wisdom of Trautman's firmness soon became evident. On the East Coast, too, a strike had been threatened. Aware of what had happened in the West, the eastern union quickly signed a similar agreement. Business there went on peacefully, without interruption. For the next two years there were no anti-Greyhound strikes of consequence.

But something else troubled the new president.

In the files Ackerman had left him he found a memorandum from one of the company's top-ranking officers—a memorandum that urged the liquidation of the company's bus business!

Trautman was shocked. "It was like recommending that we sell our soul," he said. The writer of the confidential note feared that private cars and aircraft would soon cripple bus transportation. What alarmed Trautman was the possibility that such gloom might pervade the thinking of many others. He was scowling over the thought when James Hawthorne, vice president for marketing, came into his office with a request. A big, balding man, Hawthorne said that each of Greyhound's four bus divisions would soon have its annual meeting. These meetings had never been addressed by the corporation's head and Hawthorne explained the effect he thought an appearance would make.

"If you could find the time to come to one of them," Hawthorne said, "the men would really appreciate it."

Still uneasy about company morale, Trautman said on abrupt decision, "I'll do better than that. Put me down for all four meetings."

The first occurred at the Green Oaks Inn in Fort Worth, Texas. Approximately a hundred members of the management force, representing every affiliate and every subsidiary, convened to hear Trautman's first address as chief executive officer. Grasping the lectern, he looked confident and at ease. Before all else he wanted to dispose of any doubts concerning the bus operation.

"Most people know that Greyhound is the largest intercity carrier in the world," he said. "And it must be made clear that we are not diversifying into other fields at the expense of bus operations. We will continue to promote and improve those in every possible way. The bus business has historically been our mainstay. We are the industry's leaders and we intend to keep our leadership."

In the previous year, 1965, transportation revenues had reached record-breaking heights of over $386 million. Yet Trautman said with conviction, "We are making every effort to increase those revenues. Though this must be accomplished in the face of accelerating competition from airlines and private automobiles, it is our view that it can be done through the use of modern, clean, comfortable buses; the operation of frequent and expeditious schedules; and the courteous and efficient services of our employees."

He had little need to emphasize the energy with which bus service was being promoted. The audience surely knew that Highway Tours—a Greyhound division—had been given a special award by the National Association of Travel Organizations. This was the result of bringing a group of leading European travel agents to America and giving them an exciting, revealing trip through some of the continent's most spectacular regions. That, plus the continuing offer of a ninety-nine-day trip for ninety-nine dollars, was still bringing thousands of visitors to the United States.

But at this meeting, as at the three regional conventions that followed it, Trautman stressed his personal certainty that bus transportation from city to city was more promising than it had ever been.

"For one thing, as the population grows, more and more people are traveling," he said. "For another, 90 percent of intercity travel is done in private cars. If our 'leave the driving to us' message has its effect—especially now, with the rocketing price of gasoline—I think we can easily move 1 percent of the riders out of their cars and into our buses. That 1 percent could almost double our business.

"Speaking for myself," he went on, "I have absolute faith in the future of our industry. So have our directors. That is why we have undertaken capital expenditures of $46 million for the next year. Half of that sum will go for 600 new buses, the rest for garages and terminals. That should tell you how firmly we believe bus travel is here to stay. If any of you don't feel that way, I'd say this is the time for you to get out of the business."

Nobody got out. On the contrary, in the changed expressions of the men to whom he spoke he could see that his words had rekindled confidence where it might have been ebbing.

Yet he did not underplay the importance of diversification. After all, in the past year about $135 million, fully 27 percent of total revenues, had come from nonbus activities. He reminded the audience that within the past twelve months the corporation had acquired not only General Fire and Casualty, a leading insurance company, but also Travelers Express Company.

General Fire and Casualty was licensed in fifty states to write a broad spectrum of insurance that varied from automobile coverage to worker's compensation, from fire and burglary protection to inland marine coverage. It was actually handling $5.4 million of Greyhound's own bus insurance.

As for Travelers Express, it ranked second among the nation's private organizations in the money order field. Last year, Trautman said, it had accounted for $770 million in the face value of money orders it issued through its 14,000 outlets. And money orders were by no means the only element of the company's business. It provided draft clearing services for credit unions, for banks and savings and loan institutions, and it handled a variety of other payment services.

Then he pointed out that Greyhound Van Lines—the changed name of Greyvan—was no longer a problem child. With a volume of $16 million it had become the sixth largest moving van company in the country.

And the leasing operation had expanded almost beyond belief. It now owned or had on order forty of the latest jet planes representing a total cost of $195 million. All were leased to major trunk lines. Moreover, Boothe Leasing had ordered the first of some 6,000 freight cars it would lease to railroads.

In the 1960s Greyhound's subsidiary leasing company owned 40 modern jet aircraft, like this DC-8, which were leased to major airlines.

Brewster Transport Company Limited of Banff, Alberta, Canada, a Greyhound subsidiary since 1965, provides sightseeing tours of the Canadian Rockies.

It was the kind of impressive report that made heads in the audience shake in wonder. Among the managers there were several who had recently returned from Europe, and their presence underscored the new president's assertion that "in the future Greyhound will be engaged extensively abroad."

He spoke of Canadian Greyhound Lines and of the newly acquired Gray Line sight-seeing tours in the Canadian Rockies. Then he focused on the company organized through Boothe Leasing in Europe. "This Switzerland-based company," he said, "is owned 50 percent by Greyhound Leasing and 50 percent by several excellent European banking firms. Greyhound and its European partners share the view that this company has tremendous possibilities.

"As you know," he continued, "we have also entered the bus business in Europe, though still in a modest way. VAVO-Greyhound, based in Holland, has had overtures to engage in the bus business in Ireland, Spain, Portugal, and Italy, all of them countries with great tourist attractions.

"And finally we have entered the industrial catering business in Europe through a Belgian company called Restaura. This is owned 50 percent by us and 50 percent by Au Bon Marché, a large European merchandising organization."

Having dwelt on such examples of progress, Trautman acknowledged some of the problems the company faced. First was the severe effect of ever-worsening inflation. Labor, fuel, food, equipment—all costs had risen and were sapping away the advantages of higher revenues. And the ICC was never easy to move toward needed fare increases on buses.

"That brings me to another difficulty," he said. "Overregulation and excessive interference by government. This seems to be a fact of life for all American business; we are learning to live with it, without liking it."

Yet he sounded in no way discouraged by these trials. One of those who heard him remembers saying, "I wonder how he'll talk a year from now, after he's grappled with the problems that exhausted Ackerman."

But an entirely different kind of concern—one involving laxity of morale in the Chicago office—shocked Trautman in this first year of his presidency. On his frequent trips to the city he noted that some top echelon employees were coming to work toward ten o'clock in the morning and departing soon after lunch—hardly an efficient way to run a business. The cause quickly became apparent: Frederick Ackerman was conducting affairs from San Francisco. His principal contact with the Chicago office was a daily telephone call at ten o'clock. Therefore everyone was dutifully at his desk by ten, ready to answer any question the chairman might have. After that it seemed safe to leave since there would be no further calls from San Francisco until the next morning.

Close to outrage, Trautman called in the staff. Quite forcefully he reminded them that office hours began at 9 A.M. and continued to 5 P.M. He made it clear that those who found such hours inconvenient should at once seek more agreeable employment.

Reform was promptly in evidence. Possibly it caused the new president a temporary loss of popularity; but before long the improvement in efficiency and office morale won him the staff's solid support. Nonetheless the experience gave Trautman sharp qualms about the wisdom of living in San Francisco. More and more he considered the advisability of moving to Chicago.

Another thing Ackerman had not noticed from a distance was how crowded the Chicago quarters had become. Additional personnel, essential to an expanding business, lacked the space to function at their best. So Trautman ordered a move that took the company to far more spacious offices at 10 South Riverside Plaza—a change that delighted everyone and spurred productive energy.

A succession of acquisition difficulties also required Trautman's attention. For one, the ICC refused to sanction an affiliation with Railway Express, something Ackerman had urged despite the fact that Trautman and others of the staff had opposed it. The eventual collapse of the plan caused a general sense of relief rather than of disappointment.

And there was the failure of merger negotiations with the food processing company of Libby, McNeil, and Libby. This acquisition had seemed sound and logical as an addition to the food-serving operations of Post Houses and Prophet. But the management of Libby, McNeil, and Libby voted against granting Greyhound the time it needed for thorough consideration, and the project was abandoned.

Besides, there were other pressures to face, one being the extraordinarily high interest rates of the times. These were particularly burdensome because the company was building a new terminal in Kansas City and remodeling others while financing the thriving leasing business. The corporation could not rely wholly on bus fares to defray all such expenses; it had to borrow from banks, and interest rates that climbed ever-higher could demolish growth plans.

While Trautman dealt with these problems—and there were many more—he was building his own executive staff, describing it as a "young, able, and aggressive team for now and the years to come." It was not an easy undertaking, nor was it always pleasant. There were those whom he had to replace because of their lack of competence. There were choices to be made among others of outstanding ability. The people he did choose, it soon became clear, added undeniable strength to the executive staff.

As he contemplated the future Trautman became more and more concerned about what might be called human synergy among Greyhound's 33,900 employees in 1966. How could a sense of "all for one and one for all" be created in an enterprise so widely diversified? How could someone working in a Post House restaurant or someone driving a bus be made to understand that his job was somehow connected to that of a man leasing planes to an airline? Trautman decided on a means of establishing communication among them all—a company magazine. It would report and integrate all Greyhound interests.

When its first issue appeared in the fall of 1966 he explained in an introductory message that the publication was being sent to employees and agents of all the corporation's divisions as well as to stockholders.

"It is hoped," he wrote, "that this magazine will establish a much needed channel of communications through which all of us can learn more about the growing, dynamic Greyhound of today."

Originally the publication bore the title, "Go With Greyhound." Later it was simplified to "Go Greyhound." When the president asked Donald L. Behnke of the public relations department to edit the first issue, Behnke hardly suspected that he would be repeating the assignment four times a year for the next eighteen years. What he produced was one of the most beautifully illustrated and intriguing of America's corporate publications—"binding together," as one reader put it, "all those interested in Greyhound's activities and welfare."

Another innovation, one since adopted by many other companies, related to the contents of Greyhound's annual report. General practice in presenting yearly statistics was to give a consolidated total of all corporate revenues, all corporate disbursements, rather than a breakdown of divisional figures. The Greyhound 1966 report listed the financial results attained by each division—transportation, foods, other services.

"I know it sounds perfectly normal today," said one of the company's accountants. "But in 1966 and 1967 such a step was something of a novelty for us. From the letters we received we knew it was a change shareholders and financial analysts appreciated."

In the midst of all such internal activities came an unexpected setback. This one, however, still causes some Greyhound officials to chuckle.

The Chicago Cubs, the baseball team owned by Phil Wrigley, the chewing gum tycoon, had experienced seven disastrous years. A losing club attracts meagre attendance, which meant it was playing at a financial loss. Several Greyhound executives saw a rare opportunity for the company to buy the Cubs and thereby enter a new field of diversification. But others were hesitant; could there be any synergy at all between a baseball team and the other Greyhound subsidiaries?

Absolutely, it was maintained. "We could carry busloads of people to the ballparks wherever the Cubs played."

No doubt the ball team became aware that they were in a sense being put on the auction block. Their pride wounded, their indignation roused, they suddenly began to play harder than ever. In their anger they won game after game. Astonished crowds streamed into the stadium to stare in disbelief at this transformed team. The club's gate receipts soared. The team became a source of profit and was no longer for sale. The Greyhound Corporation, swallowing its disappointment, had to accept defeat.

"Well, it wasn't really defeat," said one company officer. "As Chicagoans we felt in some measure responsible and proud for goading our losing team into a winning club. Call it a case of what was bad for Greyhound being good for baseball and good for Chicago."

•   •   •   •   •

Trautman soon discovered that well-intentioned secretaries in Chicago did not always bring important communications to his attention. Why trouble the boss with trivial complaints from disgruntled strangers? He was at his desk, glancing through the day's letters, when he learned for the first time that two Greyhound bus lines (Eastern Greyhound and Southern Greyhound) were operating in a manner that could undermine the reputation of the entire system.

"Their schedules seem to mean nothing to them," one man wrote. "We bought our long-distance tickets in good faith, feeling that where our bus had to go from one Greyhound line to another in Richmond, Virginia, this would be done in about thirty minutes, according to the timetable. We never dreamed we'd have to wait six hours in a rain-soaked, lonely spot for a new driver to take us further."

Trautman was tight-lipped when he began an investigation. Reports indicated that the charges against the two lines were completely justified. What was worse, there were many more evidences of mismanagement, almost of disinterest. As a result the head of one line was "terminated"; the head of the other was severely reprimanded.

"When you have to take such action," Trautman said, "being chief executive officer is neither easy nor pleasant. But it's something that has to be done."

Another complaint from the traveling public was lodged against Greyhound's loading platform in New York's Port Authority terminal. One man wrote, "The place is dirty, crowded, hot, and everything about it seems to need repairs." There were a number of letters to corroborate this.

On a trip to New York Trautman investigated for himself. What he saw was appalling. He telephoned two of Greyhound's directors who lived in the city, Frederick L. Ehrman, a partner of Lehman Brothers, and Charles Munson, chairman of the Air Reduction Company. He asked both of them to see what he had seen, something close to squalor. When they became as indignant as he was himself, the three went to see Austin Tobin, head of the Port Authority.

Though Tobin was sympathetic, he seemed helpless. He said he was finding it impossible to make any improvements because the City of New York would not cooperate. His pleas to Mayor John Lindsay had brought only replies of "Sorry. Not now. More important things need funds."

When Trautman offered to call on the mayor, Tobin said, "It won't do any good. Believe me. I've tried it again and again."

Thereupon Trautman rose to terminate the meeting. "I'll take care of this myself," he said.

What the others did not know was that one of his San Francisco law partners and Mayor John Lindsay had been roommates at Yale. They were the closest of friends, the godparents of each other's children. Trautman went back to his hotel and telephoned his law partner. The San Francisco attorney said he would call Mayor Lindsay immediately.

The outcome, as Trautman remembered it, was this: "The offer of the City of New York to the Port Authority was to cooperate fully in the construction of a new terminal and to indicate willingness to do whatever was necessary with streets and utilities in building the new terminal." Still, there were countless delays generally attributed to lack of funds. "But we kept after this matter," Trautman said, "and eventually, several years later, the Port Authority did provide us with a new terminal in New York City."

So it was that he learned, with crisis after crisis to confront in this first year of his administration, why Ackerman had so desperately needed someone to free him from his many responsibilities.

And now Trautman faced still another problem.

18

This rose out of the success of Boothe Leasing. (For company identification its name was soon changed to Greyhound Leasing and Financial Corporation.) Its rise was explosive. By the end of 1966 it owned more than $500 million worth of equipment. Its earnings exceeded $7.5 million. One publication called its record "the surprise of the year," and D. P. Boothe, Jr., said, "We're just starting!"

Yet Trautman was worried.

To finance its purchases the leasing subsidiary had been relying on short-term credit. At the same time it had been writing long-term leases. In other words, as Trautman put it, the company was borrowing short and lending long, and that could lead to trouble. Though D. P. Boothe, Jr., seemed to see no danger in the situation, Trautman felt he had to guard against a future crisis.

So he called a meeting of the twenty bankers most heavily involved in the subsidiary's loans. To his relief, they all came. Waiting to understand why they were here, they looked puzzled as he rose to speak.

Quite frankly Trautman expressed his uneasiness with the terms of the leasing company's loans. (Later he explained, "Our bank lines [of credit] could be cancelled virtually without notice.") Future complications could be avoided, he told the bankers, if their institutions would give the leasing company longer credit terms.

He was pleased—and perhaps surprised—when the bankers themselves rose one after another to endorse the desirability of long-term borrowing. "I am certain," he said, "this avoided many future difficulties."

The amicable and fruitful results of this first meeting posed an intriguing question: Why not hold regular annual meetings with those bankers who extended credit to Greyhound enterprises?

Within a year Trautman issued the invitations for another such conference. The bankers came. They continued to come year after year. By 1983 some seventy-five credit-line banks were invited to a meeting in Phoenix, and 108 bankers attended.

What made these gatherings truly valuable to all concerned was Greyhound's "full disclosure" policy. As Trautman described it, "We took the initiative of keeping our banks fully informed. We told them both the good and the bad. Then the meeting was turned over to them for a session at which all possible questions were discussed with the utmost candor. How often can a lead-bank have all the participant banks in a credit line in the same room to discuss freely the credit of a large company? These annual meetings have been most productive and satisfying for us as well as for the banks, and we intend to continue them as an important part of our bank relations program."

The company's relations with banks was emphasized in the early 1970s when Trautman informed a group of analysts, "In our daily operations we are one of the nation's largest users of banks, dealing with almost 10 percent of all the banks in this country. This year we maintain 2,498 accounts in 1,303 banks."

If the figure seems overwhelming, one must remember that The Greyhound Corporation and its subsidiaries operate in thousands of American communities, and many of the company's local offices have their own local accounts.

•   •   •   •   •

As a matter of historical interest one may ask: Are there any fundamental principles, policies, or philosophies that have characterized The Greyhound Corporation from its earliest days to the present? Is there a discernible bond between, say, the Wickman years and the Trautman years?

The differences between them are, of course, obvious. Half a century ago Wickman and his associates, though self-educated, began their careers with little formal education. In the Trautman slate of officers, on the other hand, there were several who represented the training of outstanding universities. Gerald Trautman himself, a graduate of Stanford University and Harvard Law School, was the recipient of honorary degrees from a number of colleges, as were other members of his executive team.

Apart from the disparity in education, Wickman launched his business with meagre savings of $600. The Trautman administration operated with hundreds of millions in cash and credit at its disposal. Wickman concentrated solely on bus transportation. Trautman's interests reached out to foods, leasing, financial services, and allied businesses.

So the differences are striking. But what of enduring similarities—those that reveal the true and lasting character of an organization?

First there is the matter of vision, the kind of vision that sees and aspires to extraordinary goals: Carl Wickman visualized bus transportation in a nationwide sense, and he achieved the goal through boldly consummated bus-line acquisitions. Trautman visualized industrial diversification in its broadest national and international sense, and he likewise achieved his goal through boldly consummated acquisitions.

Thus one constant characteristic of Greyhound must be described as a determination always to grow.

Rapid as that growth was in Wickman's day, it was even more rapid in Trautman's. The latter's sixteen-year administration increased Greyhound's annual revenues from $549 million to more than $5 billion.

Even fundamental traits, however, must have the resilience to deal with unexpected—and sometimes amusing—challenges. There was one that eventually caused Trautman to chuckle.

"You would think," he said, "that it would be easy to get our own bus manufacturing company, MCI, to paint our buses any color the management decides on, but I assure you it was not a simple matter.

"In 1964, when Greyhound had observed its 50th anniversary, our buses were painted blue and white with a big gold stripe around them in recognition of Greyhound's Golden Anniversary. By 1966 I thought it was time to stop celebrating the 50th anniversary. So, after talking with our transportation executives, I went to Winnipeg to see Harry Zoltok who was then in charge of our bus manufacturing operation. I told him I wanted to work out with him the substitution of a red stripe for the gold one. He told me he wouldn't do it; he liked the blue and gold combination, and that was the way we were going to get our buses.

"Well, I like blue and gold, too, but not as well as red, white, and blue. I might add that blue and gold are the colors of the University of California, the archenemy of Stanford where I went to college. In any event, Mr. Zoltok was adamant, and I decided there was an easier way to handle this stubborn Russian than by a face-to-face fight.

"So the next order we sent to MCI specified that the buses were to be delivered unpainted and that we would paint them in our own maintenance facilities. At the same time I called the number two man in the Winnipeg bus manufacturing plant. I asked him to come to Chicago. There I asked him if he could run the plant. Of course, this promptly got back to Mr. Zoltok, as I hoped it would. And I had no more trouble with him. Thereafter the buses came out of MCI with a red, white, and blue color scheme, and those have been our colors ever since."

19

Though the occasions for employing such Machiavellian tactics were rare, in this case they persuaded a valued associate in a subsidiary to respect company desires. Zoltok was a capable executive in his own sphere, and a temporary foible had not been permitted to deprive Greyhound of his efficiency.

Another man in the category of valued associates was the newly appointed representative for special markets, Joe Black.

These were years of racial turmoil in the United States. Riotous black demonstrations in Detroit and Newark, with sixty-six people killed and thousands hurt, were precursors to the assassination of Dr. Martin Luther King, Jr. Racial fury, aimed against many American institutions, vented itself also against big corporations. It did not matter that in these same years Edward Brooke of Massachussetts was the first black man elected to the United States Senate; that Thurgood Marshall became the first black justice of the United States Supreme Court; that Carl B. Stokes of Cleveland and Richard G. Hatcher of Gary became mayors of major American cities. Such events in no way diminished black resentment against American businesses accused of racial discrimination.

Greyhound itself was not under attack. It employed blacks at every level of operations. Yet in many ways Joe Black saved the company from becoming the target of black anger. His very presence among Greyhound's top executives was a tribute to the company's policies. In his speeches to black audiences—and he made many—Black had no need either to praise or defend the corporation. He spoke only of the needs of the black community, of its opportunities, of the importance of being self-reliant. And the respect he won was reflected in the community's attitude toward Greyhound itself.

Yet in a vicarious, though serious, way the company did feel the impact of racial conflicts. At a time of widespread rioting people were not traveling. Trautman told the press, "As a result of these disorders Greyhound had several million dollars of charters cancelled, and its regular route business in the eastern half of the United States dropped substantially for several months. It is estimated that this disruption of our business cost our shareholders about four or five cents per share."

With 31,449,750 common shares outstanding at the time, the total loss of $1.5 million was hardly cataclysmic; but added to this was the more serious drop in food revenues. This, too, was beyond Greyhound's control.

"Costly strikes of the employees of our customers in the automotive, rubber, and related industries," Trautman said, "reduced the earnings of in-plant feeding operations to the lowest point in several years."

Despite such setbacks, the company's drive for widening diversification did not cease. Every mail continued to bring brokers' suggestions for available subsidiaries, large and small. Some involved related aspects of intercity bus transportation, and as such they were synergistic with the corporation's basic interests.

Following one of these leads, Greyhound officers held preliminary telephone conversations with the Segals of Miami— Stanley, William, and Norton, respectively chairman, president, and executive vice president of their own transportation company. Through their Red Top Sedan Service they owned a valuable bus franchise for city-to-airport transportation in Miami. Similarly their Atlanta Airport Transportation owned such rights in Atlanta. They also operated a burgeoning Rent-A-Car Service in four Florida cities.

When Trautman flew to Miami to confer with the Segals, he found these entrepreneurs cordially receptive. Details were readily disposed of, and Greyhound was able to acquire the business—"An operation," shareholders were informed, "which will continue under the able management of the Segal brothers themselves."

As for the Yellow Rent-A-Car subsidiary, no one had forgotten the misfortunes into which Arthur Genet had plunged the company with his rent-a-car venture. So Trautman assured stockholders, "We intend to expand this business in an orderly manner into areas where there is a real profit potential."

• • • • •

Now that Greyhound would be transporting travelers to and from the Miami and Atlanta airports, this suggested broadening vistas of service. They were not quite new since they were in a way related to events of the past. As Trautman described what had occurred:

> Some time earlier we had sounded out the Civil Aeronautics Board [CAB] on the possibility of Greyhound acquiring an airline, even a nonscheduled airline. The staff of the CAB declared that they were never going to let a ground transportation company control an air transportation company. They threatened to take jurisdiction over Greyhound's aircraft leases if we even made a move in the direction of acquiring an airline. Faced with this inability to enter air transportation, and faced with the rapid growth of the airlines in the '60s, and our loss of traffic to them, we decided to do the next best thing. That was to acquire companies servicing the airlines—companies which might grow along with them.

This explained Greyhound's interest in negotiating for the purchase of a firm called Aircraft Services International. It was a thriving organization with almost 1,000 employees working in more than twenty American airports. Its functions were four-fold:

1. It supplied ground services such as the fueling of aircraft, providing on-ground air-conditioning equipment, and towing facilities to move planes.

2. It handled baggage and freight shipments.

3. It provided "red cap" porter service.

4. It was responsible for janitorial work at terminal areas and offices. (Eventually this broadened to include janitorial jobs at the Kennedy Space Center.)

As a result of a year of thorough negotiations Aircraft Service International was bought for 276,190 shares of Greyhound common stock. As in the case of the Segal acquisition, this company too would continue to be managed by its president, Howard Bell, and his vice presidents, Irving Rutkin and William Yates. Since Aircraft Service International had subsidiaries of its own—International Air Service of Puerto Rico and Nassau Air Dispatch—Greyhound now was operating in Puerto Rico and the Bahamas.

"A case of one step logically leading to another," wrote an analyst.

A further illustration of such synergy occurred when Greyhound acquired Dispatch Services, a vigorous and successful company run by Thomas Green and Robert Hubsch. Dispatch Services also dealt with airlines in Miami and Freeport. It provided fueling and other ground services.

In a wholly different area of business and geography, a Greyhound negotiating team was on its way to Canada to discuss the purchase of Border Brokers. These were the leading customs brokers and freight forwarders in Canada, with headquarters in Toronto. They employed some 350 people. For years they had been the agents for Greyhound's Package Express. The negotiations ran into 1968 when Border Brokers too became part of the Greyhound family.

Canada now contained a substantial part of corporate operations. In Winnipeg the Zoltok subsidiary was producing coach shells; Greyhound buses were carrying passengers through western provinces; in Alberta the Brewster Transport Company, acquired in 1965, was conducting all-expense tours through some of the most majestic scenic areas in North

America—Banff, Lake Louise, Jasper, Calgary, and the Emerald Lakes. Brewster itself had subsidiaries that operated hotels, chalets, service stations, and—a sportsman's delight—the Columbia Icefield Snowmobile Tours.

Nor was Canada the only country outside the United States where Greyhound was establishing itself. It now had a firm foothold in Belgium where the Restaura restaurant chain had forty-nine *établissements;* and their industrial catering services were steadily widening their scope.

Adding to its overseas activities, the corporation announced, "We have completed the organization and financing of our foreign leasing subsidiary, Greyhound Financial and Leasing Corporation, AG. . . . With paid-in capital of $6.75 million this company now is in a position to finance itself through foreign sources and therefore should be able to continue its profitable leasing activities throughout Europe without difficulty from the curb on U.S. investments abroad."

Surely, one would have said, all such diversifying activities were sufficient for a brief two-year period in the company's annals. But no. At the annual meeting Gerald Trautman, in reviewing events, told the audience of shareholders:

> We have an option to buy 86.4 percent of the outstanding common stock of FWD Corporation. This fifty-nine-year-old Wisconsin company makes and sells all-wheel-drive trucks. It also builds and sells vehicles used in road building, road maintenance, snow plowing, fire fighting, and oil field work. FWD has a good name and a quality product. Its products would complement our growing bus-manufacturing operations.

Then he added, "One of the highlights of the year was the appearance of our new bus, the MC-6. This bus, developed by Greyhound in its own Motor Coach Industries plant, at a cost of more than a million dollars, has been successfully road-tested and will be put into production this year, 1967. It will provide passengers with the ultimate in safety and comfort."

No wonder a stockholder asked, "Don't you fellows ever sleep?"

•   •   •   •   •

One might indeed have wondered when the company's executives rested. And their internal affairs kept them as busy as the process of acquiring outside subsidiaries.

Greyhound Leasing and Financial, for example—apart from leasing locomotives, aircraft, railroad cars, even cargo ships— was doing so well with computers that the computer business was segregated into a company of its own. It was incorporated as the Greyhound Computer Corporation. So promising was its future that fifty-seven banks joined in giving it credit lines of $56.5 million. It was independently listed on the American Stock Exchange, and over 900,000 shares of its stock were bought by the public. The rest, some 3.2 million shares worth approximately $110 million, was held by The Greyhound Corporation itself.

The Greyhound subsidiary, Greyhound Computer Corporation (now Greyhound Capital Corporation) became a major computer leasing company in the United States during the 1960s and 70s.

Almost from its inception the Greyhound Computer Corporation became the largest computer leasing company in the United States. Using IBM equipment principally, it supplied industrial, government, and other clients. Though Gerald Trautman served as its chairman, its day-to-day activities were managed by its president and chief executive officer, W. Carroll Bumpers.

Another subsidiary that was showing remarkable gains was Travelers Express, headed by Arthur S. Moore. In 1967 it sold more than 39 million money orders for a total exceeding $1 billion. It employed 15,200 agents, and after all taxes had been paid it contributed net earnings of $687,867 to Greyhound's revenues.

With so many things happening concurrently it was not surprising that the advertising people adopted the slogan, "The Action Company With A Future." Though this never achieved the popularity of "Go Greyhound—And Leave The Driving To Us," it was featured on commercials in the programs of Ed Sullivan, Jackie Gleason, Red Skelton, Andy Williams, Doris Day, Jim Nabors, Carol Burnett, and Lucille Ball.

One should not assume, however, that every subsidiary operation was successful. The Horne food enterprise, for one, soon proved disappointing. Many of its outlets were on roads that would be bypassed because of new federal highways. Their business dropped off to such an extent that Greyhound was relieved to sell the chain at its book value. At almost the same time Greyhound bought Mrs. Polly Davis' Miami Cafeteria which operated restaurants in Atlanta and southeast Florida.

Another disappointing experience occurred in Canada when a newly purchased moving van company failed to justify its potentials. This too was sold. And as if further to demonstrate the fallibility of human judgment throughout the world, there was the case of the Mercedes-Benz company in Germany.

Years later Gerald Trautman shook his head over the memory. "We were buying all our diesel engines from General Motors," he said, "and Mercedes-Benz wanted to get in on the business. They sent us some of their diesel engines, and we installed them in our buses as a test. But the test showed the German diesels to be less efficient than those of General Motors. Mercedes-Benz was not satisfied. They doubted that our testing had been accurate. So we sent an entire bus over to Stuttgart where Mercedes-Benz installed one of their engines. We then brought the bus back to the United States and road-tested it with engineers from Mercedes-Benz on board. Again the German engine got less mileage than the General Motors engine. And so we gave up all thought of using the German products."

Such isolated cases, however, never deterred the Trautman administration from furthering its diversification program. As one of his associates said, "We were now so heavily involved at airports, especially international airports, that we couldn't help noting the business done by duty-free shops. We looked into these very carefully. Then we made an offer to the leading company in the field—the Florida Export Tobacco Company headed by Alfred E. Merhige. In the Miami airport they sold tobacco, perfumes, liquors, watches, cameras, and radios to international travelers. And the firm had its own subsidiaries which we acquired in an overall purchase for slightly more than 185,000 shares of Greyhound common stock. So now you could buy all sorts of duty-free merchandise in Greyhound shops, and if you went on a cruise you could find Greyhound duty-free shops on board your ship."

While all this was happening Frederick Ackerman, now in his 74th year, surprised the directors by resigning as chairman of the board. Thus another representative of an older generation left the company. Of course, he was promptly named honorary chairman. To replace him in active service Gerald Trautman was elected to the chairmanship of the board and of the executive committee.

In its efforts to diversify, the Greyhound Corporation entered many different businesses, including duty free shops at international airports.

Various officers have their own favorite recollections of that significant year, 1967, but one event most recall—with a mixture of indignation and satisfaction—occurred when more than a hundred Greyhound managers met at a Richmond, Virginia, hotel for an Eastern Greyhound Lines marketing conference.

The group was in the lobby, registering, greeting one another cheerfully, and there was no problem until Joe Black stepped to the desk. The hotel clerk refused to let him register. Black people were not welcome.

When Trautman, already in his room, heard of this—as he did immediately—he came down in cold fury. "Get us out of this hotel at once," he told those who had arranged the meeting. "Get us into another hotel."

20

It occurred in a startling way. On a day in January 1969, Charles Munson, a Greyhound director, telephoned Gerald Trautman from New York. Munson had just talked with a close friend who was an outside director at Armour & Company. His friend was worried, Munson said, because the General Host Corporation had announced its intention to buy all the Armour stock it could acquire. In other words, General Host was aiming at a deliberate takeover.

Since Armour had experienced a few lean years, many of its shareholders might be amenable to an attractive offer. Thus General Host, a company with which Armour's executives wanted no connection, might very well seize control of the venerable food processor.

"Armour can't prevent its shareholders from selling their stock," Munson said, "but they'd hate to see it go to General Host. So they'd very much like to see a company like Greyhound, which they respect, make a counteroffer. That way, at least, they'll see their stock go into hands which they can accommodate. Also, the more shares Greyhound buys, the fewer General Host can get, which may well stop them from seizing control of Armour. Knowing that Greyhound is in the market for diversified subsidiaries, my friend is hoping Greyhound will make an offer for Armour stock."

This was hardly a casual suggestion. Considering the size and reputation of Armour—a company with gross revenues at least twice as large as Greyhound's—it was a rousing challenge.

Trautman asked, "What's General Host offering?"

"As far as I know, 7-percent debentures and there may be a one for one exchange of stock."

"No cash?"

"Apparently not. A cash offer on Greyhound's part would probably be very effective."

Trautman said, "This is something we'll have to take up with our board."

"The sooner the better," Munson urged. "Host is working fast."

Trautman at once called a special directors meeting to be held in New York. He already knew a great deal about Armour & Company. But he directed Greyhound's legal and financial people to prepare a detailed report for the board.

The knowledge about Armour that Trautman and his associates already had stemmed from a certain mutuality of interests. Greyhound, as the parent corporation of Post Houses and Prophet, which served restaurant meals, would naturally be aware of the operations of a giant food processor like Armour. Also, while Greyhound was providing airlines with ground services, Armour was furnishing them with a substantial volume of frozen meals.

So Trautman knew that Armour, through its own subsidiaries, was engaged in a wide spectrum of activities. Founded 103 years before, it was selling some $2.5 billion worth of products annually. More specific information, compiled in the report for the directors, showed that Armour now had assets of $401 million, working capital of $279 million, and long-term debt of $122 million. Some sixty subsidiaries sold a variety of products. The report listed the major ones as:

- Meat and allied food products.

- Dial deodorant soap, Dial shampoo, Dial deodorants, Dial antiperspirant, and related products.

- A vast array of drugs and pharmaceuticals, for humans and animals, through the Armour Pharmaceutical Company. One of its products, H. P. Acthar gel, popularly known as ACTH, was in use for treating some 100 diseases.

- Abrasives, adhesives, and additional items through its Industrial Products Division.

- Shoe leathers and other leather goods through its Leather Goods Division.

- Its Baldwin-Lima-Hamilton Corporation manufactured construction and industrial equipment, electronic measuring devices, specialty steels, and other heavy-duty products. It was one of the world's leaders in desalination projects, with its own network of foreign licensees and affiliates in West Germany, Belgium, Australia, and Japan.

The list went on in almost incredible detail: hydraulic cranes, thyroid medications, Parson's Household Ammonia, backing material for use inside jars and bottle caps, a synthetic aerosol ironing aid, and many more. One almost forgot that Armour had begun as a meat-packing company.

As impressive as anything else was the fact that Armour had marketing outlets in more than eighty nations. This in itself promised expanding worldwide trade for Greyhound.

The long report contained even the early history of the company when, in 1859, pioneering Philip Danforth Armour turned his back on the California gold rush. He traveled to Milwaukee where he went into partnership with the city's largest pork packer, John Plankington. Eight years later, in 1867, their ambition led them to Chicago, where they opened the first Armour & Company plant on Archer Avenue. "There," the report went on, "the world's first chilling room was built, assuring fresh meat daily." As news of this spread orders increased in such profusion that a much larger plant had to be built in the Union Stock Yards.

As further evidence of the company's readiness to pioneer, within a decade it manufactured its own refrigerated railroad cars (an investment the railroads themselves hesitated to

In 1969 Greyhound acquired Armour & Company, the giant food processing and marketing corporation founded in Chicago in 1867 by Philip Danforth Armour (above). An early Armour office at the turn of the century (top).

Gerald Trautman, chairman of the Greyhound Corporation (above, left) and Charles Orem, President of Armour and Company, at signing of acquisition papers in 1970. A famous brand name (top).

make). With the advent of this "rolling refrigeration" the Armour business spread rapidly into other regions of the country.

Surprisingly, it was not until 1965 that the company began to diversify its activities on a large scale. That was when it acquired the Baldwin-Lima-Hamilton Corporation, manufacturers of heavy machinery and microwave systems.

In all this Trautman recognized a once-in-a-lifetime opportunity for achieving an affiliation greater than Greyhound had ever before undertaken. It was as exciting as it was challenging. His enthusiasm was clear when he met with the directors.

Of the fourteen men who gathered in New York, three besides Trautman were Greyhound executives: Henry A. Montague, president of Greyhound Food Management; Jess Nicks, vice president for food of The Greyhound Corporation; and Raymond F. Shaffer, executive vice president of the corporation and also president of Greyhound Lines, Inc. These three needed no urging. The other directors may have been surprised by the enormity of the proposed acquisition, and even more surprised that a high ranking officer of Armour wanted Greyhound to bid for the company's stock. But before the meeting was over all voted for making a cash offer for the Armour shares.

And no one could foresee the problems it would engender.

•   •   •   •   •

These began when Greyhound retained a prestigious investment firm to handle its cash tender offer. General Host immediately intensified its campaign to buy Armour stock with its 7-percent debentures. In the ensuing financial battle General Host had the advantage of having been first with its publicity.

Armour stockholders, perhaps confused by the offers of the two companies, hesitated to tender their stock to Greyhound. Their offers came slowly. Some office optimists relied on a last day rush, assuring one another that "where there's uncertainty people like to wait till the last minute."

But when the last day arrived the worst snowstorm in New York's history crippled all traffic and caused the New York Stock Exchange to close. Dismayed, Greyhound had to extend the time for its offer. It did little good. The final count indicated that the company had won only 33 percent of Armour's shares, for a cash payment of over $150 million, and General Host had triumphed with 57 percent.

In an effort to become completely dominant General Host now offered to buy all of Greyhound's shares. Since 33 percent of Armour's stock could scarcely be called an acquisition in the significant sense of the term, Trautman agreed to discuss the proposal. Richard Pistell, chairman of General Host, was to represent his company at an August meeting of Greyhound directors in Seattle.

But Pistell did not appear.

The reason, proclaimed by his associates, was that he had gone to Africa "to hunt bongos." As one executive recalled, "Most of us had never heard of a bongo." The real reason for his absence, suspected by Greyhound's directors, was that his company could not raise sufficient funds to carry out its purchase offer. Greyhound, having invested $153,400,855 for its Armour holdings, was stipulating a 10-percent profit, terms to which Pistell had informally agreed.

Whether or not Pistell ever bagged a bongo, he did catch what was described as an exotic African disease that sent him flying to a Paris hospital. From there he telephoned Trautman. He maintained that his company still wished to buy Greyhound's share of Armour stock.

By this time, however, Trautman no longer wished to sell. He had a better idea in which his associates concurred. It was to buy General Host's 57 percent of Armour.

If that reversal of tactics could be achieved, Greyhound would own 90 percent of the giant Chicago conglomerate— truly the greatest acquisition in its corporate history.

But there were obstacles. First, discussions of such a proposal would take time. "Also," said Trautman, "this was a case in which we had to get the Interstate Commerce Commission's approval to buy the stock, and this too could take time." So arrangements had to be made to keep that 57 percent of shares in General Host's possession until the purchase could be made. The problem here was that General Host was obligated to pay the interest on the debentures it had issued, and it lacked the funds.

"We calculated that General Host was some $10 million short to meet its commitment," Trautman said. "So it became our job to keep General Host afloat, as it were, until our deal with them could be consummated."

New York's Citibank showed no interest in making the $10 million loan, but Trautman had better luck with Chicago's Continental Bank. There the $10 million loan to General Host was arranged with a strict stipulation. As the accounting firm of Touche Ross & Company recorded the deal:

> The Armour common stock (bought by General Host) was required to be placed as collateral for the loan. In the event of a default by Host, Greyhound Food Management entered into an agreement with the bank obligating it to purchase the note for the amount of the unpaid balance and accrued interest.

In effect Greyhound was underwriting the transaction, guaranteeing the bank against loss.

With this settled, Greyhound officers led by Gerald Trautman sat down with General Host executives to arrange terms for the stock purchase. It took some time to reach agreements, but most were concluded in September 1969. In Trautman's words, "We arranged to acquire all of General Host's shares in Armour at a price which was much lower than the price we had paid for our initial 33 percent."

Final details of the deal were left to the decision of the very top echelons of Greyhound, Armour, and General Host executives. They arranged to meet in the New York apartment of an investment banker where their privacy would be undisturbed. Greyhound was represented by Trautman and Batastini; Armour by its president, Charles R. Orem; and Richard Pistell came for General Host. In addition there were two bankers and two attorneys.

During a long afternoon session most last-minute differences were overcome. Because some of the group had dinner engagements, the men agreed to meet again at eight that evening to settle final details and sign a contractual agreement.

By eight all had returned—except Pistell.

Those present soon concurred on all items, but of course the approval of General Host's chairman was essential. And where was he? Nobody knew. Nine o'clock, and Pistell was not back. The others paced the room, scowling, frequently looking at their watches. Some were angry, some were worried. Ten o'clock, and he still had not appeared. Had he at the last minute decided to abandon the whole transaction?

Just before eleven o'clock the doorbell rang. One of the bankers hurried to open the door. Richard Pistell came in grinning, a bit unsteady on his feet.

"Sorry I'm late," he said. "Had dinner with the Duke and Duchess of Windsor. Couldn't break away."

The others could only stare at him.

As he spoke Pistell's glance turned to the piano in a corner. The sight brightened him. Still swaying slightly, he crossed the room, sat on the piano stool, and began to play. He had just started to sing in a somewhat raucous voice when two of the others lifted him to his feet and led him to the table.

The document that would bring General Host about $200 million lay there, awaiting Pistell's approval. The sight of it somehow sobered him. He took the pen that was handed to him and managed to affix his signature to the agreement.

•   •   •   •   •

This did not end all the merger problems, and one was so

incomprehensible that it stunned Greyhound's people. It occurred soon after the conclusion of the deal, when an Armour officer had been installed as a member of the Greyhound board of directors.

The shock came when it was discovered that this executive was trying to persuade the Justice Department to bring an antitrust suit against The Greyhound Corporation; he claimed Greyhound had no right to acquire Armour—a remarkable contention when one realized that he had sold his own stock to the company. Armour's officers, when they were informed of this, were as astounded as Greyhound's. As for Trautman himself, he was outraged. And he acted promptly. The executive in question was forced to resign from both Armour's board and from Greyhound's. His efforts had no results.

In May 1970 the Armour–Greyhound transaction won government approval. By virtue of its huge acquisition The Greyhound Corporation became the twenty-sixth largest industrial corporation in the United States. Hailed as a major business development, the merger was reported in publications throughout the country. It gave rise to countless commentaries, some serious, some humorous, some even imparting a malicious sting.

In Chicago, for instance, they told the story—no doubt apocryphal—of Beatrice Lillie who was in the city while performing in a British comedy. She was having her hair set in a beauty parlor when the wife of a high ranking Armour executive arrived. The Armour lady had to wait. She became impatient, irritated, finally irascible. Loud enough to be heard, she said, "When will that actress woman be done?"

Beatrice Lillie made no comment. But when at last her hair was set and she rose to go, she said clearly enough to be heard, "You may tell the butcher's wife that Lady Peale is leaving!"

21

Of course, the complicated efforts to acquire Armour could not be permitted to interfere with other interests. Many projects that had no relation to the meat packer demanded action, some of them mired in litigation. There was, for one, the unexpected legal battle with D. P. Boothe, Jr.

Boothe may have been awed by the extraordinary success of the leasing business, with 1968 profits amounting to well over $7.5 million. It must have been these spectacular figures that impelled him to leave Greyhound in order once more to launch an enterprise of his own. He called the new firm Boothe Leasing, which was a mistake; he seemed to cast aside as inconsequential the fact that in buying his original business Greyhound had bought all rights to the "Boothe Leasing" name. And he solicited business from clients he had served as a representative of The Greyhound Corporation, which was another mistake.

When Greyhound learned that its customers were being approached by a new Boothe Leasing company, many of its executives were furious. They demanded punitive action for what they regarded as reprehensible business methods as well as the illegal use of a company name. Trautman did his best to dissuade Boothe from practices he had undertaken with what seemed a lack of legal guidance. When these efforts failed, Greyhound decided to bring suit; it placed its case in the hands of an outstanding Chicago law firm.

Boothe's own lawyers must at this point have convinced him of the weakness of his case, for matters were settled out of court. He had to agree to stop using the Boothe Leasing name and to cease soliciting Greyhound's customers; and, in addition, Greyhound received approximately $1 million in a final settlement of what had been a trying affair.

Scarcely had this case been closed when another legal contest brought Greyhound's lawyers hurrying into court. This time they challenged the financial and ethical practices, of all firms, of the giant International Business Machines corporation. Thus Greyhound was pitted against the eighth largest firm in the United States, one with 1968 assets of almost $22 billion.

It was a stubbornly contested case. IBM may have decided that companies like Greyhound's computer leasing subsidiary were usurping business that ought rightfully to belong to the manufacturers of computers, in this case IBM itself. To offer more attractive terms to users it began adjusting its prices. Greyhound's lawyers charged IBM with manipulating those prices in a way designed to restrain the leasing operations of others.

In refuting the allegation IBM maintained that it was, after all, only one of many manufacturers of office appliances and machinery; people were free to buy or rent computers from any source they chose. But as one chronicler pointed out—and as any jury would be bound to concede—"IBM machines had become an industry in themselves, machines whose functions could be performed by nothing else in existence." In this particular era no one could doubt that IBM dominated the computer market.

The suit launched several years of costly, frustrating litigation that Trautman called "a battle for the very survival of the leasing industry." When the issue first came to trial in a Phoenix court, an impatient judge dismissed the jury and awarded a peremptory decision to IBM. Greyhound's lawyers were stunned. They immediately appealed to a higher court where a panel of three judges would hear the case. IBM sought delay after delay, but as Trautman said, "The higher court's eventual decision was worth waiting for because it laid down a blueprint of how to present a winning case to the jury." And though Greyhound did indeed have a winning case, IBM continued its legal maneuvers for almost five years. But in the end it accepted the inevitable. It settled the case with a payment to Greyhound of $17.7 million.

• • • • •

Obviously matters like these—and there were others—primarily concerned the legal department. They did not deter operating units from pressing on with their own activities. And some of these were dictated by national events that affected bus transportation.

On November 25, 1969, Washington, D.C., witnessed one of the most massive protest demonstrations in its history. More than 250,000 men and women, some shouting in anger and waving their fists, others silent in their thoughts, marched toward the White House in protest against the war in Vietnam. They had poured into the city in trains, in private cars, in vans, and in chartered Greyhound buses.

Waiting to take their passengers home, the buses were parked in police-designated locations. The Greyhound name and the symbolic running dog were visible throughout the national capital. They testified to the fact that the fastest growing branch of bus transportation was now the charter business. This seemed true everywhere.

In Canada the Brewster Transport Company, a sight-seeing subsidiary catering to tourists, reported "the best year ever." Record crowds were thronging to witness the annual Calgary Stampede, perhaps the most exciting rodeo exhibition on the continent. Elsewhere Greyhound's Carousel Tours were taking busloads of sightseers through California, Florida, and other regions. By 1968 the total annual revenues of charter operations reached an astonishing $126,733,125, whereupon a radio entertainer kept saying, "And you ain't seen nothin' yet."

His was only one of the programs that repeatedly exhorted the public to *Go Greyhound*. The company's commercials were appearing on the television shows of Ed Sullivan, Jonathan Winters, the Smothers Brothers, Red Skelton, and Jackie Gleason—all of them among the most popular programs of their day. Meanwhile the Grey Advertising Agency was filling national magazines with pictures of the most beautiful spots in America, all visited by Greyhound buses. Adding sightseers to the regular patrons of intercity transportation, the Greyhound bus lines were carrying some 100 million passengers a year.

"In stressing charter and sight-seeing tours we were not ignoring regular intercity transportation," said a Greyhound executive. "We never forgot that historically this has been the very foundation of Greyhound business. And we were not overlooking the opportunities of localized services, either."

What localized services?

"In New York, for instance, we bought Carey Transportation. A highly essential enterprise, this carried passengers from Manhattan to the city's three airports. We established similar services to the National and Dulles airports in Washington, D.C. Also, for local sight-seeing, we acquired the well-organized Gray Lines in city after city, and the California Parlor Car Tours in San Francisco. Bus transportation was being expanded in every possible way, and it has never stopped."

One might have said that Gerald Trautman had good reason to be pleased by the progress of the company. Yet as he sat at his desk, considering matters, studying reports of personnel, he had cause to be disturbed, too.

There was a definite sense of loss in the departure from the company of John Teets. As manager of the Greyhound restaurants at the New York World's Fair, Teets had made the concession the only profitable food operation at the exposition, grossing well over $1 million a month. He had gone on to become president of the Post House chain though he was only thirty-three, and this too had thrived under his management. Now he had left the company to become president of the J. R. Thompson restaurants in the Midwest. To replace his ability would not be easy.

So, despite Greyhound's continuing growth it was, like the nation itself, experiencing both good and difficult times. As for the problems of the nation, its shocks began in 1968 when the eighty-three-man crew of the USS Pueblo was seized by North Koreans in the Sea of Japan, and the United States was all but helpless in its efforts to rescue them. Eleven tension-filled months passed before the Americans were released. And this was also the year when Dr. Martin Luther King, Jr., was assassinated; and when, three harrowing months later, Robert Kennedy was shot to death.

Chicago, too, had its trials. The Democratic National Convention of 1968, about to nominate Hubert H. Humphrey for the presidency of the United States, attracted all types of protesting groups. From his office window Trautman could see some of them in the streets, shouting and waving placards as they might have waved flags. Historian William Manchester vividly described the situation:

> The Committee To End The War In Vietnam . . . coordinating eighty peace groups . . . came to jeer at the Chicago police. Hippies, Yippies, peace pickets, McCarthy workers, disillusioned liberals—altogether they predicted there would be 100,000 of them, and they would march on the convention in the International Amphitheatre.

Did Mayor Richard J. Daley take them too seriously? Manchester reported that the mayor "turned Chicago into an armed camp. Manholes around the Amphitheatre were sealed with tar. A chain link fence seven feet high, with barbed wire on top of it, was thrown around the hall. The city's 11,500 policemen were put on twelve-hour shifts, 5,500 National Guardsmen were alerted, and 7,500 troops of the U.S. Army, airlifted from Fort Hood in Texas on White House orders, were ordered to stand by."

When Mayor Daley flatly refused to let the demonstrators sleep in Lincoln Park, a clash between them and the police was inevitable. It dominated the nation's press and telecasts.

In such an atmosphere it might have been difficult for Greyhound executives to concentrate on other matters. Yet the truth was that nothing deterred them from concluding the largest diversification deal since the acquisition of Armour & Company. This was the acquisition of Consultants & Designers.

The very name puzzled some stockholders when they read it in newspapers. They sent inquiries by mail and telephone: "What are Consultants & Designers? What do they do?" Greyhound's public relations department formulated an answer.

"Consultants & Designers," their report began, "is headquartered in New York. It has sixty offices in major United States cities and Canada, and it is listed on the American Stock Exchange. It employs 4,000 persons, about 2,300 of them being engineers, designers, draftsmen, scientists, and computer programmers.

"These professionals address themselves to the technical needs of industry and government. In the temporary-help market their services will be in ever-greater demand because of the high cost of recruiting professional personnel, and the considerable savings to customers in not having to pay fringe benefits and other overhead expenses to temporary employees.

"Consultants & Designers recently strengthened its position in the technical field by acquiring the industry's oldest company, Design Service, and four other companies."

Outlining some specific undertakings of the firm, the report spread from the giant photographic exhibit in New York's Grand Central Station to involvement in the Apollo moonshot program at Cape Canaveral.

"Consultants & Designers," it said, "brought support services to the National Aeronautics and Space Administration [NASA] and to many other C&D clients engaged in the design, manufacture, and guidance of space vehicles. At another and completely different level of operations, we acquired Manncraft Exhibitors Service. This company installs the equipment, designs and builds the decorations, and provides all the needs of trade shows and conventions."

Clearly, Consultants & Designers was opening new areas for Greyhound enterprises. The parent company's subsidiaries, now combined with those of Armour and C&D, numbered almost 130. The Greyhound Corporation had become one of the most diversified companies in America.

•　　•　　•　　•　　•

Ask any corporate head what he considers his greatest asset, and almost invariably the answer is "people." Ask about his worst liability, and again the answer is "people." In these early years of Trautman's administration one of his most difficult duties was, as he expressed it, "To get the right people into the right jobs." Though this might bring glowing opportunity to newly promoted individuals, it could also bring pain to the officers they replaced.

"But we never terminated anyone's employment," Trautman said, "without good reason."

For example, there was a day when Armour's vice president for public relations, for purposes never explained, notified the *Wall Street Journal* that, after long consideration, the ICC had decided not to approve Greyhound's purchase of Armour stock. There was no truth in the report; the public relations man had simply invented it. Yet the published story stupefied not only General Host but thousands of people who had tendered their shares. Countless alarmed telephone calls came to the Greyhound offices. An investigation was launched.

"When we found the source of the story," said Trautman, "I instantly fired the man."

Of course the merger of Greyhound and Armour had complete government approval. As Greyhound's chairman, Gerald Trautman had the responsibility of supervising the management of both companies. And the first years of the combined operations brought some interesting results. Armour's net income after taxes was $27 million for fiscal 1970 and approximately $32 million for fiscal 1971. Trautman analyzed the figures as did Jess Nicks, Armour's vice president.

By adding the sales of Armour to those of Greyhound, total revenues of the corporation were increased from $663,118,000 in 1969 to $2,753,165,000 in 1970, more than quadrupling annual income. Since the purchase of all Armour shares had cost Greyhound something over $350 million, simple arithmetic indicated that for a payment of $350 million the company had bought more than $2.5 billion in annual revenues.

Yet, as he studied details, one thing that struck Trautman as unsatisfactory was the performance of the Baldwin-Lima-Hamilton group. "Actually," he said, "at the time we did not want to be in the heavy-industry business which Baldwin-Lima-Hamilton represented." Besides this, all its records convinced him that this subsidiary was suffering from inefficient management. The longer he amassed details, the more certain he became that its head, an Armour vice president, would have to be replaced.

But when he told this to Armour executives, they were appalled. This particular vice president, it developed, enjoyed a sacrosanct position.

"He's there," Trautman was told, "because the most powerful member of our board of directors, Bud Rentschler, put him there. We can't fire this vice president without antagonizing Rentschler, and we certainly don't want to do that."

When Trautman suggested explaining matters to this director, no one volunteered to undertake the task. It would be futile, they all maintained. So the chairman decided to do it himself. He telephoned Rentschler to make an appointment.

"We had breakfast in his apartment," he recalled, "and I told him all about the problem we were having with Baldwin-Lima-Hamilton. When I asked if he had any suggestions for handling the situation, he immediately answered, 'I certainly do. First thing you've got to do is get rid of that vice president!' "

22

Greyhound's management called the acquisition of Armour "the most significant event of 1970, and perhaps in Greyhound's history." Surely it was the most publicized. But it reached its full potential for profits only after Trautman and his associates performed what might be termed major surgery.

First, a few others like the vice president of Baldwin-Lima-Hamilton had to be released because of obvious ineffectiveness. In other cases there was a duplication of responsibilities which could be eliminated by putting one person in charge of several related operations. And there were instances where men sullenly tried to defend inadequacy by claiming, "This was his job, not mine." This could often be resolved by giving the job to the one referred to as "his."

By the time the reorganization of personnel was completed, Armour was saving over $1 million a year in executive compensation.

This consolidation of top management was, however, only one of many changes designed to bolster the company's financial status. There were still some Armour affiliates of which Greyhound wanted to divest itself, and these called for decisive action. It was undertaken after conferences with the two Armour executives who had been elected to the Greyhound board of directors, Charles Orem and David L. Duensing.

The company at once proceeded to sell those subsidiaries it did not wish to retain.

There were some that nobody wanted to buy. These were closed. As a further step toward increased efficiency and economy, it was announced that "various staff activities were coordinated, such as the use of computer operations, communications, insurance, banking arrangements, and many more."

Those company officials interested in gardening called it "a pruning operation." In any case, the money realized from the sale of the less desirable affiliates reduced Greyhound's $355 million investment in Armour to about $130 million. As a result income from Armour rose to what *Forbes* magazine rated as "a solid 28 percent on $130 million."

Even so, the value of the merger was just beginning to manifest itself. Working together, Greyhound and Armour executives inaugurated a growth program that included promotion of a line of frozen meals, Hospital Fare, to meet the requirements of hospital patients; a new facial soap, Tone; a self-basting turkey; a broader line of frozen dinner entrees.

To accommodate such growth a plant was under construction to provide shelf stable canned goods; the Armour-Dial soap factory in Aurora, Illinois, already operating three shifts a day, six days a week, was being expanded; and for the bus lines several new terminals were being completed.

The financing of all these costly projects necessitated bank loans and short-term notes amounting to $30,219,284. This raised Greyhound's total 1970 liabilities to $242,706,176, a figure that included the cost of new buses. But with assets of $445,459,721 on the other side of the ledger, The Greyhound Corporation was in sound health. This was notable at a time when American industry in general was experiencing a difficult year in an economy weakened by rising inflation. Yet Gerald Trautman said, "It is gratifying that Greyhound was able to achieve increased returns in 1970. It was expected that the combination of Armour's products with Greyhound's services would contribute to the strength of our company, and this has proved to be true."

Perhaps one could not have expected a corporate head to say anything else to his shareholders. But the figures made it clear that he was merely stating a fact.

•   •   •   •   •

In that year of continuing growth an entirely different problem confronted Greyhound management. The Greyhound and Armour personnel were scattered through many offices in a number of buildings. This made communication awkward. Efficiency of operation could be greatly heightened if the staffs of the two companies were brought close together, erasing some duplication of activities.

Once more the company's officers began to talk about moving their headquarters. Many, including Gerald Trautman himself, favored moving to another city. The question was—what city?

The Fantus organization, specialists in seeking business locations, was retained to survey the advantages of a number of cities. For months they studied San Diego, Dallas, and other communities. Their voluminous reports dealt with local taxes, the availability of labor, schools, transportation facilities, climate, hospitals, housing, cultural attractions such as theaters, orchestras, museums, and every other amenity one could question.

The first to read the Fantus recommendations were Trautman, Shaffer, Nicks, and Batastini. Then copies went to the other officers and to the directors.

According to all Fantus findings, Phoenix, Arizona, seemed to offer the most attractive conveniences, natural resources, and—not to be underestimated—the possibility of having the state government allow some welcome tax abatements. These could help defray the considerable costs of moving.

So Trautman and a few of his associates went to Phoenix to survey its opportunities. Their conferences with the mayor and other officials indicated that these men were eager to bring Greyhound to their community; the city needed a greater variety of industry than it had.

The visitors from Chicago made an inspection tour of residential districts, especially those in nearby Scottsdale. Everywhere they felt a sense of spaciousness, of invigorating air. Scenically, too, the city had its allurements. Whichever way one looked across this so-called Valley of the Sun one saw distant mountains that encircled the region like nature's promise of privacy and protection.

As impressive as anything else, and as surprising, was the presence of a new twenty-floor building just constructed by the Del Webb organization. Gleaming white in the Arizona sunshine, it was empty, waiting to welcome tenants.

The building seemed perfect for Greyhound's needs. It had ample office space for staff operations and for the headquarters of many subsidiaries. To add to its persuasiveness, it stood across the street from a new twenty-floor hotel, ideally situated for those who would come to transact with Greyhound.

By the time the executives were ready to return to Chicago they knew they had found their new home.

As might have been anticipated, however, the announcement of the impending move caused some consternation among Chicago employees. Would they lose their jobs? If not, did they really want to move their families to Phoenix, away from friends and relatives, from schools, from churches?

Trautman quickly allayed their fears. The company, he said, would assume all transportation costs and would help in finding homes. Should anyone wish to return to Chicago within a year's time, all attendant expenses would be paid. (No one ever availed himself of this privilege.)

The move was made swiftly and efficiently in 1971, utilizing the facilities of a large fleet of Greyhound vans. Through newspapers, telecasts, and municipal announcements the people of Phoenix were informed that this corporation had annual sales exceeding $3 billion. Its constant growth guaranteed an ever-increasing number of jobs for the residents of Phoenix. "Our city," said a local newspaperman, "has struck a bonanza."

•   •   •   •   •

At night, in the residential suburbs of Phoenix, one could step outdoors to gaze up at stars more brilliant than they

This company-owned Phoenix skyscraper houses Greyhound's corporate headquarters.

seemed anywhere else, and the stillness was almost awesome in its intensity. But all this peace and silence could not isolate Phoenix from what was happening in the outside world. Vietnam still embroiled half a million American troops, and in other parts of the United States mass outcries against the war were crowding cities and campuses. Vice President Spiro Agnew, contemptuous of all these dissidents, was calling them "nattering nabobs" and castigating the press for reporting their views. "Some papers," he said, "dispose of their garbage by printing it."

As for American industry in these nerve-wrenching days, its production was down, unemployment was becoming worse, inflation was rising. In an effort to cope with all this President Nixon ordered a freeze on prices, wages, and virtually everything else. As if this were not enough, the federally subsidized railroad system, Amtrak, came into existence with the proclaimed purpose of "getting people back on trains"—something viewed as a direct challenge to the bus industry.

Some editorials pointed out that because of federal subsidies to the railroads, the American taxpayer was paying over $20 for every passenger who boarded an Amtrak train, a subsidy that today has risen to $40 a ticket.

It was a challenge that had to be met by buses, and Trautman decided to treat it as a possible asset—an idea one might have regarded as impossible. Nevertheless, he discussed his plan with Greyhound's transportation executives, James L. Kerrigan, Frank Nageotte, Henry Lesko, Frederick Dunikoski, and with the company's legal staff.

The opportunity Trautman saw lay in the fact that, with the formation of Amtrak, a number of railway lines had their intercity service curtailed or eliminated. They left a gap that only buses could fill. The possibility led to talks with Amtrak officials, and Trautman reported the outcome with considerable satisfaction.

"We have been able to work out cooperative arrangements with Amtrak which can only help our business," he said. "Currently we have arrangements whereby we honor any

Amtrak tickets between two points served by both companies. The traveler can elect to go by bus or train. In another instance, combination bus–rail tickets are sold by Amtrak between two points not fully served by the railroads. And further cooperative arrangements are now under consideration."

What it amounted to, obviously, was something Trautman had been advocating for years—close and mutually profitable relations between bus lines and other carriers.

Further to promote bus travel and its attractions, advertising was intensified in every medium. And hundreds of new coaches were brought into service. The latest 102-inch-wide Supercruisers were the most luxurious on America's highways. Their advertised pictures showed smiling travelers enjoying comforts such as they had never known before.

In conjunction with all this came a "Next-Bus-Out" campaign for Package Express. "A package delivered to us thirty minutes before a scheduled departure will leave on the next bus out."

All such innovations, plus new nonstop runs between some major cities, enabled Trautman to tell stockholders that in 1972 "Greyhound had the second best earnings record in history." Gratifying as this might be, however, it could not make him sanguine about the future. Something was wrong—something that was happening in Washington.

For a long time he had been protesting against the restrictions imposed on industry by government regulations. (A Washington reporter asserted that merely to list the titles of these regulations required 1500 single-spaced typewritten pages.) Many of these orders, Trautman contended, stifled business initiative. Almost all involved long delays in obtaining official decisions.

Matters had been bad enough while Greyhound had to await actions of the ICC. Now, with Armour under the corporate umbrella, there was also the Food and Drug Administration [FDA] to cope with, as well as other agencies.

Citing some problems with government, Trautman described an illustrative case that showed how Greyhound's business had been adversely affected by what he termed overregulation.

"First," he said, "the Food and Drug Administration banned the sale of products containing hexachlorophene. This included Dial soap which contained three-quarters of 1 percent of the banned ingredient. Dial had been used in the United States for twenty-four years, and there was no evidence at all that this soap had ever been harmful to humans. Nevertheless, on approximately four days' notice, Dial soap was banned by the FDA. Since then it has been reformulated to substitute another effective antibacterial agent. But the arbitrary regulation cost our company millions of dollars in losses."

(It must be noted that some eighty other nations in which Dial was sold thereupon made their own analyses of its properties; not one found it in any way harmful. American laboratory technicians pointed to its effects on rats, whereupon an advertising man replied, "We have never tried to sell Dial to a rat.")

Trautman also reported that Armour-Dial had been trying to obtain authority from the Price Commission and the Cost of Living Council for cost-justified increases in the prices of canned food products. "For eleven months the Price Commission delayed an answer. We went from a substantial profit in 1971 to a loss of several million dollars in 1972."

Understandably, considering such experiences, his urgings for relief from government interference became more insistent than ever. In addressing security analysts, business organizations, university groups, he stressed his convictions again and again. But such talks were not enough to bring results.

Greyhound had established a government affairs office in Washington where Carl J. Fleps, vice president for government affairs, sought an easement of federal restraints. He and his staff not only took their case to congressmen, senators, and others in the nation's capital; they also testified before committees and endeavored to enlist the support of organizations and the press.

(Today the Washington office is headed by James Corcoran and George Snyder. Veteran Jack Bausch, who had represented the Armour interests for more than forty years, had retired.)

"We go out armed with facts, figures, and the best arguments we can muster," one of the staff said. "We never dissemble. For all its sophistication, Washington is a small town. Everyone knows everyone else. If you're not straight no one will trust you. No one will even talk to you. You've got to remember that a congressman wants to know why something is good for the country, not just for you."

With the drive against oppressive regulations in the hands of competent and experienced Washington people, Trautman could give his attention to other demanding matters.

One of them was the never-ending quest for sound, diversified acquisitions, and now those beneficial to Armour had to be considered. Sunshine Hatchery, in this category, was purchased to increase Armour's operations in the turkey market. Overseas the company bought LeGrys Brothers of England, another processor of turkeys. Meanwhile, also to bolster Armour, a new abattoir was constructed in St. Joseph, Missouri, and a meat processing plant in Kansas City.

When you added all these projects to the building and remodeling of bus terminals, when you considered the growth of bus manufacturing, and of sight-seeing tours, and of a contract to supply all the bus transportation facilities in Walt Disney World in Florida, and other developments, Greyhound was domestically busier than ever. Yet Trautman had to give thought, too, to foreign affairs.

A decade earlier Greyhound's interests had spanned the American continent. Now, with the advent of Armour, those interests were worldwide. They demanded attention and travel. More and more frequently he had to call in his secretary, Barbara Carr, to say, "I'll need a company plane for a flight to——." It might be someplace in Europe, in Asia, in South America, in Africa, in Australia. The company planes, acquired together with Armour, ranged the world, and some such trips brought surprising results.

Korea was one. There Trautman had lengthy conferences with public officials and businessmen. These resulted in an agreement that Greyhound would ship forty used buses to that country, to be operated by the Koreans as a joint venture with Greyhound. The arrangement proved initially successful. One of the reasons was the efficiency of Korean mechanics. They kept the buses in perfect condition, matching the skill of American maintenance crews.

On a trip to Nigeria Trautman tried making a similar arrangement. But here the unexpected happened. Wherever a parked bus was left unwatched overnight, its tires disappeared, its batteries were stolen, everything movable was taken away. Thievery was so rampant that within months the Nigerian operation had to be abandoned.

One man who must have had mixed emotions in listening to all these reports was Frederick Ackerman. In 1970, in deference to age, he had retired from the corporation and from its board of directors. Stockholders were reminded that "Mr. Ackerman started work for Greyhound in San Francisco in 1920, half a century ago. Under his leadership Greyhound's western bus operation became the model of how a bus company should be run. Later, in 1958, Mr. Ackerman was available to take over the presidency of the company when it was in difficulties. He inaugurated the diversification program and made many other substantial contributions to the Greyhound organization. His imprint upon Greyhound will be evident for many years to come."

But not to him. Within a few short years, while traveling in the Azores, Frederick Ackerman suffered a heart attack that took his life.

23

The careers of outstanding American businessmen seem to suggest that the secret of industrial leadership is to remain constantly dissatisfied. "The status quo is never good enough" is probably the best way to describe this philosophy. And it offers the only explanation of a Greyhound paradox.

Like his predecessors, Gerald Trautman annually informed shareholders that the business of the corporation was increasing, often attaining new records. This was an accurate statement as it applied to total corporate earnings. It did not imply that every one of almost 150 subsidiaries, at home and abroad, was doing as well as it could or should. In those that were lagging behind, stronger management was generally needed. It was the chairman's responsibility to find and supply such management.

This was not an easy task. The men in charge of computer leasing, for example, had for some time been yielding unsatisfactory results. "This subsidiary had a new president almost every year," Trautman said. "The business didn't really come into its own until we brought Olie E. Swanky down from Canada to run it."

Under Swanky it did indeed become a profitable operation, but the same kind of reversal could not be achieved in some other subsidiaries.

There was the case of the General Fire and Casualty Company, one of the early Greyhound acquisitions. "We had great hopes for it when this company was bought in 1964," Trautman recalled. "It had a good portfolio of securities. But it also had a miserable group of insurance risks. Its principal business was insuring taxicabs in New York City and New Jersey. You can imagine what the claims experience was on this taxi business. And there were personality problems. These concerned the men who headed General Fire. The first had certain attributes that Mr. Ackerman, then chairman, could not tolerate, and this man lasted only six months. Then others came who tested our patience in different ways."

One, despite his generous salary, lived on a much higher scale than he could afford. It soon became apparent that his expense accounts were unreasonably, even foolishly doctored. When accountants confronted him with what were obviously false expense claims, he wisely gathered his effects and departed.

To replace him a new man was installed, one whose credentials were unassailable. Under his management the insurance company saved millions in the settlement of claims. He had been promised a bonus based on profits. Judging by the funds he saved for the company, his reward would have been unusually large.

Quite a few people at Greyhound headquarters were puzzled as they studied his remarkable figures. Yet they could find nothing wrong. The man would certainly be entitled to a tremendous bonus.

And then, suddenly, on his way home from a football game he suffered a heart attack and died.

In his office his personal papers were solemnly gathered for his family. Someone opened a locked closet door to see what else might be found—and stared in amazement. The closet contained 1,700 unpaid insurance claims that had never been filed. The settlement money saved on these added hugely to the man's basis for a bonus. "He probably intended to settle these claims after he got his check," one of the accountants said. "All of them, we noticed, had come into his office in the last three months of the year."

Trautman sighed over the recollection. "By this time," he

said, "Ralph Batastini and I were beginning to think there were no honest people in the insurance business. Nevertheless, with the help of a reputable search firm, we finally chose a man who for twenty years had been a competent vice president of another insurance company. He checked out in every conceivable respect. We considered ourselves lucky for having at last found the right man for the job."

He was good. But he developed one failing.

"We eventually discovered," Trautman said, "that he was appropriating for himself the wrecked and stolen cars on which claims had been paid. Every member of his family was driving such a car. Well, after the experiences we'd been having with General Fire, we eventually surrendered. We sold part of the business for what it would bring and liquidated the rest. We had done our best—and we had failed, defeated by simple human greed."

. . . . .

In the main, however, most affiliates were doing well. Some actually provided extraordinary results. As the company approached its sixtieth anniversary Louis B. Raffel, vice president for public relations, was able to announce that Motor Coach Industries, the bus manufacturing subsidiary, had become America's leading builder of intercity buses. Incredible as it seemed, its output exceeded that of General Motors, Mack, and every other company. It was producing 765 units a year, more than two a day, and its president, Robert Borden, was scheduling even greater numbers for the years ahead; those years would see the advent of the newly designed, superluxury coaches called Americruisers.

Counting off some of the other records achieved in 1973, Raffel said, "Under the management of John W. Powell our travel agencies, the Loyal Travel chain, have become the nation's fastest growing organization of its kind. And the Segal brothers of Florida have been making such strong progress with the Rent-A-Car business that 1,000 new cars had to be bought to meet their needs of 6,600."

He went on to subsidiary after subsidiary to show how 1973 had become the best year in Greyhound's history, with total revenues of $3.4 billion.

Undeniably the chairman had good reason to be pleased. Nevertheless he still exercised the right to be dissatisfied—not so much with individual performances within the company as with endless government interference.

"While our Transportation Group did well," he admitted, "its returns were down more than 10 percent from the previous year. This was due to our inability to obtain authorization for adequate and timely fare increases to cover escalating costs. Also, profits from the leasing group were down, principally because of the high cost of money brought about by the federal government's manipulation of the money market in its effort to control inflation."

None of this altered the fact that in its sixtieth year The Greyhound Corporation was one of the largest industrial firms in the United States, and also an international organization that embraced more than 150 companies and employed more than 54,000 people.

Impressive as the record was, it did not lead to complacency. The quest for growth continued. Trautman, Shaffer, Batastini, and their associates still had to study the endless flow of suggestions for affiliates that came from brokers. Those that seemed worthy of consideration were meticulously analyzed. Greyhound representatives went to interview their officers. Nothing was haphazard. Firms that presented too many problems were put aside and forgotten.

"You would have thought," said one vice president, "that we had just begun to diversify, the interest was so great."

The result was that 1973 acquisitions included some widely dissimilar entities. Among them was the Las Vegas Convention Service headed by David Jamison. It provided the needs of business meetings, trade shows, big conventions—everything from booths to publicity, from hotel reservations to electronic communication equipment. Then there was Global Productions which produced stage spectaculars, motion pictures, television commercials, and other visual sales tools. As an aid to physicians and hospitals came the Burn Treatment Skin Bank. "Through Armour's pharmaceutical division the corporation was already in the health field," said a technician. "Burn treatment was an extension of its service."

As if these acquisitions were not enough for a single year, the company bought, also for Armour, a number of food-related firms—the Wingate Feed and Farm Service, the Rose-A-Linda Hatchery, and Graham Brothers.

Some new enterprises were not bought; they were created. Thus The Greyhound Corporation launched its Research Information Center, a full-service firm doing market research." In its relation to other Greyhound activities this too was more synergistic than might appear. "After all," said a researcher, "Armour household products were constantly being market-tested in various regions. Since we already had a well-trained staff for such investigations, why limit them to Armour's needs? Why not sell their services to others?"

Also, there was Pine Top Insurance, a company that reinsures other insurance companies by accepting part of their risk.

So it was obvious that Greyhound was not relaxing its efforts to grow. Yet it was not forgetting its obligations to bus travel, its basic business. Among the year's most successful promotions for transportation was the "Ameripass," a single ticket offering nationwide sight-seeing trips. Within twelve months it attracted 70,000 people, generating $11 million in new revenues.

In view of all this one must ask what, if anything, went wrong. Why did Trautman have to announce, in a complete reversal of his usual annual statements, "The year 1974 was not a good year for The Greyhound Corporation"?

He explained difficulties this way: "In addition to inflation which adversely affected all operations, there were three principal causes for a substantial decline in earnings. First, our Transportation Group suffered strikes—a number of them—which cost the company an estimated $4 million, or ten cents per share. Second, Armour poultry operations lost $14.4 million after tax, or approximately thirty-four cents per share. And third, the cattle feeding operation resulted in a loss of $10.2 million.

"Because we see no immediate relief from the high cost of feed and distorted market conditions," he went on, "the poultry business has been severely curtailed, and the feeding of cattle for sale on the public market has been discontinued." Then he added that the transportation strikes had ended in the signing of new and satisfactory labor contracts. Based on all such corrective actions, he predicted, "Next year will be better."

It was.

Within twelve months Trautman, addressing the corporation's stockholders, was able to say, "The year 1975 was one of outstanding accomplishment. Not only did we overcome the major problems that plagued us in 1974, but we attained the best net income in Greyhound's history, despite a national atmosphere of economic recession. Specifically, Greyhound had net income of $81.2 million on revenues of $3.7 billion, an increase of 36 percent on a per share basis. We faced the problems that faced all business—recession, inflation, the higher costs of energy and labor. More important than the difficulties, however, was our ability to overcome them and the fact that all six of our product and service groups were profitable."

Reading this, a financial writer dryly remarked, "Say what you like, they're doing something right."

24

In 1975 The Greyhound Corporation, for the first time in its sixty years, elected a woman to vice-presidential rank. Dorothy A. Lorant left a career in Boston to head the company's public relations and advertising staff, a responsibility she undertook on the first day of 1976.

One reporter asked a Greyhound officer if Ms. Lorant had been chosen in response to the nationwide pressure on corporations by women's liberation groups. The instant reply was, "Absolutely not. We made a search for the best possible person, man or woman, to fill the vacancy left by the departure of Louis Raffel. The ultimate choice—the unanimous choice—was Dorothy Lorant."

(And soon thereafter, in 1977, the company elected its first woman director, former Congresswoman Martha W. Griffiths. A distinguished Detroit attorney, the recipient of twenty-one honorary university degrees, Mrs. Griffiths had legal, political, and business experience that brought a new quality of dynamism to the Greyhound board.)

In a firm like The Greyhound Corporation, whose activities are constantly being reported in the press, a plethora of questions pours into headquarters every day of the year. The queries come from newspaper people, financial analysts, shareholders, investment bankers, brokers, editors of business magazines, and countless others. Most such inquiries are eventually directed to the chairman, and a single day's listing of them might run like this in 1976 and 1977:

Q. I see that Greyhound has bought a company called Bresnahan. What is Bresnahan?

(The chairman's answer would make it clear that Bresnahan was a computer leasing firm bought for $4,289,000
to expand the business of the Greyhound Computer Corporation.)

*Q. You also announced the purchase of the Computer Leasing Com-
pany. How does this differ from Bresnahan?*
(Computer Leasing was a worldwide company with $130
million invested in computer equipment. This was
bought to augment the computer leasing business overseas as well as at home. Moreover, the corporation also
bought Direct Dial Data Service which provides accounting and management systems available through computers.)

Q. And what is Stuart-Sauter that you acquired? More computers?
(No. Stuart-Sauter were convention and trade show con-
tractors in San Francisco and Los Angeles. They were
bought to extend Greyhound Exposition Services in those
cities. Greyhound also acquired the Cadillac Display Corporation. It manufactures display racks and other display
equipment that add to the convention and trade show
business.)

*Q. And what's this Manpower-Burley acquisition reported in the
newspapers?*
(Manpower-Burley marketed men's personal care products—deodorants, shave creams, and so on. How did this
relate to Greyhound's interests? Through Armour-Dial. It
supplemented their line of such products. Another company Greyhound added to Armour's business was Malina.
They produce yarns for knitting and handicraft uses as
well as for sweater and sportswear manufacturers.)

Q. What about business overseas? Any expansion there?
(Yes, indeed. In Belgium the Restaura chain of restaurants
was expanding. And, in another part of the world, Greyhound Support Services had won a contract to supply
food and housekeeping services to camps along the Alaska
Pipe Line.)

Q. With all such diversification in progress, hasn't Greyhound been neglecting bus travel?

(Not at all. Greyhound recently acquired both Vermont Transit and New Mexico Transportation, thus broadening its nationwide network. This is a constant process. And bus revenues for the past year were at a record high, with a net income of $40.1 million. So bus travel was certainly not being neglected.)

So it went. The most sophisticated questions came from brokers, bankers, security analysts, business writers. They expected precise dollars-and-cents replies, and Trautman had them ready.

Greyhound's pension system had its own fascination, especially for insurance companies which could see a bonanza in managing the funds. Every Greyhound employee was enrolled in the plan after he had been with the company for a year; and the company paid all costs, the employee none.

"It's an effective way to keep our people," said a personnel officer, "and far more economical than having constantly to train new employees."

As a matter of fact, not only insurance companies were interested in the pension system, but endless queries came also from employees, unions, and statisticians of all kinds. Many of these were routed for reply to the public relations department.

When Dorothy Lorant had been with the company for a few months, a newspaperman asked her how long it took to learn the widespread details of Greyhound operations. At that she leaned back from her desk and laughed. "With 150 worldwide companies making up The Greyhound Corporation," she replied, "it should take a lifetime."

•   •   •   •   •

Clearly the chairman of such an organization has much to worry about besides growth, subsidiaries, the ratio of net earnings to total revenues. Many of his concerns must probe

Greyhound has become one of the world's largest leasing companies. Its worldwide subsidiary leases aircraft, supply vessels, oil drilling rigs, heavy equipment, and trucks, as well as computers.

far beyond the company's daily operations; they are rooted in the nation's economy and in the American concept of doing business. Here Gerald Trautman had some profoundly moving and often expressed thoughts. They grew out of an aversion to excessive government regulations and to the unfounded reputation of corporate entities in the United States. Now and then some anticorporate charge might be fair enough, but most were uncalled for and infuriating. A few cartoonists in particular had long been responsible for creating unsavory visualizations of corporate affairs. In their drawings the corporation had been personalized as a fat, bloated, often obscene figure with an enormous cigar jutting from pendulous lips and dollar-signs on his watch fob and even in his eyes. The very word "corporations" had been spelled "corporation$."

Trautman reacted bitterly to such villification. Sometimes, as he read, his lips tightened and he uttered an angry obscenity of his own. There finally came a time when he decided to give vent to his feelings by expressing what he conceived to be the truth about American corporations. Someone, he felt, had to hit back at the detractors. Who? He picked up a pen and wrote "If not us, who?"

When the document came to the desk of Don Behnke, who had the responsibility of preparing annual reports, he had only to read the letter to appreciate its importance. This comment on American corporations deserved widespread attention. In an unprecedented decision he scheduled it to appear on the front cover of the 1975 annual report and to continue on the back cover.

Behnke's judgment was rewarded. Within days after it was circulated the Trautman letter brought a flood of commending mail. Most correspondents applauded Trautman for saying what had long needed to be said. The letter ran:

If not us, who?

    For some time now a savage, punitive spirit has been abroad in America, one which threatens and indeed promises to shake the pillars of our American economic system and send it crumbling down around us.

What is so alarming about these attacks is not that they are leveled but that they have gone unchallenged so long.

In this regard corporations must shoulder much of the blame. For too many years we have assumed that the excellence of the free enterprise system, a system which has so consistently and measurably enhanced the well-being of the majority of the American people, was obvious to all. In that assumption, business and industry erred. We are finding, to our sorrow, that Complacency has a friend and her name is Apathy. The three of us have been walking hand in hand for too long now.

I find it appropriate then, in this 200th year of our nation's existence, that those of us who work within and benefit by the free enterprise system engage in a little forthright drumbeating. For if we do not, then who will?

Make no mistake about it—our nation has written a remarkable chapter in the history of mankind with a pen called Profit. The American people now have over a trillion dollars in annual spending power and our Gross National Product has soared well above the $1.5 trillion mark—by far the greatest of any country in the world. America's efforts to eradicate poverty, reverse the effects of pollution, raise the socioeconomic horizons of the have-not nations—these have all been subsidized by the wealth generated by just one sector of the economy—business and industry.

But despite this, the American economic system as we know it today is an endangered species.

Corporations, which are favorite targets for attack, are being portrayed as huge impersonal monsters. Profit itself is being harangued as an immoral "win–lose" contest in which profit for the corporation inevitably means loss for someone else.

In defense of the corporate system, let me tell you something about Greyhound. The wealth generated by our operations fans out in all directions for the public well-being.

Greyhound furnishes jobs to some 53,000 employees—bus drivers, baggage handlers, meat cutters, cannery workers. It is these employees who make the corporate system work and for this they were paid $775 million in 1975.

Greyhound has also furnished the livelihood for many of its suppliers, including American farmers to whom it paid one billion four hundred million dollars in 1975. There is no way that the farmers could get this vast amount of produce to consumers except with the help of the corporate system— and entities like our Armour & Company.

A percentage of our profit goes to our 163,000 shareholders, none of whom owns as much as one percent of our stock and many of whom are those very same bus drivers, baggage handlers, meat cutters, and cannery workers. Greyhound is a means by which these shareholders can have an ownership stake in the largest bus company in the world, the very substantial food operations of Armour and our other associated operations. Finally, and perhaps most important because it is essential to the maintenance of our democratic form of government, Greyhound pays a substantial amount annually to local, state, and federal governments as taxes. In 1975 The Greyhound Corporation paid approximately $100 million in total taxes in the United States.

There is a basic lesson here for those who would destroy a system which, while admittedly not perfect, is the best that human endeavor has devised—that the corporate system in America is simply a means by which many individuals are enabled to enjoy a standard of living and form of government not equaled anywhere in the world.

And so I urge our employees and shareholders to speak up for the corporate system. If we do not, who will?

Gerald H. Trautman

25

Trautman's letter might have added that no corporation could exist independently, immune to the factors that affect all industry. In 1975 automobile manufacturers were having a disastrous year. They closed plants, laid off thousands of people. Without their factory personnel to feed, Prophet's meal services dropped again.

Nor was this the only backlash from automotive troubles. As people in the industry lost their jobs they curtailed travel plans, cancelled vacations, and bus receipts declined. Then, with fewer people traveling, the serving of meals at Post House restaurants suffered losses. For every dip in income there was an identifiable social cause outside the company. Still, Greyhound's officers could hardly be happy about the situation. They sought remedial activities.

In an effort to stimulate food sales the company completed two years of negotiations for a "pooling of interests" with Faber Enterprises. This firm, managed by Milton Faber and Donald Murphy, operated restaurants in a number of large Chicago office buildings. The astuteness and vigorous enterprise of Faber and Murphy made this one of the most successful of Greyhound's acquisitions in its field.

And so, with more than $119 million flowing into the corporation from its food group, Greyhound could have been forgiven if it had simply decided to settle down to await better times. But that would have been a static response to circumstance, and Greyhound had never been static in more than sixty years. The challenging problem now was—how could the growth of food services be further stimulated in this period of national recession? Was there a need for management with fresh ideas?

As he sat at his desk, grappling with the question, Gerald Trautman remembered another period of trying times. His thoughts went back to the New York World's Fair of 1964, recalling that the Post House restaurants within the fairgrounds had been the only profitable food concession at the exposition; they had actually grossed more than $1 million a month. And they had been managed by John Teets.

Unfortunately Teets had left Greyhound in 1968 to accept that attractive position with the John R. Thompson restaurants, from which he had gone on to become corporate vice president of the Canteen Corporation and then chief executive officer of Bonanza International.

"At the time," said Trautman, "I could think of no one whose record in food management was more impressive. We should never have allowed him to leave Greyhound, but it was too late to bemoan that. The question now was—could we bring him back?"

There was only one way to get an answer. Trautman located Teets in Dallas, telephoned, and immediately flew down to see him. As the chairman reported their meeting:

> He met me at the plane, very cheerful, and before all else I had to go see where he jogged. As we drove past the place I assured him that there were plenty of good jogging places in Phoenix, too. Next he wanted me to see his office, which was quite attractive. I told him we had a better office for him in Phoenix. Then we went to the place where he did his aerobic exercises and got weighed under water. At that point I was defeated. 'John,' I said, 'we don't have any place in Phoenix where you can get weighed under water. What's more, I don't know anyone in Phoenix who wants to get weighed under water. If that's an important consideration, I'm licked.' He laughed at that, and we finally went to his home. After a good lunch we got down to business. By the time we rose a deal had been made. We shook hands, and I flew back to Phoenix, feeling much better.

Teets rejoined Greyhound in 1976. He assumed the posts of

chairman and chief executive officer of Greyhound Food Management as well as head of the entire Food Service Group.

From the time he strode into his large new Phoenix office—a tall, lean, tousle-haired figure exuding an athlete's energy, his eyes bright and restless behind their glasses—he created a new sense of excitement. Almost at once he began meeting with district managers. Later, when the publication, *Restaurant Hospitality,* sent an interviewer to question him about his policies, Teets answered with characteristic ferver, "I meet with our district managers monthly." For emphasis he repeated, "Monthly! Before I came back to Greyhound these people hadn't seen each other for years. Now we get together to solve common problems. People want to be involved in problem solving. They want to make a contribution. They are managers. They have as much right to be involved in the decision-making process as I have.

"At these meetings everyone contributes. You present a problem. What action did you take? How successful was it? Did anyone else face a similar problem and take different action that resulted in a better solution? Our meetings turn out to be amazingly successful learning experiences."

At a cost of about $25,000 a month these gatherings necessitated the expenditure of about $300,000 a year. But in the very first year of Teets' leadership the profits of food service leaped to $6.2 million, virtually doubling the $3.6 million of the previous year. So the price of meetings was hardly worth discussing.

"I have expert analysts working for me," he said. "They tell me what's happening with the industry, with our competition, with our own units. When I see the district managers every month I'm armed with all this data, and I share it with our people."

As to his personal relations with his district managers, he had a philosophy that must have startled them. The good men might confess a bit awkwardly that they had received offers of jobs elsewhere. "I congratulate them," he said. "I tell them

From 1978 through 1982, under the management of John Teets, right, many of the company's Post House restaurants were converted to fast food operations. Touring the Sacramento operation with Teets is the then chairman, Gerald Trautman. Teets became corporate chairman in 1982.

very frankly that if they are not getting a job offer at least once every six months, then they're doing something wrong."

The improvement of service in bus-stop restaurants—that is, giving people what they most wanted to eat—resulted eventually in the introduction of franchised Burger King restaurants. Greyhound could no doubt have launched a fast-food operation of its own. But Burger King, as Teets said, "already had an established performance of high earnings and steady growth, and had presold its concept on TV to millions of Americans."

What he came to deplore, however, was the dependence of these places solely on bus travelers. If traffic lessened, food sales dropped. So he changed menus to appeal to nontravelers, the neighborhood trade. Local advertising proved surprisingly effective, and business boomed.

Seeing all this, Trautman probably felt that the flight he had once made to see Teets in Dallas was one of the most productive trips he had ever undertaken.

•   •   •   •   •

When Raymond F. Shaffer announced that he would retire from the presidency of The Greyhound Corporation because of mandatory age stipulations, he ended a career that had kept him in the company for thirty-one years. With no immediate successor in mind, the directors asked Trautman to assume the presidency while continuing as chairman.

He agreed. Also, he recommended three promotions to which the board at once consented. Ralph Batastini, executive vice president for finance, Clifford Cox, executive vice president for Armour, and James Kerrigan, executive vice president for transportation, were all elected vice chairmen and members of the board. This, Trautman felt, would give these three men and their abilities greater exposure to the directors who, presumably, might eventually elect one of them to the presidency.

Simultaneously he brought Carl Fleps in from the Washington office of government affairs to serve as his administrative assistant.

(It was a year of change among the company's directors, too. Following the retirement of William R. Adams and James W. Walker, this was the time former Congresswoman Martha Griffiths joined the board, as did John B. Connally, who had been governor of Texas as well as Nixon's Secretary of the Treasury and Secretary of the Navy. The third new director was Samuel A. Casey, chairman of the Great Northern Nekoosa Corporation, a leading paper manufacturer.)

The activities of the Washington office, under James Corcoran, largely reflected Trautman's responsibility as head of an influential American corporation. As always in the past, he felt an obligation to speak out on what he considered unfair burdens being heaped upon the American people.

For instance, he had never stopped emphasizing the harmful effects of unnecessary federal regulations. "Among other excesses," he now said, "we have over 1,000 domestic assistance programs in existence today, versus only 100 in 1961." (This superfluity of regulatory agencies, it had been reported, was costing the American consumer over $130 billion a year.) "If we don't soon address ourselves to the task of controlling and containing both the size and the spending habits of government," he warned, "we can look forward to chronic inflation of a type that will make that of 1973 and 1974 look positively benign."

In connection with this he stressed a point aimed directly at legislators:

> Government is not a generator of wealth but only an allocator of the wealth created by others—specifically by the working men and women of this country. The only source of wealth that I know of for financing all the altruistic pursuits of government lies in the taxes paid by employed people working for profitable businesses. To sandbag, penalize, and restrain the profit-making ability of the private sector is the worst sort of politics. Many companies simply cannot absorb the cost of complying with excessive regulations and end up cutting staff or going out of business, throwing thousands of people into the category of the unemployed.

Furthermore, Trautman inexorably opposed what he termed double taxation. This was something he constantly urged the company's Washington representatives to stress with legislators.

"In 1976," he said, "The Greyhound Corporation paid to its shareowners, in the form of dividends, over 62 percent of its 1976 net income. Here is a problem that Greyhound shareowners face in common with America's 25 million other shareowners. It is the unfair double taxation of the same earnings, once at the corporate level and again at the shareowner level."

Such economic concerns did not lessen Trautman's concentration on the immediate needs of the corporation. The bus industry in particular required attention.

In this 200th year of the nation's history Bicentennial celebrations were in progress throughout the land. Every community, large or small, held its parades. In New York the "tall ships" spread their sails like wings and slid majestically past

Navy vessels moored in the Hudson. In Philadelphia crowds gathered at the Liberty Bell to hear orators proclaim the greatness of America. Every town in the United States bedecked itself in flags and exhibited attractions as varied as the Virginia City, Nevada, Camel and Ostrich Races; and the Morgan City, Louisiana, Shrimp and Petroleum Festival.

Since thousands of people might wish to witness some of these spectacles, Greyhound offered fifty-dollar one-way trips to any point in the country, and equally alluring round-trip fares. These bargains were widely advertised by the company's new agency, Bozell and Jacobs. In broadcasts Greyhound's principal voice was that of Pearl Bailey, "America's First Lady of Song." Appearing on millions of television screens, she sang, "Say Hello To A Good Buy—Go Greyhound."

And of course the buses that sped passengers to the festivals also carried shipments of packages. For the first time, in 1976, Package Express achieved revenues that exceeded $100 million. Indeed, it was the very growth of transportation that posed new problems, for now more coaches were constantly needed. In Winnipeg and Pembina the manufacturing of buses, now under the aegis of Executive Vice President Frank Nageotte, was thriving. In that single year 1,096 new coaches rolled out of the plants. Of these, 514 became part of Greyhound's own fleet; the rest, 582, were sold to other companies. "Our MC-8 bus, the Americruiser," the manufacturing group announced, "is bought by more independent carriers in the United States and Canada than all other makes of intercity buses combined."

It has been recognized as early as 1974 that even more buses could be sold if production space were available. Merely to enlarge existing facilities would not do; an enormous, completely modern new plant was necessary.

A search committee, setting out to study possible factory sites, traveled from city to city only to encounter a variety of obstacles. In some places local taxes were too high; in others a labor pool of sufficient size was unavailable; or energy costs were prohibitive; or civic conditions were disappointing.

But when the committee descended from a plane in Roswell, New Mexico, their spirits quickly brightened. Roswell's mayor and civic leaders welcomed the visitors with warm handshakes. They had limousines waiting. The Greyhound men were driven to inspect a huge building, formerly an aircraft hangar, that was empty, clean, ready to be converted to a bus-manufacturing facility.

It was not the sale of the building that primarily motivated the people of Roswell. (As a matter of record, the ultimate sale was negotiated for a token price of $100.) Their interest lay in creating new jobs for their community.

"That place was exactly what we wanted," said Frank Nageotte. "We installed equipment and began operations late in 1976. Transportation Manufacturing Corporation (TMC)— the name we coined for the plant—had a great capacity which reinforced our position as the leading manufacturer of motor coaches. TMC was a success from the start."

Yet, for the Transportation Group, it was by no means the only visible evidence of growth. At a cost of some $50 million it was, constructing new terminals and garages in Atlanta, Albuquerque, Denver, Cincinnati, and Little Rock. All told, the Transportation Group was making a significant contribution to the corporation's total 1976 revenues of $3,738,000,000.

Nevertheless, in Trautman's opinion, buses were not fulfilling their real potential. This was, he told shareholders, "because of the failure of the Interstate Commerce Commission, on two occasions in 1976, to approve fully justified price increases. Our obligations to the public and to our shareholders make it unconscionable for management to sit idly by and suffer the United States bus industry to go the way of the rail industry. We are therefore determined to obtain adequate fares through, we trust, the present regulatory system but, if necessary, through deregulation."

And the struggle continued.

26

Twice a month, as a regular procedure, chief officers of The Greyhound Corporation met with Trautman to discuss urgent affairs. It was a small group. Basically it included Ralph Batastini, Clifford Cox, and James Kerrigan. Others were brought in when their special interests and expertise were involved—men like W. Carroll Bumpers, group vice president for leasing; or John Teets on questions concerning food services; or Armen Ervanian, vice president for real estate.

Though all corporate affairs were weighed at these bimonthly sessions, the problems of subsidiaries were among the most frequent. With well over two hundred affiliates now operating domestically and abroad, there were always some that developed shortcomings and disappointments. These had to be analyzed. Was management at fault? Had Greyhound itself been overly optimistic in making the acquisition? Or were there uncontrollable extraneous circumstances? In some cases government edicts could rob an affiliate of its profits.

In such instances, where corrective measures could not be taken, intelligent corporate progress could dictate the divestiture of acquisitions.

The year 1977 produced two such situations. One dealt with the Armour Pharmaceutical Company. It was fairly lucrative; no disputing that. But unfortunately, as stockholders were informed, it had often to endure long delays caused by "the ponderous procedures of the FDA for the approval of new drugs and processes, and the difficulties of doing pharmaceutical business overseas, exemplified by unstable foreign governments and fluctuating exchange rates."

In addition, Armour Pharmaceutical was too small to compete successfully with the giant firms in its field. Greyhound would either have to buy another pharmaceutical company to augment Armour's size, lifting it to a size capable of challenging all others; or else it would have to sell this subsidiary.

For these reasons the Greyhound executives gathered in Trautman's office to give serious thought to an offer from Revlon. The cosmetic manufacturer was willing and ready to buy Armour's pharmaceutical division.

The decision on Greyhound's part was solidly affirmative. Armour Pharmaceutical was sold to Revlon for $87,342,000. The price yielded a profit of $24,246,000 over the cost of the affiliate (reduced to something over $12 million after the payment of income taxes). Apart from the profit it produced, the sale relieved The Greyhound Corporation of constant irritation with government procedures. Companies like Revlon were accustomed and willing to accept the FDA's deliberate pace in approving new products. For Greyhound the pace had been far too slow.

In another category of subsidiary problems was the Korean joint venture in bus operations. Uncertainties of exchange rates, of political changes, and other imponderables in a business 12,000 miles from Phoenix finally eroded a good deal of Greyhound's enthusiasm for the project. It was profitable enough; but when a suitable offer was made, the company sold its Korean interests to a Korean firm for $3.5 million.

On the domestic scene, in still another aspect of divestiture, two of Armour's slaughtering plants were closed as being no longer essential. All such negative actions, if one could call them that, were more than balanced by positive strides in the continuing quest for sound diversification. Even while selling some subsidiaries, the company acquired others.

One was the Bucilla Company of Long Island, highly successful under the management of its president, Sidney G. Wasch. This was bought for $11,632,000. Like Malina, it manufactured textile handicraft and art needlework materials.

Combining the outputs of Bucilla and Malina, Greyhound at once became the leading producer of such materials in the United States.

Also in 1977 it completed negotiations begun a year earlier for the purchase of Shorrock Developments of Blackburn, England. Admittedly this venture carried Greyhound into wholly new fields. Shorrock specialized in the design and construction of "sophisticated security systems." Thus the corporation now became a guardian of banks, museums, office buildings, shops, and every other target of thievery. Its overall management was assigned to the Greyhound Computer Corporation of which Batastini was chairman and Olie Swanky president.

With this completed, Greyhound turned to the demands of one of its biggest deals. It made a tender offer to buy, for $100 million, the stock of the Verex Corporation of Madison, Wisconsin.

One hundred million dollars. Not long ago, when the company's current executives were still schoolboys, such an expenditure would have been breathtaking. Some stockholders might have protested against undertaking so tremendous a debt, for the money would have to be borrowed from banks.

Yet in 1977 nobody thought the amount unreasonable. A good part of American business was dealing in billions. Besides, Verex, an insurer of private mortgages, was earning substantial profits. If the long-term bank loans were paid out of Verex's own earnings—which was quite feasible—one might say that the company was costing Greyhound nothing at all.

The eventual price of the purchase was $109,372,000—a sum that gave Greyhound full ownership of a leader in its industry. Trautman and his associates had high hopes for the continued growth and profitability of their newest acquisition. "We favor companies like Verex in the financial services area," they said, "because they are not labor intensive, have no inventories, and are good generators of cash."

* * * * *

At the same time there were those at Armour who spoke of the common frankfurter, the American hot dog, as a perennially reliable producer of cash. "Americans," they said, "consume 1.5 billion pounds of frankfurters every year. That's an annual average of eighty hot dogs per person."

How did something with so odd a name become popular? How did it acquire the name? The answers relate to one of the country's wittiest sports cartoonists of past years, Tad Dorgan.

There was a summer day when Tad sat in the press box at Ebbets Field, the Dodger baseball stadium in Brooklyn. He was watching a dull game that offered no inspiration for the day's cartoon; he kept on yawning and wishing that something exciting would happen. It did not. By the seventh inning he gave up all hope of finding some good subject matter.

Then, looking around, he was struck by the number of people who were eating frankfurters on rolls streaked with mustard. Hawkers went up and down the aisles, shouting, "Get 'em hot here! Get 'em hot!" That roused Tad. He bent over a paper and hurriedly sketched a frankfurter embedded in its roll; the cartoon itself would be completed at home. Perhaps he meant to call it something like, "Today's most satisfying offering at Ebbets Field."

Now he added a typical Tad touch to the sketch. He shaped one end of the frankfurter to resemble a dog's head. This made the frankfurter itself suggest the long, low-slung shape of a dachshund.

In view of the Germanic source of the word "frankfurter" Tad may have meant to caption the drawing something like "Hot dachshund! Come and get it!" What checked him was uncertainty of how dachshund was spelled. He tried several versions, not one of which looked right. In the end he gave up and wrote simply, "Hot dog."

Tad could not have realized he was enriching the English language. "Hot dog" found its way into dictionaries. It found vendors and buyers everywhere. In New York's Coney Island, for instance, Feltman's made a specialty of hot dogs, became famous for them, attracted long lines of buyers day after day.

By 1974 the company was widely advertising "the dogs kids love to bite." Shareholders must have been amused as well as delighted to learn that Armour "had continued growth in hot dogs and had furthered its position as the number one deli supplier in this fast-growing segment of the meat industry." To publicize the growth of hot dogs there were photographs of "a continuous stream of fat, luscious frankfurters pouring down a series of stainless steel chutes toward final vacuum packaging under the familiar Armour Star label."

Despite the success of hot dogs, however, the food business as a whole did not yield similar results. The poultry business in particular was disappointing. As management put it, this operation "had a swing from a profit in 1973 to a loss in 1974 amounting to $14.4 million after tax. And because we see no relief from the high cost of feed and distorted market conditions, the poultry business has been severely curtailed."

But in a more optimistic vein the report pointed out that in spite of various setbacks "overall Armour returned a substantial profit in 1974."

•   •   •   •   •

In the case of Prophet Foods, strikes and layoffs in many industries were recurrent plagues. Whenever a closed plant cancelled food service it became a drain on Prophet's revenues. The staff to service the account had to be retained on the chance that the factory would soon be reopened. And since Greyhound could not justify any long-term absorption of losses, something effective, even drastic, had to be done. That was when John Teets took remedial action.

He selected the ten accounts that were yielding the poorest results, then set a date by which they must show improvement. If no improvement became apparent, Greyhound Food

Services would have to resign from the account. It would then undertake the same analysis of the next group of ten clients.

Through this policy of resigning from the most hopeless cases the corporation saved more than $1.5 million. Yet this was only a beginning.

The company now introduced a novel method of soliciting new accounts. A committee of three or four service experts studied a prospective customer's needs. They had to decide whether a contract could benefit both parties, and how these benefits would be achieved. Such preliminary surveys helped to avoid what Teets described as "inadvertently taking on accounts that are unprofitable and from which we would have to extricate ourselves at a later time."

To strengthen this policy the company concentrated on prospective clients who were not influenced by cyclical changes as was, say, the automobile industry. Greyhound now sought contracts with such comparatively stable institutions as schools, hospitals, banks, and colleges. This approach enabled Prophet to announce that its new 1977 customers would include a major school system in New York State and, in the Phoenix area, the feeding of 1,000 elderly people at fifteen neighborhood centers—a program funded by the federal government.

How successful were these new approaches? In a single year, from 1975 to 1976, Food Service earnings increased by 77 percent, soaring from $2.5 million to $4.5 million. And by the end of 1977 the profit figure rose to a formidable $7 million.

The way Greyhound was now handling its Food Service business must have impressed potential clients, for in 1977 the company signed the largest feeding contract in the world. This was a three-year undertaking to serve 40,000 meals a day at Lackland Air Force Base in Texas. Teets had to hire and train a large new kitchen staff.

As the company continued to seek contracts among institutional and government clients, it assured Greyhound stockholders: "The Food Service division is confident that profits will never again cycle with anything like the deep fluctuations that characterized some results in the past." A lesson had been learned.

Unfortunately the increasing success of the Prophet type of Food Service found no echo that year in the plight of Armour Foods. Companies like Armour, all of them, were enduring a time of extremely short supplies in hogs. Their prices went so high that consumers flatly refused to pay them. Simultaneously the cost of feed grain rose to levels that made it impossible to feed cattle with any expectation of profit.

Both of these circumstances were beyond cure in Phoenix headquarters. The causes lay in the laws of supply and demand. In 1977 Armour Food's profits dropped from $13 million to $7.8 million.

But the slump did not prevent the company from marketing new products, especially in the prepared meals sold to airlines. And a unique new customer joined the Armour list—the United States Department of Agriculture. The Department ordered frozen meals for the frequently isolated men in its Forestry Service. As an Armour cook said, "If we don't feed 'em right, they'll quit and go home."

•   •   •   •   •

One area of diversification that created earnings without too many headaches was the Financial division.

By 1977 the Greyhound Computer Group, for example, had $500 million worth of computer equipment that it was leasing in more than 600 worldwide locations. According to Olie Swanky, its president and chief executive officer, "our computers were performing services which ranged from accounting to telecommunications, to payroll and tax computations, to manufacturing schedules, to inventory records, to air-traffic control, to nuclear research."

Meanwhile the more generalized Greyhound Leasing and Financial Company, of which Robert W. Bertrand was president and chief executive officer, provided equipment, to both the New York and American Stock Exchanges, for recording bid and offer quotes. It leased $3 million in oceangoing barges to a California shipping company; $2 million in refrigerating units to a New York importer of Australian lamb; a 747 jet plane to a Luxembourg firm; the list went on and on with an incredible variety of transactions.

Still, not every subsidiary attained spectacular heights of earnings. The Rent-A-Car business, for one, suffered from another drop in Florida tourism. But with all divisions taken into account, Greyhound's net income in 1977 was $82.5 million, or $1.88 per share, as compared with $77 million, or $1.76 per share in 1976. And Gerald Trautman was able to say, "In terms of net income and per share earnings it was the best year in the company's history."

27

One morning the people of Phoenix saw in their newspapers the picture of a gruelling marathon race. It had been sponsored by Armour-Dial. Among the leaders, making a final sprint toward the tape, was Greyhound's John Teets—disheveled, spent after the long run, every sinew of his lean body straining to give its ultimate bit of energy. He was not the winner. Yet here was testimony that some of the company's officers did more than encourage and support athletic events: they participated.

Sports have long been a special interest of Armour-Dial. Its public relations director quite frankly told a reporter, "We use our sponsorship of sports as a major publicity effort for Dial and Tone soaps because there is a natural relationship between these products and athletics. In an era when brand awareness is so important in a highly competitive market we have delivered the Dial and Tone brand names to millions through media coverage of our sports events." At the outset, some years ago, Armour-Dial sponsored only a modest gymnastic program. "But we soon adopted a much wider scope of interests," he added. "It made sense to recognize other sports."

The extent to which the program was broadened was reported by the trade publication, *Household & Personal Products,* which said, "Greyhound now has one of the most comprehensive sport programs in the United States. It is involved in sports twelve months of the year in all regions of the country, from women's ski racing to college basketball, from baseball to tennis. It even sponsors the search for the National High School Athlete of the Year."

It might have added the establishment of football and basketball camps in summer, as well as activities designed for the handicapped. "Together with several Pennsylvania Elks Clubs," another Armour representative said, "we've even conducted such things as a handicapped children's fishing tournament on the Delaware River."

Today such undertakings are, of course, part of a corporation's sense of responsibility to its community. They are taken for granted. Virtually all major corporations in the United States recognize civic, philanthropic, and social obligations, and their rationale is quite pragmatic: "We cannot survive by constantly taking from our environment and thus draining it of substance. We have to support the society that supports us, or it will disappear."

In addition Greyhound, like others, had long been involved in campaigns for the public welfare. These continue today. Some are local—the support of hospitals, educational institutions, orchestras, theatrical groups and such, not only in Phoenix but throughout the United States. Others are of a national scope—campaigns for everything from the United Way to cancer research.

And too, Greyhound has some very special interests. One of these, usually expressed through Joe Black, deals with the needs of minority groups. In 1977, as in other years, Black had ample reason to show the reality of that concern. On one occasion, facing a large audience, he announced that 126 black students in sixty-seven universities were being granted Greyhound scholarships—a procedure repeated annually; only the figures change.

Elsewhere he attended gatherings at which Greyhound honors and awards were bestowed on the Black Woman of the Year and the Black Father of the Year; in truth, he appeared at so many functions honoring America's black population that one newspaperman commented, "It's a way of life at Greyhound."

It has often been suggested that modern concepts of corporate responsibility would not have been understood a century ago. Social historians like to point out that for a time even John D. Rockefeller thought that the best way to illustrate his company's concern for others was to hand out dimes. The change has been so diametric that if a corporation fails to support worthy causes, shareholders may indignantly demand to know why.

And this increase in support of the welfare of others has of course been accompanied by increased support of a corporation's own people. Bertram E. Thomas, president of the Batelle Memorial Institute, once said to a Rochester audience of scientists:

> Within corporate walls are found many of the elements of social organization for which men have been striving for decades. Men can spend their entire lives under its protection. Its program of social security is far more realistic than any the government is likely to develop. It offers old age security and hospitalization protection to employees and their families. It offers paternalism to those who desire it. But more important, it offers ever-greater opportunities for creative thought and action to those who have the necessary talents and wish to develop them. The competitive structure of our economy ensures to each individual the freedom to leave the shelter of one corporation and to seek that of another—or even to "go it alone" if he aspires to create a corporation of his own making.

Greyhound is certainly not unique in its concern for its employees. Like other major corporations, it maintains pension plans available to all (their cost in 1978 was $70,409,000); it offers insurance coverage, stock purchase options, incentive plans for key personnel—indeed, all those social and economic advantages that American corporations and American unions have through the years forged for their mutual benefit.

But in 1978 the company assumed a new public stance: political.

This was neither Republican nor Democrat. It existed solely in support of candidates who, like Trautman and his associates, sought to further the cause of free enterprise. Explaining this innovative step to Greyhound stockholders, Trautman said:

> The Greyhound Good Government Project is a political action committee which solicited voluntary contributions from Greyhound executives and distributed these funds to political candidates supportive of free enterprise and responsible government spending. Of the 222 candidates we supported 54 percent were Republican, 46 percent were Democrat, and a very encouraging 90 percent of them were elected to public office, state and federal. At Greyhound we recognize that our future is linked with that of the general economy, and we feel that the actions we took help position the company for a new era of growth.

Another Greyhound group, BARK, sought deregulation on a nationwide basis. (Originally BARK was not an acronym. It was intended to symbolize the voice of the Greyhound dog, his bark. But nobody grasped the symbolism; so a few good minds invented a phrase to suit the letters: Becoming Active with Ready Knowledge.) They wanted deregulation achieved "by federal legislation which would preempt state action." They explained, "For both the carriers and the public, patchwork deregulation state by state would be chaotic."

While the Greyhound Good Government Project and the BARK program operated from Phoenix, the Government Affairs office in Washington pressed the issues in the nation's capital. In the meantime the company could only hope for results while it concentrated on its day-by-day business.

And there was much to be done.

•   •   •   •   •

Perhaps the most surprising management decision of 1978 was this: For the first time in years—indeed, in its history—the company planned no new acquisitions.

The fundamental reason lay in the country's extraordinarily high interest rates. In October, when the Federal Reserve Board raised the discount rate to 9.5 percent, the stock exchange reacted with the worst week in its annals. Nine-and-one-half percent was considered a "record high" and ruinous. No one could foresee or even imagine that before long the Federal Reserve would be countenancing rates of 16 and 17 percent, and that the prime borrowing rate at banks would rise even higher.

For Greyhound, as for many companies large and small, the cost of borrowing capital to acquire subsidiaries became prohibitive. Therefore the chairman said:

> Our resources will be directed at helping our existing businesses meet their own growth objectives. We'll be trying to maximize the returns on what we already have, improve our asset management, increase our profit margins, and seek higher productive levels. This is the only route within everyone's grasp to assure that the gains we make are substantive in nature, not just inflation-fed dollars.

And so, though an outside observer might have said the corporation was doing quite well with total revenues of $4.4 billion and a net income of $58.4 million, Trautman exercised the chairman's right to be dissatisfied. Improvements had to be made.

Did he have a personal motive? Some of his colleagues suspected he had. In August 1977 he would reach the mandated retirement age of 65. No doubt he wanted to leave a heritage of maximum efficiency, an organization that fulfilled its highest potentials.

The directors too must have been thinking of the day when Trautman retired. Who was to succeed him? To have one man serve as both chairman and president, as Trautman was doing, seemed too great a personal burden to impose on anyone. To give themselves time to find a successor, they persuaded him to revise his contract and stay on to the age of 70. With this accomplished, the board began to consider various candidates for the presidency, seeking someone who could work with Trautman for the next few years, preparing himself for the responsibilities of the summit.

The chairman himself, however, soon had something else to worry about—worsening conditions in bus transportation. In shirt-sleeves and tieless, in deference to the Phoenix heat, he paced his office, planning remedial measures. Again and again he discussed these with James Kerrigan, vice chairman for bus operations. Kerrigan had his own ideas, and while these were debated bus returns continued to deteriorate. Inevitably the time came when Trautman had to act on his responsibility to some 200,000 stockholders and some 60,000 Greyhound employees. Diminishing bus returns simply could not be accepted. He had to ask the board to relieve Kerrigan of his transportation duties. The directors acceded—on the understanding that Trautman himself accept the responsibilities.

"That same day," he said, "I telephoned Frank Nageotte and asked him and Fred Dunikoski to meet me in our office on Saturday morning. When we got together, uninterrupted by telephone calls or other distractions, we planned a program of things that had to be done. First we realized that a number of transportation executives had to be replaced. Then authority for running the lines had to be put back in the field, where it belonged, rather than have all matters decided and handled at a distance in Phoenix headquarters."

This, it had become clear to Trautman, had been one of the weaknesses in the management of bus transportation—the attempt to substitute absentee supervision, as it were, for on-the-site leadership.

"Also," he continued, "terminals and garages had to be cleaned up, and morale had to be improved among our employees, as did our relations with the union. So we laid out a program which would meet all these needs."

To carry it out Trautman himself became chairman of Greyhound Lines. Nageotte became president and chief executive officer, and Dunikoski was named executive vice president. As one of their associates said, "At that point they assumed full responsibility for rescuing bus transportation. Trautman made it his chief concern. He traveled wherever bus problems had to be solved."

Trautman remembered, "I visited innumerable garages and terminals and talked with hundreds of employees. I wanted to get an intimate understanding of their beefs and needs, and that meant spending a good deal of time with them. Once—," he smiled at this recollection, "I even played in the bus drivers' annual golf tournament."

Not that everything he found it necessary to do was as pleasant. He had to arrange a termination agreement with Kerrigan who then left the company. In the main, however, this whole year with its changes did lift the transportation business back to a profitable and satisfactory level. Once that was accomplished, Trautman relinquished the bus line chairmanship to Frank Nageotte; and Fred Dunikoski became president.

Still, though a more efficient team of executives could not have been chosen, it was not an easy year for transportation. First, winter blizzards had buried the entire Northeast under thirteen inches of snow. Businesses had to close, automobiles were stranded, bus travel was crippled. A few days later fifteen inches of snow covered the Middle West, and there, too, bus routes became impassable.

And yet, despite all setbacks, the improved status of the bus lines was not undermined. By the end of the year all bus terminals, it was reported, had been raised to "unprecedented standards of cleanliness and efficiency." A team of examiners made spot checks in every state to ensure the best possible service. Reclamation centers, reduced to two in the East and two in the West, again shortened the time of delivering emergency equipment. And 400 new red-white-and-blue buses of the MC-9 class—"the most modern, highly engineered in the industry"—sped over the highways of America, carrying the emblem of the Greyhound dog to every section of the United States.

With the immediate future of transportation thus improved and entrusted to Nageotte and Dunikoski, Trautman looked next at the ailing food business.

It needed his attention—desperately. Armour's once vaunted

profits had been sliding down into what financiers termed "negative cash flows," a euphemism for losses. One of the things that disturbed—indeed, shocked—Trautman was an announcement made by Armour's president, Donald J. Shaughnessy. He had said:

> We reorganized Armour into six distinct operating companies. We realized we were no longer dealing with one homogenous market but with six different segments, each requiring its own market strategy and its own special management. . . . We felt we were following the most intelligent course we could take.

Intelligent? Trautman, appalled, considered the reorganization a disaster. In its first five-month period the reorganized executive staff posted a loss of $21 million, and further deterioration continued month after month. Shaughnessy's reliance on outside consultants to support his methods proved futile. Losses could not be stemmed.

Inevitably an alarmed board of directors came to share Trautman's lack of faith in Armour's reorganized management and its head. The Armour operation simply had to be rescued, and rescue would require drastic measures.

First, Donald Shaughnessy was reassigned to other duties. He was instructed thereafter to report directly to Trautman, who took over the post of Armour's chief executive officer and chairman. The two men continued to meet; but Shaughnessy—insisting on maintaining his reorganized staff—constantly opposed Trautman's plans for change. As a company Fact Book later reported:

> The net effect was devastating, and the Processed Meat operation, which had never previously lost money and which, in fact, for a decade had reported an average annual pretax profit of nearly $17.5 million, reported a pretax loss of $7.7 million for 1979 and $25.3 million for 1980.

How long could such a situation be tolerated? There was only one course to take. On July 18, 1980, Trautman relieved Shaughnessy of all his duties and arranged for the termination of his association with the corporation. A veteran Greyhound officer, Wallace L. Tunnell, then president of the Armour Fresh Meat Company, was summoned to replace Shaughnessy.

And, as one of Trautman's associates said, "He rolled up his sleeves and took on the job of making Armour profitable again—a task to which he devoted the next full year." What he did later was summed up in the corporation's Fact Book:

> Deeply concerned over the deterioration in the Processed Meat operation, Greyhound's chairman directed in August of 1980 that the Processed Meat operation be consolidated with the Fresh Meat Group under a new management team. Immediately profit responsibility lines were reestablished and a number of other steps taken aimed at turning around the operation.

> These methods included the reestablishment of our second-line brands which had been dropped; a major push to regain the private label business we had abandoned; the revamping of vital distribution systems and the reopening of communication with former customers; a policy of advertising and promotion at the local level to meet specific local needs; and renewed attention paid not just to our branded products but to the significant number of high grossing items in which we enjoy almost an exclusive market.

> As a result of all these steps, for 1981 Processed Meat operations reported a positive swing of $37.4 million and a pretax income of $12.1 million.

Put briefly, the endless losses of a misguided policy were within a single year converted to heartening profits. In all probability even some experienced security analysts raised their brows in wonder, not quite understanding how it had been done. Only the insiders knew.

•   •   •   •   •

The history of Greyhound, like that of many an American business, was often a paradox of expansion on the one hand and contraction on the other. A significant integration oc-

The evolution of the famous Greyhound manufactured MC buses is shown on these pages. From the top are the MC5, 1963; MC7, 1968; MC8, 1973; and, top right, the MC9, 1979.

curred when Trautman merged Greyhound Exposition Services with Greyhound Exhibitgroup. This created a single entity, Greyhound Convention Services, headed by Leo S. McDonald, Jr. Its 1978 operations rose to a memorable climax when it managed the tremendous trade show of the American Mining Congress. One of the largest such trade exhibitions ever held, it had 500 participants whose booths filled more than a million square feet of space in the Las Vegas Convention Center, and spilled over into an outdoor area and into a hotel. By any standards it was a landmark achievement.

International operations, however, could not be so dramatically shaped by actions taken in the offices of Greyhound subsidiaries—or, for that matter, in the Oval Office of President Jimmy Carter. In country after country the American dollar was being mercilessly buffeted. Its value declined immediately after the disclosure of America's $3 billion overseas trade deficit. Seeking a more stable monetary base than the dollar, the world bought gold—and sent its cost soaring.

Yet all this did not inhibit Greyhound from listening to the offerings of some foreign markets. Aramco, for one, sought the company's cooperation in Saudi Arabia. Its delegations sat with Greyhound's representatives in round-table session after

Greyhound buses are a familiar sight the world over, including this one on a desert highway in Saudi Arabia.

session. The outcome came with the announcement that "Greyhound has been selected to be a partner with Aramco and certain Saudi Arabian interests to participate in a substantial bus venture in that country. Documents have been signed under which Greyhound's subsidiary, Motor Coach Industries, will sell approximately 200 new MC-5 buses to the joint venture. Greyhound will have a 40-percent interest in the venture and, in addition, will conduct the bus operations under a management fee arrangement."

With so many domestic and foreign matters demanding his attention, Trautman must have been a weary man by the end of 1978; but also a gratified man. The Greyhound Corporation was yielding greater returns than ever before. Yet the chairman had no opportunity to be complacent, for unexpectedly the company found itself in an awkward situation.

28

It occurred when the board of directors ended its search for a new corporate president. In the ordinary course of events he would be expected to succeed Gerald Trautman as chief executive officer after the chairman's retirement in 1982.

A research firm of reliable reputation was employed to help in the selection of a candidate. They found a man whom they recommended highly—Robert K. Swanson who had held important executive positions at General Mills. After formal personal interviews Swanson was employed as president and chief operating officer of The Greyhound Corporation.

He held the position for only eight months.

What went wrong? Was it a matter of temperament, of inability to reconcile his way of doing business with that of Greyhound? Whatever the reason, Swanson's ways managed to alienate most of Greyhound's top executives. It also irritated a number of the company's outside directors.

It hardly required eight months to indicate that Swanson would not be selected as chief executive officer when Trautman retired. Robert Swanson must have realized that too, and a mutually agreeable termination was arranged.

So the board once more had to seek a replacement.

For Gerald Trautman, who was now expected to make new presidential recommendations, this presented a special problem. If the Swanson experience emphasized anything at all, it was—as had the selection of Arthur Genet twenty-four years earlier—that an outsider would find it difficult to integrate his methods with those of Greyhound. The best appointment to the presidency would be that of someone who understood the company's varied operations, someone who had long been familiar with them. As he considered people who fulfilled such qualifications—and there were several—three struck him as being qualified above all others. They were financial vice president Ralph Batastini, transportation chairman Frank Nageotte, and food chairman John Teets.

Which of them would most impress the board? Again Trautman's way of seeking an answer was to have all three elected directors, each with the status of vice chairman of the corporation. In this way all three would be working closely with the other directors. During the next two years they would be thoroughly appraised by their colleagues. By 1982 the board should be in a position to make an intelligent and enduring choice.

Trautman's plan was adopted; and thereafter, of course, the work of all three candidates was closely watched by their fellow directors.

Batastini's financial acumen was evident in the corporation's surprising annual report. High interest rates and the inflated cost of everything Greyhound had to buy had cut deeply into earnings. Nevertheless, "net income for the company again reached an all-time high, 47 percent better than it had been in 1978. And although we increased capital expenditures 22 percent to keep our equipment and facilities up to date, and increased dividends to an annual rate of $1.20, these were accomplished without an appreciable increase in debt." Undeniably Batastini's department was being well managed.

What must have impressed many stockholders and employees was, too, the amount of contributions the company made to its pension funds. These rose from $74,982,000 in 1979 to $82,938,000 in 1980—an eloquent commentary on corporate responsibility.

Frank Nageotte's report on transportation, for its part, noted among other things that the nation's severe gasoline shortage, creating long lines at pumps, had discouraged many motorists from driving their cars. They had turned to bus travel.

"Even with the tremendous demands put on our facilities by an overnight surge of travelers," he said, "Greyhound Lines was positioned to respond with ready buses, improved terminals, and skilled people. Almost every day we had an average of 200 more buses on the road than the prior year. The result was that our 1979 net income reached $39.5 million compared to last year's $22 million.

"We also inaugurated a pilot program in conjunction with the Department of Energy to test under actual road conditions a series of developmental turbine engines fitted into Greyhound Americruisers. These turbine-powered buses are operating in regular service between New York and Washington, generating test data for our own and Department of Energy transportation experts."

John Teets had his own impressive progress to report. It started with the fact that in the past four years the income from Food Services had soared from $3.7 million to $9.1 million.

"Our operations are now global," he said. "They cater to the cultural, ethnic, national, and special dietary needs of a clientele that ranges from Navajo school children in Arizona to diamond executives in Belgium and to Greyhound passengers in the United States."

During the year Greyhound Food Services had added a volume of some $5 million in new accounts. They included Goodyear Tire and Rubber Company's plant in Danville, Virginia; public school systems in Illinois and Texas. Also, seven new Burger King restaurants had been opened in terminals, and the one in Omaha won the City Beautification Award presented by the Women's Chamber of Commerce.

True, none of these activities constituted a major new acquisition in 1980, but the year did witness the divestiture of one large subsidiary.

This was Border Brokers of Canada.

The move must have puzzled many shareholders. The company explained it quite explicitly: "Changes in Canadian law clearly limited the extent to which we could expand this operation in the years ahead, and the decision was made to divest the company and invest the proceeds in other, more profitable areas."

•　•　•　•　•

It would be erroneous to suggest that Greyhound—or any responsible corporation in a leadership position—concentrated wholly on "more profitable areas." Frank Nageotte once said, "The trouble with a financial yardstick is that it was never intended to measure intangibles—like our pride in certain activities."

He was speaking of the company's Helping Hand innovation. This originated after various bus drivers told of their difficult experiences with handicapped people who had to be helped into and off a bus. To cope with this the company announced that henceforth every passenger so handicapped could be accompanied by an attendant at no extra cost.

In a detailed communication to the public, Vice President Dorothy Lorant made it clear that:

> Helping Hand Service applies to all Greyhound adult fares, allowing travel over all Greyhound routes. Greyhound carries your nonmotorized wheelchairs and certain other aids and devices as baggage without cost.

> To get started, simply phone your local Greyhound terminal. Ask for Helping Hand Service. Give your name and your companion's name. . . .

> We ask that you call early and that you arrive at the terminal at least thirty minutes before your scheduled departure. This enables us to make arrangements for your seating and other details. Wherever possible we'll arrange "first on" seating and try to set aside a front seat for your comfort and convenience.

Another new public service feature she announced was that of a telephone Information Center in Allentown, Pennsylvania. This would facilitate and expedite information on bus travel throughout the country.

"Everyone expected it to be a successful operation," Ms. Lorant said. "But we certainly did not foresee that it would handle 5 million calls in its very first year. We had to increase its staff again and again. By the end of the year we had 109 trained operators working on each shift."

Such innovations naturally won the acclaim of Greyhound employees as well as of the general public. But by far the most spectacular event of the year, and the most exciting, occurred at the Winter Olympics in Lake Placid, New York.

More than a year before the Games were scheduled to begin Frank Nageotte had tried to negotiate the bus concession with the Olympics Committee. He pointed out that Greyhound's unique transportation experience at various world fairs— surely greater than that of any other company—enabled it to provide all the essential services for Lake Placid. But the Committee, as was no doubt its obligation, was studying the competitive bids of other companies. Those with the least experience seemed to be offering the lowest terms. Would Greyhound meet such terms? Rather than diminish necessary services by lowering his bid, Nageotte withdrew Greyhound's offer.

What happened thereafter made history.

For one thing, the popularity of the Games had been underestimated. Attendance soared beyond the most optimistic predictions. As throngs tried to drive into the town it became evident that preparations had been woefully inadequate. Lake Placid is small. Its limited parking space was filled days before the formal opening of the Games. Subsequent visitors who arrived by car were in many cases forced to park miles from the town—only after they pushed their vehicles through heavy traffic jams on every narrow road. Many people found themselves miles from the Games with little hope of reaching them on time. Buses? These had to sound their horns constantly in the hope of pressing through the mobs. More and more frequently they were as hopelessly stalled in the jams as was the rest of the traffic.

Confronted by this almost frantic situation, the Olympic Committee seemed helpless. Visitors were howling their protests, blaming both the committee and the state of New York for gross ineptitude in making adequate preparations. Throughout the country editorials, too, were mercilessly berating those who had so badly planned the great international event.

At this point a harassed official telephoned Frank Nageotte. Was there some way, he asked, that Greyhound—with its wide bus and fair experience—could reconsider and bring some order out of the Lake Placid chaos?

Nageotte, having greater faith in the permanence of New York State than in the permanence of the Olympic Committee, came to a quick agreement with the state itself. "This was to be a rescue operation," he said later.

He promptly dispatched 200 Greyhound buses to the Lake Placid area. They came from New York City, from Boston, from every surrounding Greyhound base. They brought a small army of traffic experts—supervisors, dispatchers, all the rest. Pouring out of the newly arrived buses they began using whistles and waving arms to clear choked roads. They turned many side roads into diagonal parking areas. Somehow— newsmen described it as a miracle of experience and efficiency—traffic jams were relieved. The big red-white-and-blue Greyhound buses, with the roads opened before them, were able to run crowds of visitors to the sites of the games.

One may feel that such experiences are peripheral to the growth of a corporation, that they have little relation to the forward sweep of its history. Yet these very experiences, peripheral or not, are often the most vividly remembered by those who shared in them; and in all probability that was true not only of Greyhound personnel but of those thousands of people they "rescued" and carried to the Winter Olympics.

29

The start of a new decade was an apt time for stockholders to assemble at an annual meeting to hear how The Greyhound Corporation and its subsidiaries were faring. Facing an audience of several hundred people, Gerald Trautman could speak with pride. This year, 1980, the corporation—now among the giants of American industry—had grossed revenues of $5,136,000,000. It had showed net earnings of $118,300,000, the equivalent of $2.67 per share.

Though the foundation for all this had been laid long before Trautman himself had joined the company, Greyhound's major growth had unquestionably occurred during his administration, largely because of his insistence on diversification.

Diversifying, however, had never meant merely accumulating. The company had been rigidly selective. In fact, it had rejected far more opportunities than it had accepted. Moreover, the creation of a profitable diversified corporation had often entailed selling a subsidiary, or liquidating it, or trading it off in order to acquire something else.

Thus in its time General Fire Insurance had been sold; many of the Armour affiliates had been disposed of, including its pharmaceutical division; Border Brokers was gone, as were the bus lines in Korea. Yet each divestiture had in its way added to Greyhound's basic strength. Each had helped to build the original business into this $5 billion multifaceted industrial enterprise with outlets throughout the world.

Nevertheless, in 1980 the records of some acquisitions were less than brilliant. As an example there was the generally quiet and self-effacing Shorrock.

In its early years Shorrock had been selling burglar alarms to shops, homes, warehouses, and similar customers in the United Kingdom. After the company became part of the Greyhound organization it showed moderate growth in other countries, but much of its progress continued to be in England. By this year, 1980, it had some 20,000 alarm systems in use and it employed 700 people. Certainly this was not a bad record, but Shorrock was hardly the most lucrative of Greyhound subsidiaries. One might have argued that it made up in dignity for what it lacked in revenues. After all, it had the honor of guarding the library of Windsor Castle and the palaces of several Mideast potentates.

(When Don Behnke investigated the operations of Shorrock for a *Go Greyhound* article, he learned that one potentate had ordered TV cameras to survey every chamber in his palace, and he wanted a security system that could be operated "from a pen in his pocket." He got what he ordered. In addition, it developed that, for all its modest attainments, Shorrock was protecting nuclear power plants, missile sites, hydroelectric generators, oil refineries, research laboratories, water reservoirs, and other industrial properties. In other words, its achievements were impressive in the services it performed rather than in the immediate profits they yielded.)

In financial contrast, the Greyhound Leasing and Financial Corporation had a record that was almost incredible. It now owned equipment whose total value exceeded $1 billion. During the year it had purchased, at a price of $50 million, a McDonnell Douglas DC-10 capable of seating 315 passengers. This it leased to a Mexican airline. Spread more widely than ever, the properties it leased included not only aircraft but railroad cars, oil tankers, barges, ocean-depth drills, heavy industrial machinery of all kinds. This subsidiary was producing an annual net income of $33 million.

"Not bad," an accountant remarked, "for a business we originally acquired for an investment of $14 million."

Equally remarkable was the recent growth of the Transportation Group. In two years its net income had increased by 150 percent, climbing from $21.5 million to $54 million. Could such growth rate be sustained? Frederick Dunikoski, president of the Greyhound Bus Lines, expressed the company's confidence in the future by pointing out that in 1980 it had invested $79 million in new buses and new facilities.

"In addition," he said, "in every category from driver to baggage handler we have hired more people than at anytime in our history. And in our Package Express operation, which grows larger every year, we have just added a door-to-door pickup and delivery service. So when you ask if we can continue our growth rate, the answer is we are continuing it and we expect to go on continuing it."

Perhaps the most notable development of the ensuing year, one which must have brought relief and reassurance to Greyhound shareholders, was the restoration of Armour's profitability. The methods Gerald Trautman had taken—the antithesis to what Shaughnessy had attempted with his staff reorganization—proved to be the remedy Armour had required. By February 18, 1981, he felt his job of resuscitation had been accomplished, and, with the approval of the directors, the task of heading Armour was turned over to John Teets.

Armour-Dial, too, was subjected to rejuvenation. Trautman said of this: "We brought back another veteran, David Duensing, as president. I considered him to be the best executive in the business. New marketing strategy, vigorous new product development, and the capacity to make sound, incisive decisions now mark Armour-Dial operations under Dave Duensing's leadership."

In sum, the immediate future for Greyhound now seemed bright with promise. There was every reason for optimism and cheerfulness in the Phoenix offices. Yet there were some who frowned and shook their heads and predicted that the company would soon suffer a disappointment because of a miscalculation.

•　•　•　•　•

This, they said, would occur in 1982 at the Knoxville World's Fair. Greyhound, having won the contract to be the exposition's Official Motor Coach Carrier, had committed itself to arrange more than 2,000 charter bus trips. So the doubters were saying, "Knoxville isn't New York or Chicago. It won't attract the same crowds."

Frederick Dunikoski, speaking for Greyhound Bus Lines, disagreed. "Knoxville's location in the heart of many resort areas like the Great Smoky Mountain National Park," he said, "will draw many visitors."

The pessimists still insisted, "Knoxville doesn't offer anything like the Grand Canyon or Yosemite."

"But it offers a World's Fair. Don't underrate that."

(In time his optimism was justified. After a slow start Knoxville did attract crowds. Greyhound's charter buses brought so many visitors to the exposition that Tennessee's Governor Lamar Alexander, at a public ceremony, presented a Certificate of Appreciation to the company.)

But the most spectacular bus achievement of 1981 had no connection with Knoxville. It was, on its own, a triumph of planning and organization.

This happened on September 19, designated as Solidarity Day by American unions. Thousands of people were coming to the nation's capital to stage a demonstration of labor unity. Since this occurred in the midst of the widely publicized air controller's strike, many union members refused to fly; to board a plane would have been tantamount to crossing a picket line. They preferred bus transportation.

In anticipation of the occasion Greyhound had signed contracts with the unions to take their members to and from Washington, D.C. The company marshalled 560 Americruisers—12 percent of its entire fleet—to transport some 24,000 people who came from states as far away as Texas. And the problems they posed were staggering.

The first challenge was: Where in the city can you park 560 huge buses while they wait to take passengers home?

Days before the event Greyhound sent a logistics team to Washington. Led by J. O. Whitt, the company's regional director, its task was to make all necessary traffic arrangements. These had to be coordinated with the plans of the police.

The answer to the parking problem was found in the immense, twenty-acre parking lot behind the JFK Stadium. There Greyhound buses could be aligned in symmetrical rows—not in any haphazard fashion, but each coach assigned to a clearly numbered spot. Greyhound officials would be on hand to direct drivers to the prearranged locations. Before passengers left their bus they would be given cards with the numbered position of their coach; this would eliminate confusion and searches when these people returned.

While the demonstrators' parade was in progress a staff of attendants would clean the buses, inspect tires, and do everything else to expedite return trips in safety.

One Washington observer told the press, "I couldn't help wondering how drivers from other states, approaching Washington from every direction, would go straight to the parking area without blundering into other parts of the city. They couldn't all be familiar with the capital."

He soon discovered the solution. The logistics team had posted cars on all the main approach roads where turns had to be made. On the roof of each car was a large Greyhound sign with a giant arrow pointing the way.

That day not a single driver went astray. Later Washington's police chief declared that he had never witnessed anything as flawlessly planned and organized as "Greyhound's conquest of the capital."

• • • • •

The fact that in 1981 such a demonstration could be held at all suggested that the country was trying to cope with its normal day-to-day concerns. For it could hardly be called a normal year.

In March a fanatic gunman shot President Reagan in the chest, sent another bullet into the head of Press Secretary James S. Brady, and wounded Secret Service Agent Timothy J. McCarthy and police officer Thomas K. Delahanty. It was an act of senseless violence that shattered the emotions of the entire nation. By a miracle of good fortune the shot that hit the President was not fatal; otherwise the history of the times might have taken another course.

As things were, the President recovered only to be assailed by the country's inflation, unemployment, high interest rates, an ever-mounting national debt, and an unequal balance of trade overseas.

So it was truly notable—impressive not only to Greyhound's stockholders and employees, but also to bankers and security analysts—that Trautman was able to say of 1981: "It was an excellent year for Greyhound in a disastrous year for the economy."

30

Because 1981 was the last full year of his administration—Gerald Trautman would be retiring in August 1982—this could have been a saddening time. Yet he had ample cause to be gratified, too. His sixteen years as Greyhound's chief executive officer had succeeded beyond anyone's expectations. Not only was 1981 a good year; in truth, financially it exceeded every other year in the company's annals. Net income reached $138 million or $3.06 per share. Simultaneously long-term debt was reduced by $80 million, in itself a notable achievement at a time when inordinately high interest rates were undermining earnings.

A year earlier, in a message to stockholders, he had said, "Our goal is to free our resources and redirect them to areas that enhance the value of our shareholders' investment in the company. Our current strategy is based on building on our existing businesses rather than reaching far afield for growth. We are convinced that it is not just earnings that count, but the quality of earnings."

And his strategy had been successful.

Yet these were not the things that brought Trautman his deepest satisfaction. In the annual report he used his final message as chairman and chief executive officer to tell the company's shareholders:

> There is something more than net income that influences a company's present and future. For some years now my primary concern has been to assemble the kind of management team that could be entrusted with the job of moving Greyhound into the future. I have worked too long beside the fine men and women of Greyhound to leave their aspirations and their well-being in uncaring hands.

For that reason it is with considerable satisfaction that I report that upon my recommendation the board of directors selected John W. Teets to be chief executive officer. I have known John Teets for some twenty years and have watched his progress through the Greyhound organization, rebuilding the Food Service operations of Greyhound Food Management and helping in the revitalization of Armour. He has the attributes to move Greyhound ahead in the '80s and beyond.

He spoke of a new labor contract that John Teets arranged with the United Food and Commercial Workers International Union. This agreement would have a powerful effect on Armour since it provided for a four-year freeze on wages and cost-of-living increases. It was a truly significant achievement. To both labor and management it brought time to adjust intelligently to the economic uncertainties of the era. For the next four years there would be cooperation in the pursuit of mutual interests.

Trautman then referred to other corporate matters.

"I am pleased to report," he said, "that shareholder equity reached $942 million by the end of 1981, and the total assets of Greyhound and its consolidated subsidiaries amounted to nearly $2 billion. What this means for the future is that Greyhound has the financial ability to support the expansion of its existing operations and, if deemed desirable, to acquire other businesses."

Having covered these and other matters, Trautman reverted to a personal note. "I want to tell you I have thoroughly enjoyed the opportunity to participate as chief executive officer in Greyhound's growth over the last sixteen years. What has been achieved has been done through the work and integrity of thousands of Greyhound people. That continuity of excellence, that passing on of pride from one generation to another, is why this company is such an enduring part of the American scene."

•   •   •   •   •

If this was Trautman's final message as chairman, it was also the occasion of John Teets' first message as chief executive officer. He devoted that message entirely to a tribute to Trautman.

Surely he could have discussed important corporate developments. He could have reported his trials at the long, difficult negotiating sessions with the United Food and Commercial Workers International Union. Also, he could have dwelt on the fact that in December 1981 the company had begun to purchase Greyhound common stock on the open market. According to a company spokesman, "We did this because we believe our stock was undervalued at the time and did not reflect the quality of our business and our prospects. In addition, it enhances the per share earnings of our stockholders. From time to time in 1982, when market prices make such investments attractive, we may make additional purchases of our common stock to cover reserved share requirements or for other corporate purposes."

Though this was to be a most significant corporate undertaking for Greyhound, Teets did not mention it in his first message. He chose instead to say with quiet eloquence:

> In August of 1982 Gerald H. Trautman will retire as chairman of the board of The Greyhound Corporation, a position he has filled with distinction.

> During his years as the head of Greyhound his was the vision that took the company from a basically single industry entity—bus transportation—to the vibrant, diversified corporation it is today. It was his resolve that shaped a company that looks quite different today from what it was in the mid-sixties when he assumed the helm.

> A private man, one who does not talk easily of his own accomplishments, Jerry Trautman is probably the most reticent executive of a Fortune 100 company. For that reason it is necessary to chronicle precisely what his stewardship of Greyhound has wrought, because if left to him it would go unsaid.

The record is this: He leaves The Greyhound Corporation in the best and strongest financial position in its history. In a scant decade and a half he has taken the company from assets of $385 million to nearly $4 billion, and shareholders' equity from $210 million to $942 million. In the sixteen years he has served as chairman revenues went from $500 million to over $5 billion, and net income has more than tripled from $43 million to $138 million.

In 1966 the bus company, which had been the workhorse of the corporation for over half a century, had its detractors all too eager to write it off as an obsolete business. Jerry Trautman was not one of them. He built it back into a company to be proud of, and moved the company into bus-building as well, making Greyhound the most respected name in intercity bus manufacturing in the world.

He was also the architect of Greyhound's diversification, starting with the expansion of the Financial Group, which in the early sixties consisted primarily of just a small leasing company and which is today the largest contributor to corporate net income.

Under his aegis Greyhound also entered the food and consumer products businesses; expanded food service operations to embrace fast-food facilities and hotel management; and broadened financial services to include mortgage insurance and electronic funds transfer. And in each of our businesses we are not only in them, but are a preeminent name in them.

For many of us at Greyhound we are what we are today as a consequence of Jerry Trautman's talent for bringing out the best in people. His way always has been to give a long tether and something more—his trust, patience, and approval. Rarely was the trust misplaced, and when it was no one felt it more keenly than he did, but it didn't sour him from readily giving trust and approval again. Greyhound today is filled with people whose talent and self-confidence, whose executive skills and ability, were nurtured under this man's support and encouragement.

Those of us who know him as a friend and colleague recognize the deep personal concern he has shown over the

Gerald H. Trautman, chief executive officer of Greyhound from 1966 to 1982.

years in building a company that would survive the discontinuities of time. He has done that well; and in the doing he has carried responsibility with integrity and worn authority with grace and lightness.

It is with both tremendous respect and affection that we cite the record of these sixteen years. The respect is based on the accomplishments of the executive; the affection is for the warmth and humor of the man.

For those of us who will lead the corporation in the '80s, we inherit a corporation that is poised for even more growth, and no one is more excited by the prospects than I am. We will be working from an enviable base—strong financial condition, strong consumer franchises, strong management. My objectives for the '80s are very ambitious; not just growth, but quality growth, not just profitability, but enduring profitability.

The concept of change, as we have witnessed it over these sixteen years and benefited by it, is even more than just desirable. It is absolutely essential. Because no matter how good things are today, we nevertheless cannot be content with a continuation of things as they are. We have in our grasp the ability to shape our own destiny—as Jerry Trautman so often proved—but more than that, we have the will to make it happen.

Thus, for the first time, a message in an annual report bore the signature of John W. Teets, Chief Executive Officer.

A few months later, on August 19, 1982, Gerald Trautman officially retired as chairman of The Greyhound Corporation. The board of directors, meeting that day, elected Teets chairman to succeed Trautman. It also elected Frank Nageotte to the presidency and announced that Ralph Batastini would continue as vice chairman and chief financial officer. As for Trautman himself, he was named honorary chairman, to remain a member of the board of directors and of its executive committee.

31

"Starting from a strong base," as Teets had put it, the company was indeed in a solid financial position when he became its chairman.

If ever the power and wisdom of diversification were evident, it was in the fact that 73 percent of the corporation's total revenues now came from nontransportation sources—and this despite the Transportation Group's own revenues of $1,045,953,000.

Moreover, bus income was increasing every year as 3,400 commission agents sold Greyhound tickets throughout the country. The company's buses now linked 138 major terminals. The people who wrote the advertising messages were using every phrase they could invent to convey the idea that by Greyhound you could go anywhere from any place.

Still, by far the largest source of corporate revenue lay in the foods sold by Armour, a total of over $2,302,241,000. Added to this was the sum of $444 million for meals served in plants, schools, offices, and various institutions through Food Management Services.

The fastest growing of the company's divisions, however, was its Financial Group. The Greyhound Leasing and Financial Corporation now had 800 major customers scattered through the United States, Canada, Switzerland, England, Hong Kong, Japan, and Latin America. Verex-insured loans aggregated $3.9 billion, and Travelers Express was annually issuing more than 75 million money orders.

"Any one of these companies," said an officer of the Financial Group, "was in itself a thriving business."

And yet there were some subsidiaries that were suffering because of events beyond Greyhound's control. Airport Services was an example.

Everywhere in the nation airport activities had been affected by the long and bitter strike of the air-traffic controllers. Even President Reagan's intervention, outlawing the union, could not immediately restore normal airport operations. The airlines changed schedules and cancelled a number of flights. This reduced the amount of ground services required, and Greyhound's Airport Services Group had to share lean times with the airlines.

"Actually, we showed no losses," an executive said. "We simply held our own while we waited for better times."

Other victims of uncontrollable circumstances were Florida's hotels and travel agencies. Local tourism was being undermined by the country's weakening economy. All rent-a-car companies were slashing prices, and Greyhound's Rent-A-Car subsidiary could not escape the general slump.

If one tried to find an industry that gained anything from a period of hard times, the closest one might come would be temporary help services. The reason was a matter of practicality. To hire permanent salaried people involved all the expenses of maintaining Social Security records, pension benefits, insurance requirements, and other regulatory functions. Many firms preferred to rely on temporary employees; this absolved them of endless responsibilities and expenses. And so Greyhound's Temporary Personnel Services did well. In 1981 it added to its business by signing a $4.5 million contract with New York City and additional contracts with others, including the General Electric and Union Oil corporations.

Weighing all such factors, good and bad, one had to conclude that Greyhound's 200,000 shareholders had ample reason to be pleased. This was a vital, fast moving, successful company John Teets had risen to lead. The question he faced, as had all his predecessors, was: Where do we go from here?

•　•　•　•　•

Where Greyhound went would obviously depend to a great extent on the character, the methods, the plans of its new head. Yet the future could not be wholly his to control. As always, much of it would be shaped by economic conditions in the United States and abroad. In August and September of 1982 these could hardly be called bright.

American unemployment was at a record high. With more than 10,790,000 people jobless, one could not expect them to be thinking of spending their savings on vacations. There would be fewer passengers on buses, fewer stopping to eat at Post Houses, fewer taking meals in factories and office buildings.

Just as bad was the inflated cost of foods, clothing, housing, and every other commodity. Greyhound could not avoid feeling the effects of all this. Nor were conditions better in other nations to which the company's interests had spread.

So stockholders were certainly entitled to ask—what were John Teets' attributes as a chief executive? What talents did he bring to his new responsibilities in these trying years? In brief, what could one expect from this new administration?

On September 1, 1982, John Teets himself answered those questions; it was his first day in office.

That morning he strode briskly, tall, lean—with the slimness of an athlete—his curling dark hair showing spots of gray. He settled at this desk, ready for the many interviewers who wanted to see him. All of them probably knew that he had often described himself as "before all else a manager."

He had in truth been a skillful manager ever since his first participation in Greyhound's food industry. As far back as the New York's World's Fair, when he had made the Post Houses the only profitable restaurant venture at the exposition, he had demonstrated the power of intelligent, imaginative management. Much had been said at the time of the million-dollars-a-month that Post Houses were garnering. But how had that been accomplished?

When this question was asked by the first interviewer of the morning, Teets removed his glasses, toyed with them for a moment, then explained:

A survey we made of fair employees indicated there were over 7,000 of them, and they would be eating at the fair every day in good weather or bad. That was the group I wanted to attract—regular, dependable customers who would come back again and again. The other restaurants were appealing to tourists and charging fairly high tourist prices—say $3.50 for a chicken-in-a-basket lunch. I undertook to provide a high-grade lunch for $1.69. To meet that price I made low cost-plus deals with my suppliers. They agreed because they could foresee it would mean steady, day after day deliveries. The result of serving high quality meals at reasonable prices, for the most part to fair employees, was that we had lines waiting to get into our restaurants every day of the week. Tourists came too, of course, but the bulk of our business was with the regular customers who were fair employees. Catering to them paid off.

Teets' innovative methods proved successful wherever he went after the fair. In 1980, in recognition of his efforts as a food manager, he won the prestigious Golden Plate Award, the highest honor the food industry can confer. Some 1,200 industrial leaders applauded him when he rose to accept the Plate in Chicago's Conrad Hilton Hotel; he was applauded even more enthusiastically when he returned to Phoenix.

And yet, when he was chosen to head The Greyhound Corporation in 1982, there were a few questioning reminders from press people—generally addressed to Gerald Trautman—that Teets' background lay wholly in food management. He had never been involved in Greyhound's other interests, specifically bus lines, leasing operations, financial services, and the rest. Was he equipped by experience to handle this widely diversified company?

Trautman waved such doubts aside. "Teets has proved his management ability time after time," he said. "He knows how to indoctrinate himself thoroughly in new areas of business. He has a quick grasp of details and he is not afraid to make decisions. I am confident his management skills will become evident in all our operations."

One personal characteristic made the new chairman unique among corporate heads, and often astonished those who came to see him. This was his utter devotion to biblical precepts. A Bible lay in his desk drawer; it was always at hand, and he never hesitated to take it out, open it to well-marked sections, and quote its wisdom in support of a business conviction. He maintained that his faith in biblical guidance invariably helped him in making difficult decisions. (For years he had done his utmost to pass this faith along to others by teaching Bible classes on Sunday mornings. "Respect for the Bible," he argued, "leads to a healthy mind, while physical exercise leads to a healthy body. Put the two together, and you have the secret of a good life.")

With that kind of philosophy he might have been expected, when discussing Greyhound's character, to talk loftily of ethics, of honesty in all dealings, with frequent reference to the biblical injunction to "Do unto others———." But he did not speak like a preacher. He was crisp and businesslike.

"The basic character of Greyhound lies in constant change that leads to growth," he said. "First it changed from a one-car operation to a nationwide holding company that spread over all aspects of motor transportation. Then, through diversification, it changed to a worldwide organization interested in many forms of business. Change has been a governing factor of its past and change will continue to shape its future."

The interviewer asked, "Does that mean there will now be acquisitions in fields you never touched before?"

"No, not immediately. For the next year or so we will consolidate our present holdings. We will probably sell off those that are not completely satisfactory and thereby strengthen the corporation as a whole. And we will concentrate on expanding those subsidiaries that show real promise."

As he had done years earlier when Armour subsidiaries had

been sold, he called such selling "a pruning process." And this evoked a boyhood memory that made him smile.

He recalled his dismay, his actual pain, when he watched his father lop off branch after branch of a beautiful old peach tree. It seemed cruel and wanton until he discovered that the pruning of dying branches resulted in more and better peaches than the tree had ever before yielded.

"Pruning of loss-factors in a business like ours," he said, "can be as remunerative as making new acquisitions. We earn by eliminating losses."

Did that mean that pruning would soon occur in The Greyhound Corporation?

"Where it improves efficiency it should occur," Teets said. "We are a company with almost seventy years of background. In a situation like ours there are always a few people who feel that, in their particular jobs, they ought to leave well enough alone, they ought to follow established routine. Some of them have lost the sense of excitement and achievement that comes with finding ways to add to growth. They may be functioning, but they are no longer striving. The only way our company can grow is through the energetic efforts of all its people. I consider my responsibilities to Greyhound, to its shareholders, to its employees, are to make this as vital and profitable a company as I can. And that may well entail pruning off some personnel. But where that becomes necessary we plan to make it as painless as necessary."

"By what means?"

"In the case of people in their late fifties or early sixties, we may offer them early retirement, something many of them actually welcome if it doesn't involve a great financial sacrifice. We'll try to help them in every possible way, not only with liberal pension benefits but by adding a monthly sum equal to the Social Security payments they will receive at age sixty-five. If any other company does this, I haven't heard of it. I think Greyhound is extraordinarily generous in the terms it plans to offer those who are encouraged to take early retirement, and I think most of our people will agree."

(Teets was not the only corporate head to encourage early retirement at various levels of management. Many corporations, including major oil companies, had been reducing operations as well as the size of their staffs. In some cases such "pruning" was attributable to improved technology. As one chief executive explained, "New office equipment, including information systems never dreamed of in the past, increases the productivity of executives and their staffs, making it feasible—even obligatory—to reduce the size of management." So Teets was by no means alone in his thoughts about increasing efficiency.)

His associates learned long ago that he is a blunt man. "He doesn't try to hide behind soothing phrases," one of them asserted. "He says exactly what he means. At times he may sound tough because of this directness, but you have the advantage of knowing precisely what he has in mind. There is no guessing, no need to wonder if there is more or less in what he says. You get it straight, and he expects the same from you."

This expectation of candor on the part of others includes their right to point out any error he may make. Again and again, according to his colleagues, he has acknowledged with thanks the correction of some misinformation on which he may have acted.

But if there has been one thing Teets has refused to tolerate, it has been any suggestion of threat. There was the case of an angry vice president who objected to one of Teets' directives. He strode into Teets' office and snapped, "John, if I can't handle this my way I'm quitting!"

Teets at once extended his hand across the desk. "Good-bye and good luck," he said. "We're sorry to lose you."

The man stared. "What are you talking about?"

"You just resigned. I'm accepting your resignation."

John Teets, chairman of the Greyhound Corporation, is pictured with a wood sculpted greyhound for a corporate advertisement that appeared in major financial publications.

The bewildered vice president protested, "But I didn't mean it that way!"

Teets motioned to the door. "Then why don't you go out and come in again, ready to discuss this intelligently instead of threatening me?"

Very much subdued, his associate actually did start again. They discussed the problem and settled it. Thereafter, as far as Teets was concerned, the incident was closed and forgotten.

Then there was the case of a badly overstaffed subsidiary. Careful analysis had made it clear that this operation should divest itself of eleven people whose duties could easily be handled by others. The change would make for "a leaner, more efficient operation." Teets called in its supervisor and asked him to cut down his staff by eleven people in low-level management.

Within a day the supervisor was back, shaking his head. "The most I can release is two," he declared. "Can't go any further."

Teets promptly said, "That makes three."

"Three? I said two."

"You make three. If you can't manage eleven, bring in your next in command and he'll take your place. If he can't manage eleven, we'll go to the next in line. We'll get eleven."

The shaken supervisor mumbled, "Let me go over my list again."

"By all means."

Before the day ended the man was back with eleven names. As matters developed, the reduction in staff did indeed convert a static operation to one that became vigorous and profitable.

If John Teets seems tough, say those who work closely with him, he is also fair. His toughness is exerted only to fulfill his obligations as chief executive officer. Those who have known him through the years add that they have never found him insensitive to the feelings of those he has had to oppose or overrule. Many a subordinate had been startled by an evening telephone call at home, a call expressing Teets' own reactions: "What's past is done with. I've forgotten it. I hope you will, too."

In the days after he assumed the chairmanship more than one interviewer asked about his plans for future acquisitions. For each of them he had to repeat his original reply: "We'll be ready to consider the next big acquisition in a couple of years."

"In what field?"

"It's far too early to say. We'll have to see what the economy does and what opportunities arise."

"Meanwhile, what are the problems you foresee?"

Teets gave this silent consideration. Then he said, "There's this about our bus industry. For years we've been demanding deregulation. Now at last we're getting some of what we wanted. But there's a price to pay. Deregulation enables hundreds of would-be bus operators to get into the business. That takes us back to the kind of competition, open to everybody, with which Greyhound's founders had to contend. Over and over they had to fight fierce price-cutting wars. Say what you like about the evils of bureaucratic regulation, it did serve for a time to protect us from wildcat, cut-throat competition. Now we'll have to learn all over again how to compete with wildcatters in a free and open market. It may be a graver problem than we had bargained for."

"A Pyrrhic victory?"

"Call it a partial victory. There's still a struggle ahead. But we'll handle it."

Perhaps the outstanding impression one gathered of John Teets in these first days of his administration was his firm confidence. Greyhound's future would depend on sound management; and, as he had said, he was before all else a manager. In Trautman's words, the company was in capable hands.

•   •   •   •   •

So, Gerald Trautman could retire with faith in the future and with deep satisfaction in his own sixteen-year record. As he leaned back in his desk chair he looked relaxed, happy, content. On the Saturday of his retirement some two hundred of his colleagues had honored him at a farewell dinner. The affair was attended by civic leaders and noted industrialists. What all of them had stressed was that he had richly earned the leisure and pleasure that lay before him.

Yet what pleased him most, he revealed as he chatted in his office, was the quality of the executive staff he had organized to carry The Greyhound Corporation into the years ahead. All were people of proven ability. All had long experience in the company.

On this particular morning one of his associates, coming into Trautman's office, speculated with some amusement on what Carl Eric Wickman might have said, had he been able to envision the size of the corporation as it was in 1982.

The comment caused Trautman to smile. Perhaps his thoughts went back to the old Hupmobile that carried passengers between Hibbing and Alice for fifteen cents a ride. Perhaps, by contrast, he thought of Greyhound's modern presence in the world. After a moment he chuckled and said, "I imagine that he might have remarked that his little venture had at last spread out as he knew it would—going from Hibbing to *everywhere*."

32

Trautman could not foresee—nor could Teets in the first days of his administration—what the vicissitudes of the American economy would do to the company. There was little reason to be worried. Respected analysts were assuring the nation that it was at last recovering from the severe economic setbacks it had sustained. Inflation, they pointed out, was being held in check. Unemployment, though still rampant, was no worse (despite the fact that some 10 million Americans were still seeking jobs).

But The Greyhound Corporation, especially in its Armour division, had to contend with something few of the experts mentioned: The high and still escalating cost of beef was drastically reducing meat consumption. A number of packinghouses were being shut down. Others were operating at a fraction of their capacity and were suffering serious losses.

Matters were even worse for the Armour turkey-breeding facilities. They were at a virtual standstill. In Phoenix one company official somewhat grimly, if poetically, observed, "Armour storm clouds are hiding our sun."

Teets saw the need of immediate changes if Greyhound was to be guided past the misfortunes of the economy. In the case of Armour's faltering enterprises the sixteen-year era of diversification would have to yield to a series of divestitures (a matter of lopping off the dying branches of a tree in order to stimulate the growth of the tree itself). At the end of 1982, after his first full year in office, Chairman Teets told Greyhound stockholders exactly why the company was divesting itself of certain Armour interests.

"We found ourselves in the untenable position," he said in his annual report, "of supporting businesses showing marginal returns—or marginal prospects—at a time when those resources were needed to assure the growth and expansion of our other businesses."

He was acting on the simple principle that profitability can be achieved by ridding oneself of the source of losses. But it was not an easy process. It would be painful for those who lost their jobs. Teets was well aware of this. "The dilemma for all managements," he said, "is the age-old choice between being a guardian of orthodoxy or a champion of progress." He chose the latter course. This, as he saw it, demanded freeing the company of segments that were causing financial losses.

And so he reported that in 1982 "A number of our businesses and assets were divested at book value or better, yielding $42 million in cash and notes . . . and freeing an additional $15.4 million in working capital. These included two Armour turkey-raising facilities, a beef abattoir, and the filament yarn business of Armour Handicrafts. It also included the closing of six Armour branch houses in the East."

Yet all these were merely preliminary steps to the complete divestiture of the Armour Food operations. Teets finally sold Armour Food to Conagra of Omaha for $160 million. As a reflection of how the financial community regarded this, the *New York Times* reported: "With this sale Greyhound spins off a low-return, high-cost subsidiary in a troubled industry." Clearly, it was seen as a sound move.

Yet it was not the only such move in the process of "yielding to the demands of progress." In 1982 the company divested Walters Transit, Carey Transportation, American Sightseeing, Gray Line of New York, and Red Top Sedan, and in 1983 sold Greyhound Rent-A-Car.

Inevitably there was the question of how stockholders and employees would react to this "dismemberment" of the conglomerate Trautman had so carefully assembled. To explain

"STRIKES, PICKETS — WHO NEEDS THE AGGRAVATION WHEN I CAN HOP A FLIGHT TO MIAMI BEACH FOR EIGHTY-EIGHT BUCKS.?"

Two newspaper cartoons that reflected editorial reaction to the Greyhound strike of 1983.

what was happening Teets said, "In its simplest terms Greyhound is changing. It is happening without upheaval and it is happening as a consequence of meticulous planning. There are no drawbacks to the changes—just sound professional management of our assets."

He might have referred, though he did not, to a statement Trautman had issued two years earlier: "Management will continue to review the strengths, weaknesses, and market positions of each of our businesses. We will be looking at the long-term value of each, whether it is a generator or a user of cash, and its return on assets employed. Our goal is to fill up resources and redirect them to areas that enhance the value of our shareholders' investment in the company."

In other words, the divestitures of 1982-83, dramatic as they might be, could be said to adhere to the principles that had long guided Greyhound. The sale of Armour unquestionably bolstered the health of those businesses that the corporation retained. One might have expected a return to normal conditions.

And then came the explosion—the sudden, violent bus strike of 1983.

33

Over the years, Greyhound Bus Lines had, of course, experienced several strikes. For much of its history the company's nationwide bus service had been operated by a number of regional Greyhound bus companies, each with its own union contract. Consequently, strikes were generally localized and were settled without any injury to the company, to the unions, or to the 14,000 American communities served by intercity bus lines. All in all, the long-term relationship between Greyhound and its unions had been harmonious and both sides had prospered.

But the negotiations of 1983 and the strike that ensued were dramatically different. By 1974 all of the separate Greyhound bus line companies had been brought under one management, and a single union—the Amalgamated Transit Union—represented the majority of Greyhound Lines employees.

As a result, when the strike came on November 3, 1983, it erupted on a nationwide basis. It not only isolated thousands of small towns that depended wholly on bus transportation to connect them with the outside world; it also affected the millions of people in the larger towns and cities who had come to depend on Greyhound as their basic means of travel. The strike involved not only bus drivers but maintenance personnel, baggage carriers, ticket sellers, janitors. All told, some 12,700 workers walked off the job.

From the start it was a strike that led to angry, physical confrontations between strikers and nonstrikers, as well as clashes between picketing demonstrators and police. In some places where nonstriking and new-hire employees tried to move buses, windshields were spattered with eggs, a few were shattered by rocks. *Business Week* described it as "the bitterest walkout in Greyhound history—unprecedented and frightening."

Throughout the seven long weeks of the strike, newspapers and magazines besieged Greyhound headquarters for statements; radio and television newscasters clamored for interviews with John Teets and Frank Nageotte, chairman of the bus division. Television cameras covered the nation for scenes of angry, fist-brandishing, sign-waving strikers.

"The wildest days I've experienced in all my years with the company," one senior officer declared, and his was a mild way of putting it.

As in all conflict situations, there was no single element that triggered events. Rather, it was the confluence of many factors: First was the fact that the Amalgamated Transit Union, in early 1982, had granted a wage freeze to Greyhound's principal competitor, Trailways. Trailways immediately took this wage advantage, added it to its already considerably lower labor rates, and initiated a fare war against Greyhound.

At the outset, Greyhound chose to ignore the fare discounting by Trailways. But by the spring of 1983 passenger counts were down drastically as riders, alert to a bargain, began treating bus transportation as just another commodity to be purchased at the lowest possible price. The best buses, the best schedules, the best terminals and the best personnel had all been persuasive factors in favor of Greyhound so long as fares were equal. But 1983 proved that the one thing riders were looking for—lowest fares—Greyhound was not providing.

Faced with the prospect of seeing its share of the market being eroded by this tactic, Greyhound had no alternative but to drop its fares to meet the competition.

Another factor converging on events was bus deregulation

which served as an invitation to hundreds of new entrants into the business. The *Chicago Tribune* reported that the ICC had received some 2,000 applications for authority to operate "chartered or scheduled services." These new entrepreneurs, hungry for patronage, operating with low maintenance costs while paying minimal wages, also could drastically undercut Greyhound fares. And they did.

Lastly, there was the effect of airline deregulation on competition. Deregulation had relieved the airlines of former strictures and the result was an influx of new, feisty, low-cost carriers. They too became major competitors of Greyhound. Some, like People Express and Southwest Airlines, were able to undercut bus fares to an alarming extent. As examples, People Express charged twenty-three dollars for a flight between New York and Buffalo; Greyhound buses, to cover expenses, had to charge forty-one dollars and fifty cents for the same trip. Between Phoenix and San Francisco, Southwest Air charged sixty dollars; the Greyhound fare was seventy-nine dollars.

Fighting against the price-cutting war in every part of the United States, Greyhound Bus Lines posted an operating loss in 1982 of $16 million; and by mid-1983 it had racked up operating losses of some $18 million.

How long could any bus line continue to sustain such a drain? What could be done about it?

Attempting to raise income by increasing fares would not solve the problem. It would simply drive more passengers to the cheaper bus lines and air carriers. Nor could the company cut the multimillion-dollar cost of fuel and other materials it had to purchase; control of those prices lay with the suppliers. The only possible area where cuts could be affected was employee wages and benefits which constituted 62 percent of Greyhound operating costs, and which in the case of Greyhound were 30 percent to 50 percent higher than the wage costs of other major bus carriers.

In salary and benefits, Greyhound drivers were earning an average of \$35,744 a year, while drivers of other Class I carriers were averaging \$27,437. Thus, Greyhound drivers were annually receiving \$8,307 more than their counterparts elsewhere. With nearly 7,500 drivers on its roster, the company was expending some \$62 million a year more than other bus operators were paying.

Wage differentials were equally striking in every category of employee. Greyhound's mechanics and service personnel were earning an average of \$28,110 a year; the same type of worker in other companies was getting \$20,190. And so the figures ran. Greyhound's terminal personnel were averaging \$26,614 as contrasted with \$17,746 elsewhere; Greyhound office workers were earning \$22,079 in jobs for which other companies were paying \$14,660.

It was true that Greyhound Lines had always prided itself on paying the highest wages in its industry. But in view of the heavy losses that were being incurred since the advent of deregulation, could the luxury of maintaining such high salary levels be continued? To go on operating at a loss would be an unpardonable disservice to stockholders and to the employees themselves, for the ultimate collapse of the bus division would entail the loss of all their jobs.

So Teets—together with the bus division's chairman, Frank Nageotte, and its president, Frederick Dunikoski—came to the difficult but inescapable conclusion that to remain solvent in its industry, Greyhound would have to cut its wages and benefits to levels approximating those of its competitors.

Parity of labor costs thus became the overriding issue of the 1983 negotiations, and it was on this basis that Greyhound employees were asked to accept a wage cut of 9.5 percent.

The request caused immediate consternation and outrage among union leaders. They demanded that the company rescind so unthinkable a plan. When Teets insisted that the pay cut was absolutely essential and that he was determined to see it enacted, he was called "tough, intransigent, stubborn." But the opposition of the union heads was just as unshakable, and thus the historic strike was precipitated.

Management was ready for it. As they told an interviewer from *Fortune:* "Our Number One assumption was that we'd have to operate during the strike. Lawyers were designated in 150 cities to get temporary restraining orders or injunctions where necessary. We trained 500 new drivers. We dug holes in the ground so that rent-a-fences could be put up overnight around our buses. We moved 300 executives to the field to help, and kept seventy-five key ones here to man the command center twenty-four hours a day. We had hand-held video cameras at every terminal so that if anyone damaged our property we wouldn't get into arguments. It's a federal violation to interfere with a moving intercity bus, and we wanted firsthand evidence."

Such precautions, however, did not deter the strikers. As picketers continued to walk in front of every bus terminal—a human barricade that sent potential travelers to other lines— the strikers denounced the company's efforts as an attempt to take away gains for which labor had struggled for years to achieve.

This accusation was immediately refuted. In full-page newspaper advertisements the company declared:

> Greyhound Lines has the highest labor costs of any carrier in the intercity bus industry.

> Our labor costs are 30 percent to 50 percent higher than other major bus companies in America. Our principal competitor, for example, has contracts with the ATU (Amalgamated Transit Union) which are more than 30 percent lower than our prestrike labor costs. That fact makes it impossible for us effectively to compete against both the new regional airlines and against other bus companies, both of whom can cut their fares and still prosper.

PARITY IS VITAL TO OUR SURVIVAL!

When the strike continued without any sign of yielding on the union's part, Teets demonstrated the toughness of his determination. He announced that on November 17—two weeks after the strike began—the company would institute Phase I of its plan to begin operating its buses in spite of the strike. This partial start-up involved maintaining service to some 501 cities in twenty-seven states, primarily in those areas that traditionally had provided the greatest number of passengers. Along with a supervisory staff, the corps of drivers and other personnel on hand to provide this service was made up of both those union members who had continued to work and of some 1,300 new hires, including a large group of experienced drivers from other bus companies who had been recruited and trained by Greyhound in anticipation of the strike.

Additional phases for further expansion of service were also ready for implementation as the company's manpower resources increased. The goal was to have full service restored within ninety days.

Greyhound also announced that it would replace all striking drivers and other personnel with new employees who would be hired at the lower, prevailing industry rate.

That announcement brought an amazing result. Long lines of job applicants immediately appeared at every Greyhound office. As one of the company's public relations officers said, "We had at least a hundred applicants for every available job." Remember, this was happening at a time of nationwide unemployment. Over 60,000 jobless people applied for work at Greyhound Lines, eager to grasp the pay the company was offering.

But new drivers, as well as the other essential personnel, had to be trained, and that required time. So Greyhound decided on another attempt to persuade the striking employees to return to work. It lowered the projected pay cut to 7.8 percent.

Even though this proposal meant that Greyhound workers would remain the highest paid in the industry, the union leaders still refused to accept the terms. Some continued to label Greyhound a "union buster." Nevertheless, they agreed to put the new offer to a vote of their 12,000 constituents, while actively and publicly denouncing the offer and conducting the vote in as public a forum as possible. As expected, an overwhelming 9,181 out of 9,522 employees rejected the plan.

This time Teets showed that he could indeed be tough. "We will go ahead full force," he avowed. "If we cannot do it with our current employees, we will do it with new hires."

Deeply concerned, the international ATU leadership sought the help of the AFL-CIO and federal mediators who called a meeting in Washington. On Friday, December 1, the federal mediator invited Greyhound Lines negotiators to meet with the ATU, and late Saturday evening, December 2, a tentative agreement was reached.

Once more the offer was put to the union's membership. This time the tentative agreement their leaders had worked out with the company was sent to each employee's home for secret voting, and they were asked to return their ballots by mail. December 19, 1983, was set for the counting of the vote.

One may ask: Was it that after seven tortuous pre-Christmas weeks of striking—payless weeks—employees were weary of going without checks? Were they secretly fearful of losing their jobs to the rapidly increasing number of newly hired replacements? One possible influence on their ultimate decision was the company's demonstrated ability to operate its service with new employees and with the increasing number of veterans who were willing to work at the reduced wage . . . as well as the ever-increasing passenger loads being carried daily by Greyhound Lines.

Whatever the motivation, on December 19 the membership of the Amalgamated Transit Union voted to accept the new terms—with 7,404 employees out-voting 2,596. And the bitter strike came to its end.

John Teets, standing behind his desk as he spoke to reporters, announced, "We will restore full service at once."

And so the new day in intercity bus transportation arrived—a day that promised more equalized opportunity for all those in the industry. Commenting later, Teets said, "Unquestionably, the month-and-a-half-long strike was the most difficult time ever experienced by our bus company. However, had we continued to operate, burdened as we were with labor costs far in excess of other bus lines, and against increasing competition from the airlines, there is little doubt that Greyhound Lines would have eventually withered and died. What we accomplished not only saved the jobs of 16,000 bus company employees, it also guaranteed that Greyhound Lines has a future and can continue its proud, nearly three-quarters-of-a-century-long tradition as 'America's Bus Line.' "

And old-timers at Greyhound could smile again and say, "We carry people from Hibbing to everywhere."

INDEX

*Page numbers in italics
indicate illustrations.*